Case Studies

THE DOCTOR OF NURSING PRACTICE DrNP

Setting a New Standard in Health Care

Columbia University School of Nursing
2005

In Conjunction with the Hope Heart Institute

First Edition
Printed in the United States of America

Published by Columbia University School of Nursing
639 West 168th Street
New York, NY 10032

Published in conjunction with the Hope Heart Institute
1710 E. Jefferson St.
Seattle, WA 98122

ISBN 0-9777051-0-2

Foreword

The cases assembled for this reader are examples of current evaluation and management of sophisticated clinical issues drawn from neurology to pediatrics and cardiology to psychiatry. What makes them unique is that they represent the work of the new professional practitioner, the Doctor of Nursing Practice. They are the case studies written by the first of the faculty for this new clinical doctorate. How do they stand apart from the work of young physicians completing the Doctor of Medicine? They emerge as integrating the science and current practice with a disciplined interest in the evidence that underscores it. The authors use powerful understanding, not only of the pathophysiology of disease and its therapies, but the current understanding of the organization of health care and its delivery. Elements of medical ethics and care dilemmas of innovative therapy are elucidated in the traditional case format.

Reading of the cases provides a first insight into the advantages to patients managed by both MDs and DrNPs. The ability to synthesize a longitudinal medical experience necessitated by the need to provide ongoing follow-up in the face of specialty interest is evident. In this era of greater specialization, the ease with which a patient with complex problems is shuttled into a singular diagnostic category because of the proclivity of the physician is too familiar. The Doctors of Nursing Practice shun such ready narrowness. Furthermore, the extraction of the individual from the disease is rarely seen in the reports; the DrNP is empowered to view the patient in the context of illness. Whether perspective will be altered as interaction in the medical model continues is unclear; generally, the firm foundation they have entered with will provide a buttress against reductionism.

Support has been provided by the Hope Heart Institute. From its origins 46 years before, this institute from the Pacific Northwest has emerged with a dedication to serving humanity through research and education. It has had national impact with its particular emphasis on vascular biology research directed to translation to clinical problems as well as robust preventive education. The innovation reflected in the studies supported by Hope Heart Institute parallels the professional innovation reflected in these collected case studies of Doctors of Nursing Practice.

Joseph Tenenbaum, MD
Edgar M. Leifer Professor of Clinical Medicine

Columbia University Medical Center

Introduction

Columbia University School of Nursing's Doctor of Nursing Practice (DrNP) program is designed to provide nurse practitioners with the knowledge and skills necessary for fully accountable health care for patients across clinical sites over time. This degree is consistent with the 1996 Institute of Medicine's definition of primary care as the "provision of integrated, accessible health-care services by clinicians who are accountable for addressing a large majority of personal health-care needs, developing a sustained partnership with patients, and practicing in the context of family and community." This clinical doctoral degree is the natural evolution of master's prepared, site-specific nurse practitioner education.

Columbia's DrNP curriculum was developed utilizing advanced clinical competencies, empirical evidence from outcome studies, and the Columbia University faculty practice model. This level of practice requires knowledge and understanding of the health-care system, legal and ethical implications for practice, as well as sophisticated clinical diagnostic decision making, practice management, and business skills. The DrNP curriculum provides students the opportunity to assimilate and utilize in-depth knowledge of biophysical, psychosocial, behavioral, and clinical sciences, and sophisticated informatics and decision-making technology to develop context-specific collaborative strategies to optimize patient health.

DrNP courses are divided into three clusters: 1) support core, 2) clinical core, and 3) residency. Support core courses provide the scientific knowledge needed for this level of practice and include Informatics and Evidence-Based Practice, Quantitative Research Methods, Principles of Epidemiology and Environmental Health, Legal and Ethical Issues, Advanced Clinical Genetics Seminar, and Practice Management. Clinical core courses include didactic courses, clinical application seminars, and advanced clinical experiences. Upon successful completion of DrNP course work and a comprehensive examination, students enter the DrNP residency. During the residency, students participate in clinical seminars and assemble the DrNP portfolio.

The portfolio is the capstone project submitted in partial fulfillment of the requirements for the DrNP degree. The portfolio is a scholarly quantitative and qualitative document, which in its entirety presents evidence of mastery of comprehensive care of patients across clinical settings over time. Portfolio components demonstrate the attainment of scholarship evidenced by primary authorship in a peer-reviewed journal and presentation at a professional meeting; self-evaluation; quality assurance; and a plan for future continued learning.

Case studies, the main component of the DrNP portfolio, enable the DrNP student to demonstrate mastery of clinical competencies and provide the Portfolio Review Committee a basis for evaluation of care delivered. Case studies include patient assessment and the clinical decision-making process, citation of the biophysical underpinnings and evidence for the plan of care provided, and discussion of the intervention outcome. Each student's portfolio requires a minimum of 15 complex case studies to provide sufficient evidence of achievement of this level of comprehensive practice.

This reader contains examples of individual portfolio case studies submitted by Columbia University School of Nursing's first graduating class in 2005. They serve as a basis for discussion and a guide for those who will follow.

Janice Smolowitz, DrNP, EdD
Associate Professor and Associate Dean for Practice

Columbia University School of Nursing

Table of Contents

Contributors to the DrNP Reader

The following contributors to this book are all members of the first Doctor of Nursing Practice class which graduated from Columbia University School of Nursing in 2005.

Joyce K. Anastasi, DrNP, PhD

Karen S. Desjardins, DrNP

Jennifer Dohrn, DrNP

Judy Honig, DrNP, EdD

Ritamarie John, DrNP, EdD (c)

Patricia A. Maani, DrNP

Lori Rosenthal, DrNP

Josephine Guide Sapp, DrNP

Janice Smolowitz, DrNP, EdD

Edwidge Jourdain Thomas, DrNP

Portfolio cases are based on student-patient encounters. The introduction to each narrative explains the reason the case was selected. Some case studies depict a single encounter while other case studies demonstrate provision of care over time. All cases include a discussion of the assessment and the clinical decision-making process, and cite the biophysical underpinnings and evidence for the plan of care. To enable the reader to differentiate case narrative and clinical evidence, the cases are written using two fonts. The case narrative is written in a regular font. *Evidence for scientific underpinning is cited in an italic font after the appropriate section in the case narrative.*

CHAPTER I:
About the DrNP Case Studies Reader

by Mary O'Neil Mundinger, DrPH
Dean and Centennial Professor of Health Policy
Columbia University School of Nursing

This Reader is a reflection of the competency achievements of the graduates of the first clinical doctorate in nursing in the country. The Doctor of Nursing Practice degree represents the profession's current evolution and a new opportunity for nurses to assume positions in society and the health-care system where they can better meet the needs of their patients. As you read through these remarkable case studies, the nursing acumen and comprehensive care provided to these patients become clear; neither would have been possible in a conventional system in which nurses do not have education beyond the master's level and have limited accountability and authority for patients across sites and over time.

Columbia University School of Nursing developed the clinical doctorate following a decade of innovations and partnerships with physician colleagues. This degree was designed to prepare students for the kind of practices pioneered by our faculty, and then carefully evaluated by a panel of distinguished external scientists. Looking back at the process, our success was founded on a constellation of resources and a special window of opportunity.

Twenty years ago, in 1986, Columbia University School of Nursing was experiencing a crisis of confidence within the University. Functioning largely as a nursing unit within the medical school, the School's national presence had eroded. It faced budget deficits, low enrollments, and minimal faculty scholarship. Within a year, a radical plan had been developed and implemented. Serendipitously the School had strong support from the chairman of the University trustees and the vice president of the Health Sciences (both physicians whose medical education had included clinical training with strong, smart nurses). Without these two advocates in our camp, we might never have been able to launch the plan or bring it to fruition.

The goal was to develop a faculty with more depth; in addition to teaching, professors would engage in scholarly research or sophisticated clinical practice. To formalize this, we devised a then unique faculty practice plan. It requires every faculty member to be engaged in a full professional role. Everyone would continue to teach, and then add either research or clinical practice as another dimension to their scholarly role.

Explicit reduction of teaching loads occurs in proportion to the percentage of time devoted to practice or funded research. Those opting for a practice role initially had six months to contract for a practice. Those choosing research (and who were doctorally prepared) had six months to draft proposals and begin pilot work and two years to obtain funding.

During these early years of innovation the School obtained full school status, and the practitioner faculty began showing up in medical school departments and clinics where their value was soon established. We filled a need in an academic health center, where patients require comprehensive primary care as an adjunct to the broadly accessible medical specialties. We also developed a research doctoral program, which was launched in 1993.

That same year, as all of our initiatives were succeeding, the hospital faced a crisis. Desiring New York State funding in order to construct a new building, the hospital was required by the state to open several new primary care sites for the surrounding underserved community. It did not take long for the hospital President to visit and ask our now visible and highly regarded nurse practitioner faculty to provide primary care in the new clinics.

The School agreed, with the proviso that faculty would carry out this new role within a research framework to assess the value of nurse practitioner primary care. We then set out to design a study comparing nurse practitioners and physicians in primary care. In order to reduce the variables between the two groups and to assure a valid study, we asked the hospital medical board to grant our practitioners admitting privileges at the University hospital. We knew our measurements — including patient outcomes, satisfaction, and cost — would be compromised unless the nurse practitioners had the same authority for patients and the same hospital access as the primary care physicians. It took a full year to educate and convince the 16 medical department chairmen of the validity and safety of this approach. All but one department concurred and offered to provide informal tutoring and access to resident education programs for faculty learning to admit and co-manage hospitalized patients. This admitting authority was intended to last for the two-year period of the research.

Following two months of orientation, the new nurse-run clinics (named Columbia Advanced Practice) opened. Nurse practitioners provided pediatric, adult, family, and geriatric services. Because the community had long been underserved, significant pathology was diagnosed, and several hospital admissions occurred. Our physician colleagues provided extraordinary support. We spent many weeks orienting the hospital nursing staff to this new model; we wanted them as partners without setting up hierarchical competition. The process worked flawlessly.

During the time we sought medical board approval, the hospital received their preferred mortgage approval from New York State, and the School received a New York State Workforce Improvement Grant to fund part of the research. With evaluation funds from U.S. Health and Human Services and implementation funding from the Robert Wood Johnson Foundation and the Fan Fox Foundation, we conducted a randomized trial — the first ever in nurse practitioner evaluation history — comparing nurse practitioner and physician outcomes in primary care.

As we had more admissions than expected, and as most required co-management with a specialist, physicians soon became comfortable with our new authority and model of care. Long before the randomized trial was complete, the medical board changed the hospital by-laws to make admitting privileges a statutory right for nurse practitioners with a Columbia University School of Nursing faculty appointment.

We appointed a distinguished scientific advisory board, which included the chairman of the Presbyterian Hospital Medical Board, to oversee the study; all were nationally known physicians. Having an all-physician advisory board provided credibility in the physician and payer communities. The study showed no significant differences between nurse practitioners and primary care physicians in any of the parameters of care examined. Almost all the patients were enrolled with Medicaid, and the claims tapes showed that patients were staying where they were randomized. That neither cohort "jumped ship" validated the study outcomes. In the end, the advisory board was so satisfied with the conduct of the trial that they all contributed to it and signed on as authors. The report was published as the lead article in *The Journal of the American Medical Association* in the first issue of 2000.

Before we knew the results of the study, we began planning our next project — an independent nurse practitioner clinic for commercially insured patients. By locating it in a site with an abundance of physicians, we would learn whether patients, if given a choice, would choose a nurse practitioner.

Nurse practitioner access to Medicaid and Medicare patients, which had occurred within seven years of the 1965 inception of the nurse practitioner role, was never a threat to physicians. Most physicians were happy to share those populations. But would they be as magnanimous with mainstream commercially insured patients? As we designed the new practice, the major insurer for Columbia physicians, Oxford Health Care, agreed to credential our faculty as primary care providers.

As full primary care providers at the medical center, we asked to join the physicians' contracting group. This newly formed organization brought a coordinated physician network to contracting negotiations with managed care companies. The founding president was also the chair of the department of medicine, and our major ally during the admitting privileges discussions. He welcomed the nursing school faculty practitioners into the organization. They now pay the same dues, receive the same fees, and are listed as primary care practitioners by all managed care organizations as medical center physicians.

We opened our practice in the fall of 1997 in a Columbia building, just off Fifth Avenue across from Central Park and the Plaza Hotel. Many Columbia specialists practiced in this site, and we had ready access to them, and to lab and X-ray services.

We didn't think this would be an easy step, but we weren't ready for the immediate onslaught. The president of the New York State Medical Society threatened to step down so he could work full time to close down our practice. The New York State Office of Professional Discipline paid a surprise visit to see if we were practicing medicine without a license; they decided we were not. Our Columbia physician colleagues never wavered. They publicly signed on as our collaborators, took our referrals, and recognized the quality of our care. We called the practice CAPNA for Columbia Advanced Practice Nurse Associates.

Our faculty practitioners carried on their informal learning — use of sophisticated informatics, business and legal ethics, new fields of genetic risk, practice management strategies, detailed evidence-based practice assessments of the literature, research training to identify valid design and methods in order to make appropriate determinations of evidence in the literature, and continual study of pathophysiology and emerging pharmacotherapy. The learning was constant, and patient outcomes kept getting better.

By 1999 we knew this model could be replicated, could be taught, and would be enormously attractive to seasoned nurse practitioners everywhere looking for ways to advance their practices. We also knew that the Columbia prototype had to be part of a national model in order to achieve broadly accepted standards and reliable excellence. We therefore founded a council composed of leading nursing school deans and an equal number of eminent physicians active in health policy with the mission of advancing the scope of doctoral nursing practice.

This Council for Advancement of Comprehensive Care (CACC) has met 10 times since 2000. Our goal is to set the national standard by developing a single model and offering it to a firm coalition of nursing schools. The educational model for this new practice paradigm borrows from medicine, public health, and business but adds dimensions not now regularly available to patients from any practitioner. It prepares nurses to provide basic medical and health care, including disease prevention, risk reduction, incorporation of patient desires and values, accountability for coordination, and consultation across site and over time. The kind of practice is not encounter- or episode-based but patient-focused and is founded on two current guides for excellent practice. One is the Institute of Medicine studies and publications issued over the last decade, recommending content and outcomes of a quality-driven health-care system. The other, broader focus, is to base clinical decisions on the best evidence.

As I write this in the summer of 2005, the clinical nursing doctorate is spreading like wildfire, fast and in a relatively uncontrolled fashion. Dozens of colleges and universities are creating this new degree, sometimes as hybrids with research, sometimes upgrading MS programs, sometimes just changing the title of an existing degree program, and sometimes ignoring clinical practice components and using the DrNP title for degrees in administration or education. Thus far only Columbia has developed a comprehensive clinical program de novo. Standardization by title is currently not happening. But standardization by competency is still possible and lies at the core of quality assurance. The Council's mission is to determine and promulgate the clinical competencies required for the DrNP degree, and it will develop and offer a prototype certification. Our public, the payers, and policymakers who can advance this level of practice need to know what these nurses can do in a reliable, distinctive, and high-quality way. Certification of core clinical competencies will accomplish this. Our ultimate goal is to improve the nation's health using these new doctoral clinicians as the instrument of such a plan.

The case studies in this Reader comport with scientific evidence for best practices at the time they were written. Part of the challenge of adopting evidence-based practice as a guide for clinical decision making is the fact that evidence changes, and the dynamic nature of this kind of quality assurance requires diligent and continuous assessment of the science informing practice. There is no longer a defensible basis for "conventional wisdom" in practice decisions.

As you can see from this narrative, Columbia Nursing is a work in progress. We hope and expect other nurses to learn from and improve our work, promising our collective patients the very best care.

Mary O Mundinger

CASE ONE:

A 92-year-old woman with multiple chronic illnesses on admission to a skilled nursing facility

I have selected this case to illustrate chronic illness management and coordination of care for a patient with complex comorbid conditions at the time of her admission to a skilled nursing facility.

ADMISSION NOTE

Source: Patient who seems reliable.

Mrs. Jones is a 92-year-old Caucasian female with multiple chronic illnesses. She requires nursing home admission because she is experiencing increasing difficulty conducting activities of daily living.

CC: "I am moving here because my family says I cannot take care of myself at home anymore."

Mrs. Jones lived in New York for most of her adult life. She moved to an adult community in Florida 29 years ago with her husband after his retirement. He died seven years after their move. Mrs. Jones stayed in the community because she and her husband had established many friendships and she enjoyed the weather. Her children continued to live in NY and Connecticut and visited her regularly with the grandchildren. In the past year, many of her friends died or entered nursing homes. Her daughter visited six months ago and found Mrs. Jones had increased difficulty in dressing, bathing, and walking. They spoke about moving to NY. After much discussion, Mrs. Jones agreed to return to NY to be near her daughter but was not comfortable about living with her. Mrs. Jones states that she could not walk up the steps at her daughter's apartment building and thought she would feel secluded. Mrs. Jones' primary care provider agreed that a skilled nursing facility would be appropriate and facilitated admission to this facility.

CURRENT HEALTH

Current Medications
    Norvasc 5 mg PO qd
    Lisinopril 30 mg PO qd
    Atenolol 25 mg PO bid
    Lasix 20 mg PO bid
    Imdur 30 mg PO qd
    Plavix 75 mg PO qd
    Lovastatin 50 mg PO q hs
    Docusate 250 mg PO qd
    Niferex 150 mg PO qd
    Fe SO4 325 mg PO qd
    Artificial tears 2 gtts os tid
    MVI 1 tab PO qd
    Vitamin E 400 IU PO bid
    Calcium with Vit D 500 mg PO bid
    Acetaminophen 500 mg, 2 tabs PO qid prn

CURRENT HEALTH PROBLEMS

Dyslipidemia x 20 years. Tries to watch diet with low-fat foods. + sedentary lifestyle. Denies abdominal pain or myalgias which she knows can be an adverse effect of Lovastatin.

Hypertension x 20 years. Taking medications for 20 years. Doesn't recall names of previous meds.

Angina x 10 years. Has had chest pain with walking more than two city blocks or one flight of stairs. Used to take nitroglycerin sublingually but now takes Imdur. No history of MI.

Congestive heart failure (CHF) x five years. Was hospitalized five years ago for increasing shortness of breath at rest and with exertion. Had increased swelling in legs with more fatigue than usual at that time. Denies syncope, palpitations, or hemoptysis. The cardiologist told her she had a "congested heart." She last saw the cardiologist six months ago and he said she was "okay." There were no changes in medications.

Following low Na+ diet. No added salt at table. Avoiding canned foods, soups, and cold cuts. No regular physical activity. Prior to admission walked one block to shop. SOB and occasional chest pain when walking more than two blocks, or climbing more than one flight of stairs. Would stop and rest for a minute or use oxygen from tank when she felt SOB. No episodes of chest pain or SOB in past month. Sleeps on three pillows x three to five years, gets up one to two times/night for urination, has slight swelling around ankles. Denies claudication, palpitations, sudden sensory motor deficits.

Anemia for a few years. Doesn't recall circumstances surrounding diagnosis or diagnostic tests performed. Her doctor told her she "needed iron." She doesn't like the medicine because it makes her feel constipated. Denies history of ulcers, liver or gallbladder disease, folate or B12 deficiency. Denies exposure to toxins, never had blood transfusion. Dark brown bowel movement every other day. No rectal bleeding or pain. Denies bleeding, excessive bruising, jaundice, hematuria, post-menopausal bleeding.

Osteoarthritis/osteoporosis x ~30 years. Mild pain in feet and hips. No radiation down legs. Attributes pain to arthritis. Limited physical activity due to SOB and a feeling of unsteadiness because of pain in feet and hips. Uses front-wheel walker for steadiness. Denies previous fractures, falls, other joint pain, stiffness, joint swelling, deformity, limitation of motion. Has lost at least 2 inches in height over unknown time period.

PMH: Denies glaucoma, thyroid disease, diabetes, tuberculosis, and cancer.

Childhood illnesses: Without significance. No h/o rheumatic fever, scarlet fever, croup, pertussis, or polio.

Operations/hospitalizations/accidents: Denies.

Allergies: Penicillin causes shortness of breath and rash. No known allergies to other medications, food, or environment.

Habits: Coffee, two cups per day. Alcohol, one to two drinks per week x 40 years. Stopped 10 years ago except for one drink on "holidays." Never smoked cigarettes.

Sleep/rest: Bedtime 10:00 p.m. Difficulty falling asleep, wakes up during night several times to urinate. Able to return to sleep without difficulty. Feels refreshed when awakens at 6 a.m. No sleep aids.

Exercise/leisure activities: Reads books, knitting.

Nutrition: Unable to recall food intake of yesterday. No food intolerances.

Use of safety measures: Always uses front-wheel walker, nursing home has handrails in halls, needs help with showers.

Screening tests: PPD, negative last year. Does not recall last pelvic exam. Does not recall last mammography, refuses examination.

Immunizations: Yearly flu vaccine, pneumococcal five years ago. Doesn't recall date of last DT.

> *Diphtheria and tetanus toxoids, combined (DT) for protection against diphtheria and tetanus, should be given every 10 years for continued immunity.*

> *Pneumococcal vaccine (Pneumovax 23) (23 of the most prevalent or invasive pneumococcal types stimulate active immunity through antipneumococcal antibody production) (Karch, 2005).*

> *Influenza virus vaccine (inactivated virus antigens stimulate an active immunity through production of antibodies specific to the antigen used; antigens vary yearly) used as prophylaxis for people at high risk of developing complications from infection with influenza (Karch, 2005).*

FAMILY HISTORY

Denies family history of cancer, glaucoma, TB.

SOCIAL HISTORY

Born in Germany. All family Holocaust victims during WW II, four sisters, three brothers, and both parents. Immigrated to America in her 20s and became a seamstress. Married at age 21, has one son and one daughter. Husband deceased x 20 years. Daughter is married with three young children; her son is married with two children. Both live in the area and will visit "frequently." Has lived alone for the past 20 years. Believes self able to perform all ADLs but needs help with shoes and shower. Uses front-wheel walker for ambulation.

REVIEW OF SYSTEMS

General health: Reports fatigue daily, usual health "OK." Denies weakness, fever, sweats.

Skin: No history skin disease. Denies change in skin color, pigmentation, nevi, pruritus, rash, or lesions. Denies change in hair or nails.

Head: Denies unusually frequent or severe headaches, head injury, dizziness, or syncope.

Eyes: Difficulty with vision due to bilateral cataracts both eyes. Wears glasses, not sure of last exam. Denies double vision, eye pain, inflammation, discharge, lesions.

Ears: Reports excess wax in ears, needs drops and cleaning frequently. Denies hearing loss, discharge, tinnitus, or vertigo.

Nose: Reports constant postnasal drip over the past few years that is irritating to throat and voice, made better when drinking hot liquids. Denies discharge, sinus pain, nasal obstruction, epistaxis, or allergy.

Mouth and throat: Hoarseness due to postnasal drip, no tenderness in throat. Denies mouth pain, bleeding gums, toothache, dysphagia, sores, or lesions in mouth. Full dentures.

Neck: Denies pain, limitation of motion, lumps, or swollen glands.

Breast: Denies pain, lump, nipple discharge, rash, swelling, or trauma. No past surgery. Does not do breast self-examination. Does not want mammogram.

Respiratory: No past history lung disease.

Cardiovascular: See HPI, cardiac.

Peripheral vascular: See HPI, cardiac.

Gastrointestinal: See HPI, anemia. Appetite fair. Denies food intolerance.

Urinary: Up several times a night for urination. Occasionally loses some urine when coughs hard. Denies dysuria, urgency, hesitancy, or straining. Denies pain in flank, groin, suprapubic region.

Genitalia: Gravida 2/Para 2/Abortion 0. Menarche as "teenager." Last menstrual period around age 48. She has not been sexually active since her husband died 20 years ago. Denies vaginal itching or discharge, sores, or lesions.

Musculoskeletal: See HPI, osteoporosis/osteoarthritis.

Neurological: Denies history of seizure disorder, stroke, fainting. Denies weakness, tremor, paralysis, difficulty speaking or swallowing. Denies numbness or tingling. Reports memory good.

Hematologic: History of anemia. See HPI.

Endocrine: Appetite fair. Denies increase in hunger, thirst, urination, problems with hot or cold, change in skin, or nervousness.

Psychiatric: Expresses sadness about deaths in family history and husband. Not aware of memory problem, nervousness, mood change, or depression. Denies any suicidal ideation.

PHYSICAL EXAM

Height: 163 cm (5' 1")
Weight: 68.6 kg (110 lb)
BMI: 20.8 (normal)
B/P:
    140/96 right arm, lying
    138/98 left arm, lying
    142/100 right arm, sitting
    144/100 right arm, standing
Temp: 37° C
Pulse: 64, regular
Respirations: 18

General survey: Ms. Jones is a 92-year-old, thin, white female, who walks and moves slowly with walker and responds quickly to questions. She talks freely but appears somewhat tense. She wears no makeup. She is neatly groomed.

Skin: Uniformly tan pink in color, warm, dry, intact, turgor good. Hair, normal distribution and texture, no pest inhabitants. Nails, no clubbing or discolorations. Nail beds pink and firm with prompt capillary refill.

Head: Normocephalic, no lesions, lumps, scaling, parasites, or tenderness. Face, symmetric. No weakness, involuntary movements.

Eyes: Conjunctivae pink. Sclera white, PERRL. No lesions, redness, ptosis, lid lag, discharge, or crusting. Visual fields full by confrontation. EOMs intact, no nystagmus. Fundi: Not observed due to cataracts.

Ears: Pinna; no mass, lesions, scaling, discharge, or tenderness to palpation. Canals with moderate amount of dark amber cerumen. Tympanic membrane pearly gray, landmarks intact, no perforation. Whispered words heard bilaterally.

Nose: No deformities or tenderness to palpation. Nares patent. Mucosa pink, no lesions. Septum midline, no perforation. No sinus tenderness.

Mouth: Mucosa and gingivae pink, no lesions or bleeding. Full dentures. Tongue symmetric, protrudes midline, no tremor. Pharynx pink, no exudate. Uvula rises midline on phonation. Tonsils 1+.

Neck: Neck supple with full ROM. Symmetric, no masses, tenderness, lymphadenopathy. Trachea midline. Thyroid nonpalpable, nontender. Jugular veins flat @ 45 degrees.

Thorax and lungs: Respirations shallow. Chest expansion symmetric. Lung fields resonant. Breath sounds vesicular with no adventitious sounds.

Breasts: Symmetric; no retraction, discharge, or lesions. No masses, tenderness, lymphadenopathy.

Heart: Precordium, no abnormal pulsations, no heaves. Apical impulse at 6th ICS left AAL, no thrills. Carotid arteries 2+ = bilaterally, no bruits. S_1, S_2 present, no S_3 or S_4. Systolic murmur, grade III/VI, loudest at 2nd ICS no radiation, present supine and sitting.

Abdomen: Flat, symmetric. Skin smooth with no lesions, scars, or striae. Bowel sounds present, no bruits. Tympany predominates in all quadrants. Liver span 7 cm in right MCL. Abdomen soft, no organomegaly, masses, or tenderness, no inguinal lymphadenopathy. No vascular bruits. Aortic pulsations ~3.0 cm. No CVA tenderness.

Peripheral vascular: 1+ pitting ankle edema bilaterally. All peripheral pulses present, 2+ and = bilaterally.

Musculoskeletal: Vertebral column no tenderness, slight kyphosis. Arms and legs symmetric, extremities have full ROM, tenderness over base of thumbs bilateral. No crepitation. Muscle strength, 5/5.

Neurological: Alert and cooperative, thought coherent, oriented x 3. CN II-XII intact. Sensory: pin prick, light touch, vibration, stereognosis intact. Motor: normal strength, bulk, and tone. Cerebellar: finger-to-nose and heel to shin smoothly intact. RAMs and point-to-point intact. Negative Romberg's sign, no pronator drift. Gait: uses walker — steps are short, somewhat uncertain, and almost shuffling. The legs are flexed at hips and knees. DTRs 1+ throughout with downgoing toes bilaterally.

Genitalia: Refused.

Rectal: Refused.

Psychiatric: Appearance, behavior, speech appropriate. Remote and recent memories intact. Affect appropriate, somewhat tense without evidence of hallucinations, delusions. No suicidal or homicidal ideation.

Review of labs (patient has copy of labs drawn by PCP 3 months ago):

Sodium	140 mEq/L	(136-145 mEq/L)
Potassium	4.3 mEq/L	(3.5-5.2 mEq/L)
Chloride	101 mEq/L	(96-108 mEq/L)
Bicarbonate	23 mEq/L	(24-30 mEq/L)
BUN	27 mg/dL	(6-26 mg/dL)
Creatinine	1.0 mg/dL	(0.7-1.3 mg/dL)
Glucose	97 mg/dL	(65-110 mg/dL)

ASSESSMENT

Mrs. Jones is a 92-year-old woman being admitted to a nursing home facility, as she is reported to no longer be able to live independently. Mrs. Jones is receiving treatment for hypertension, angina, CHF, and high cholesterol. She has never smoked cigarettes, stopped drinking alcohol 10 years ago except for an occasional "holiday," and maintains a sedentary lifestyle due to unsteady gait, SOB, and occasional chest pain after walking more than two level city blocks or climbing one flight of stairs.

Angina/hypertension/CHF treated with Norvasc, Lisinopril, Atenolol, Imdur, and Lasix. She does not describe symptoms of CHF or angina at this time. On examination her BP was 144/86 without postural hypotension, lungs were clear, neck veins were without distention, displaced apical impulse, systolic murmur III/VI heard best at second intercostal space, no S_3 or S_4, and mild bilateral ankle edema. Clinically stable with regard to CHF and angina. I will obtain old records from cardiologist.

Angina pectoris occurs whenever myocardial oxygen demand exceeds oxygen supply. Chest discomfort caused by transient myocardial ischemia is the clinical manifestation. This clinical diagnosis has a 90% predictive accuracy for the presence of coronary heart disease (CHD). Stable angina is chest discomfort that occurs at a certain level of exertion and is relieved with rest or nitroglycerin. The goals of the therapy of stable angina include: relief of symptoms; prevention or slowing of disease progression; prevention of future cardiac events, such as MI, unstable angina, or the need for revascularization; and the improvement in survival (Kannam, Aroesty, & Gersh, 2005). This patient is stage II — "slight limitation of ordinary activity." Angina occurs on walking or climbing stairs rapidly; walking uphill; walking or stair climbing after meals; in cold, in wind, or under emotional stress; or only during the few hours after awakening (Kasper, 2005).

Hypertension is common, asymptomatic, easily detected, and usually easily treatable. It often leads to lethal complications if untreated (Kasper, 2005). In evaluating patients with hypertension, the initial history, physical examination, and laboratory tests should be directed at 1) ruling out correctable secondary forms of hypertension, 2) establishing a pretreatment baseline, 3) assessing factors that may influence the type of therapy, 4) determining if target organ damage is present, and 5) determining whether other risk factors for the development of arteriosclerotic cardiovascular disease are present (NIH, 2004). Epidemiological studies show that there is a gradually increasing incidence of coronary disease and stroke and cardiovascular mortality as the blood pressure rises, with some differences in risk based upon age and underlying comorbid conditions. The correlation between the risk of adverse outcomes (including death) and blood pressure is a continuous variable, rather than based on blood pressures above a certain point. Diastolic blood pressure greater than 90 mm Hg or systolic blood pressure greater than 140 mm Hg should be treated. According to the Hypertension Optimal Treatment (HOT) study, a reasonable goal is 140/90, especially in the elderly, as long as there is no diabetes. Treatment is focused on the relief of stress, dietary management, regular aerobic exercise, weight reduction, and control of the risk factors contributing to the development of arteriosclerosis (Kasper, 2005).

Heart failure is a condition in which an "abnormality of cardiac structure or function is responsible for the inability of the heart to fill with or eject blood at a rate commensurate with the requirements of the metabolizing tissues." Hypertension is the primary cause in many patients. Ischemic heart disease is responsible for about ¾ of all cases in Western Europe and the United States. It is more common in the elderly. Signs and symptoms include circulatory congestion, dyspnea, fatigue, and weakness. The severity is based on criteria developed by the NY Heart Association. There are many precipitating causes, including but not limited to infection, myocardial infarction, anemia, aggravation of hypertension, and arrhythmias. There are many forms of heart failure (systolic vs. diastolic, right-sided vs. left-sided, etc.), but the differences are often blurred in the course of chronic CHF (Kasper, 2005).

For patients with established CHF the increased left ventricular wall tension raises myocardial oxygen demand. Treatment of CHF with ACE inhibitors, diuretics, and digitalis reduces heart size, wall tension, and myocardial oxygen demand which, in turn, help to control angina and ischemia. Transient left ventricular failure with angina can be controlled by the use of nitrates (Kasper, 2005).

Dyslipidemia x 20 years. Treated with Lovastatin and diet, no adverse effects from medication reported. Lipid status unknown. Will re-evaluate.

Several epidemiologic studies have shown a strong relationship between serum cholesterol and CHD. Randomized controlled trials have documented that lowering plasma cholesterol reduces the risk of clinical events due to atherosclerosis. The treatment of dyslipidemia is needed for long-term relief from angina, reduced need for revascularization, and reduction in MI and death. The control of dyslipidemia can be achieved by combination of a diet low in saturated fatty acids, exercise, and weight loss. Frequently, statins are required (Kasper, 2005).

The Third Report of the Expert Panel on Detection, Evaluation, and Treatment of High Blood Cholesterol in Adults (Adult Treatment Panel III, or ATP III) guidelines are based upon observations that showed a graded relationship between the total cholesterol concentration and coronary risk. They are influenced by the absence or presence of pre-existing CHD. A meta-analysis of 38 primary and secondary prevention trials found that for every 10% reduction in serum cholesterol, coronary heart disease mortality was reduced by 15% and total mortality risk by 11%. According to the ATP III 2004 Guidelines from the NIH and the National Heart, Lung, and Blood Institute: 1) determine lipoprotein levels by obtaining complete lipoprotein profile after 9 – 12 hour fast (optimal LDL <100, desirable total cholesterol <200, and high HDL >60) and treat elevated triglycerides (National Heart, Lung, and Blood Institute [online]).

Anemia. Treated for iron deficiency anemia x a few years, etiology unknown, will re-evaluate for presence of anemia and evidence of iron deficiency. It is unclear if Mrs. Jones has been adherent with iron replacement. If anemia is found, will evaluate underlying etiology and therapeutic intervention. If no evidence of anemia, will discontinue medication and follow.

*At least 75% of all anemia cases are hypoproliferative due to mild to moderate iron defi-
ciency or inflammation. Other causes include ineffective erythropoiesis and blood loss or
hemolysis. In general, these anemias are characterized by normocytic, normochromic red
cells, although microcytic hypochromic cells may be observed with mild iron deficiency
(Kasper, 2005).*

*It is necessary to evaluate the patient's iron status fully before and during the treatment of
any anemia. The development of iron deficiency is dependent upon the individual's initial
iron stores. In affluent countries the major cause of iron deficiency is blood loss, either
overt or occult. Overt blood loss is often easy to discern, whereas occult blood loss may be
more difficult. Reduced gastrointestinal absorption of iron and a diet deficient in iron can
also cause iron deficiency (Schrier, 2005).*

Osteoarthritis/post-menopausal osteoporosis functionally controlled. No history of falls
or fractures. Uses walker for stability. Will continue acetaminophen regimen and assess mobility
to maintain best function with particular attention to safety.

*Osteoarthritis is joint pain described as a deep ache localized to involved joint, aggravated
by joint use and relieved by rest. There may be stiffness after a period of inactivity that
usually lasts <20 min. Reducing pain, maintaining mobility, and minimizing disability
are the main treatment goals. Patients are instructed to use proper body mechanics, take
rest periods during the day, and apply heat to affected joints to reduce pain and stiffness.
Drug therapy is palliative with acetaminophen. Risk factors include age, trauma, repetitive
joint use, and obesity (Kasper, 2005).*

*Osteoporosis is a disease of the bones caused by a loss of bone mass as well as a change
in the bone structure. Risk factors include: age over 30, non-Hispanic white and Asian
ethnic background, small bone structure, family history, previous fracture following a
low-level trauma, estrogen deficiency, anorexia nervosa, cigarette smoking, low dietary
intake or absorption of calcium and vitamin D, sedentary lifestyle or immobility, medications including glucocorticoids, heparin, Synthroid, and phenytoin. Osteoporosis is
diagnosed by a bone mineral density test, the dual energy X-ray absorptiometry (DEXA)
(National Institutes of Health Osteoporosis and Related Bone Diseases National Resource
Center [online]).*

Health maintenance: Pneumococcal current, flu shot yearly, refuses mammogram and Pap.
Will discuss colonoscopy given history of anemia as well as preventive screening examination.

PLAN

Admission: Admit to skilled nursing floor.

Vital signs: Weekly, weekly weights.

Diet: Step 1 American Heart Association diet. No added salt at table.

*Hypertension, CHF — Dietary management should include sodium restriction, caloric
restriction for overweight patients, and cholesterol and saturated fat restriction (Kasper
et al.).*

Activities: Activities as tolerated, OOB with walker, shower with assistance weekly.

Medications:

- Nitroglycerin 0.2 mg SL every 5 minutes during chest pain.
  A maximum of 3 doses in a 15-minute period.

  Sublingual nitroglycerin remains the treatment of choice for an acute anginal attack. Chronic nitrate treatment is used to prevent recurrent anginal episodes (Kannam, Aroesty, & Gersh, 2005).

- Imdur 30 mg, 1 tab PO/day

  Chronic nitrate therapy, in the form of an oral preparation, can prevent or reduce the frequency of recurrent anginal episodes and improve exercise tolerance. However, tolerance to long-acting nitrates can develop and has limited their use as first-line therapy. The extended-release preparation of isosorbide mononitrate, which is administered once per day, may be preferable to improve compliance. The starting dose is 30 mg once daily and can be titrated to 120 mg once daily as needed. This preparation is particularly useful in patients who have effort-induced angina. However, since the effect lasts only about 12 hours, some patients may develop nocturnal or rebound angina. Such patients require twice daily dosing or additional antianginal therapy (Kannam, Aroesty, & Gersh, 2005). Isosorbide mononitrate (Imdur) relaxes vascular smooth muscle with a resultant decrease in venous return and decrease in arterial BP, which reduces left ventricular workload and decreases myocardial oxygen consumption. Used for prevention of angina pectoris (Kasper, 2005).

- Atenolol 25 mg, 1 tab PO bid

  Beta-blockers relieve anginal symptoms by inhibiting sympathetic stimulation of the heart, thereby reducing both heart rate and contractility. Lower doses of the cardioselective beta blockers, such as atenolol, block beta-1-receptor mediated stimulation of the heart and are therefore the preferred treatment for stable angina (Kannam, Aroesty, & Gersh, 2005).

- Norvasc 5 mg, 1 tab PO/day

  Calcium channel blockers prevent calcium entry into vascular smooth muscle cells and myocytes, which leads to coronary and peripheral vasodilation, decreased atrioventricular (AV) conduction, and reduced contractility. In patients with angina, these effects result in decreased coronary vascular resistance and increased coronary blood flow. Calcium channel blockers are used in combination with beta blockers when initial treatment with beta blockers alone is not successful (Kannam, Aroesty, & Gersh, 2005).

- Lisinopril 30 mg, 1 tab PO/day

  Angiotensin converting enzyme (ACE) inhibitors are not typically used as a treatment for angina pectoris. However, most patients with angina will be treated with an ACE inhibitor for other reasons including previous infarction, left ventricular dysfunction, or hypertension. ACE inhibitors are first-line therapy in all patients who have heart failure, anterior wall MI, ST elevation MI, diabetes, or systolic dysfunction, and in patients with proteinuric chronic renal failure (Kannam, Aroesty, & Gersh, 2005).

- Lasix 20 mg, 1 tab PO bid

  Sodium and water retention lead to the common congestive symptoms of pulmonary and peripheral edema. Fluid overload can typically be controlled and symptoms improved by diuretic therapy within hours to days. Loop diuretics should be given to control pulmonary and/or peripheral edema. The most commonly used loop diuretic for the treatment of heart failure is furosemide (Kannam, Aroesty, & Gersh, 2005).

- Lovastatin 1 10 mg tablet and 1 40 mg tablet PO q hs

  Statins are the most powerful drugs for lowering LDL-C, with reductions in the range of 20 to 60 percent. The effects of statin therapy are additive to those of a controlled diet. There is risk of hepatitis, so liver transaminases should be checked every six months. Statins are also used to slow the progression of atherosclerosis in patients with CAD. Maintenance dose 20 – 80 mg/day, adjust dose q four weeks as needed.

- Plavix 75 mg, 1 tab PO/day

  Both antiplatelet and anticoagulant therapy have been used for the management of acute ischemic stroke and for the prevention of stroke. Antiplatelet therapy reduces the incidence of stroke in patients at high risk for atherosclerosis and those with known symptomatic cerebrovascular disease. A meta-analysis published in 2002 by the Antithrombotic Trialists' Collaboration (ATC) compared antiplatelet therapy, primarily with aspirin, with placebo in the prevention of stroke, myocardial infarction, and vascular death among high-risk patients with some vascular disease or other condition implying an increased risk of occlusive vascular disease. There was a 25% risk relative reduction in nonfatal stroke in patients treated with an antiplatelet agent (Kasner & Dashe, 2005).

- Docusate 250 mg, 1 capsule PO/day

  A stool softener to be used in patients who should avoid straining during defecation and constipation associated with hard, dry stools. It is a safe agent for use in the elderly. Stool softeners are unnecessary if stool is well hydrated, but there is usually some constipation with use of iron preparations (Karch, 2005).

- Niferex 150 mg, 1 capsule PO/day for iron deficiency anemia (hold pending results of a.m. bloods)

  Iron-polysaccharide (Niferex-150) is a mineral used to prevent and treat iron deficiency that is safe, inexpensive, and effective (Karch, 2005).

- Fe SO4 325 mg, 1 tab PO/day for iron deficiency anemia (hold pending results of a.m. bloods)

  Oral iron usually provides a safe, inexpensive, and effective means of restoring iron balance. Iron is a mineral used to prevent and treat iron deficiency.

- Artificial tears 2 gtts each eye tid

  Tear replacement by topical artificial tears and lubricants is currently the most widely used therapy for dry eye. The goal of tear substitution is to increase humidity at the ocular surface and improve lubrication. In addition, artificial tears smooth the corneal surfaces of dry eye patients (Karch, 2005).

- MVI 1 tab PO/day

  A supplement to a low-fat diet full of fruits, vegetables, and whole grains to help counteract the harmful effects of stress, aging, lack of exercise, and illness.

- Vitamin E 400 IU PO bid

  Antioxidants such as vitamin E act to protect your cells against the effects of free radicals, which are potentially damaging by-products of energy metabolism. Free radicals can damage cells and may contribute to the development of cardiovascular disease and cancer. Studies are underway to determine whether vitamin E, through its ability to limit production of free radicals, might help prevent or delay the development of those chronic diseases. Vitamin E has also been shown to play a role in immune function, in DNA repair, and in other metabolic processes.

- Calcium with Vit D 500 mg, PO bid

  There is accumulated evidence that positive calcium balance — promoted by adequate calcium and vitamin D intake — is beneficial in the prevention of bone loss in older people. Stronger bones should result, and stronger bones should be more resistant to fracture if older people fall.

- Acetaminophen 325 mg, 2 tabs PO qid prn for arthritic pain. No more than 12 tablets in 24 hours.

  Acetaminophen belongs to a class of drugs called analgesics (pain relievers) and anti-pyretics (fever reducers). The exact mechanism of action of acetaminophen is not known. Acetaminophen relieves pain by elevating the pain threshold, that is, by requiring a greater amount of pain to develop before it is felt by a person. It reduces fever through its action on the heat-regulating center of the brain. Specifically, it tells the center to lower the body's temperature when the temperature is elevated.

Labs: Fasting in the morning
- Electrolytes
- CBC with indices
- Serum iron and iron-binding capacity, serum ferritin
- Lipid panel
- ALT and AST
- TSH
- Urine analysis
- Stool guiaic x 3
- Pulse oximetry in a.m. for baseline data and weekly for oxygen use

Health maintenance: Influenza vaccine

  Influenza virus is typically brought into the nursing home by staff or visitors and spreads rapidly among the residents who share rooms and eat in a communal dining room. Hospitalization rates soar during epidemics as the frail elderly develop cardiac compli-cations, principally myocardial infarction and congestive heart failure, and pulmonary complications, particularly bronchospasm and pneumonia. In addition, many nursing home residents affected with influenza infection experience a subsequent decline in func-tional status, including a decrease in independence in bathing, dressing, and mobility. Every effort should be made to vaccinate both residents and staff against influenza in the early fall (Barker, 1998).

Education/counseling:
- Reviewed sodium and fat dietary intake.
- Explained ischemia (demand vs. supply) and reassured about angina.
- Explained reason to hold iron and Niferex until blood test results obtained.

Referrals:
- Nutrition — to individualize diet.
- Ophthalmologist for admission baseline to evaluate for hypertensive retinopathy and cataracts.
- Physical/occupational therapy consult to maximize independence and safety.

  Better physical functioning reduces their risk of hospitalization. Conditions and factors that place frail older patients at risk of being hospitalized are CHF, DM, and anemia, tak-ing several medications, low BMI, and emergency department in the past year (Damish et al.).

Records:

- Request summary of care and previous diagnostic test reports from Mrs. Jones' cardiologist for coordination of care.

Oxygen:

- O_2 at 2 l/min by nasal cannula as needed for shortness of breath prn.

  Supportive oxygenation is essential to ensure adequate O_2 delivery to peripheral tissues, including the heart (Kasper, 2005). Current indications for long-term oxygen therapy are as follows:

  General indication:
  If PaO_2 <55 mm Hg or SaO_2 <88

  In the presence of Cor Pulmonale:
  PaO_2 55 – 59 mm Hg or SaO_2 >89 or EKG evidence of pulmonary hypertension or Hematocrit >55% or clinical evidence of right heart failure

DNR

Discussed end-of-life care decisions with Mrs. Jones, who feels she has had a "good life." She doesn't like being on oxygen but finds it helpful when short of breath. If she develops an irreversible condition, where there is little hope of having her current quality of life, she does not want CPR, dialysis, or a ventilator. She has designated her daughter as her health-care proxy.

  All DNR orders in New York State must be written on a form (form #DOH-3474) provided by the New York State Department of Health. All nursing home residents are required to fill out advance directives upon admission.

References

Damish, T., Smith, D., Perkins, A., et al. *Risk factors for nonelective hospitalization in frail and older adult outpatients.* Gerontologist, 44 (1): 68 – 75.

Karch, A. (2005). *Lippincott's Nursing Drug Guide.* Philadelphia: Lippincott Williams & Wilkins.

Kasner, S.E., Dashe, J.F. (2004). *Antiplatelet agents for stroke prevention.* Up-to-Date. Retrieved Nov. 9, 2004, from http://www.utdol.com/application/topic.asp?file=cva_dise/_12856&type=A&selectedTitle=6~111.

Kasper, K., Braunwald, E., Fauci, A., Hauser, S., Longo, D., Jameson, J. (2005). *Harrison's Principles of Internal Medicine,* 16th ed. New York: McGraw-Hill, Medical Publishing Division.

Kannam, J.P., Aroesty, J.M., Gersh, B.J. (2004). *Overview of the management of stable angina pectoris.* Up-to-Date. Retrieved Nov. 9, 2004, from http://www.utdol.com/application/topic.asp?file=chd/5855&type=A&selectedTitle=5~423.

National Institutes of Health Osteoporosis and Related Bone Diseases National Resource Center (2004). *Osteoporosis.* Retrieved on Nov. 9, 2004, from http://www.osteo.org/_osteolinks.asp.

National Heart, Lung, and Blood Institute, U.S. Department of Health and Human Services, National Institutes of Health (2004). *National Cholesterol Education Program.* Retrieved online Nov. 10, 2004, from http://www.nhlbi.nih.gov/about/ncep/.

National Heart, Lung, and Blood Institute, U.S. Department of Health and Human Services, National Institutes of Health (2004). *High Blood Pressure.* Retrieved on Nov. 9, 2004 from http://www.nhlbi.nih.gov/health/dci/Diseases/Hbp/HBP.

Schrier, S.L. (2004). *Causes and diagnosis of anemia due to iron deficiency.* Up-to-Date. Retrieved Nov. 10, 2004, from http://www.uptodateonline.com/application/topic._asp?file=red_cell/5132.

A 34-year-old woman with advanced emphysema secondary to alpha-1 anti-trypsin deficiency referred for lung transplant evaluation

This case study presents the care provided for a 34-year-old female with advanced emphysema secondary to alpha-1 anti-trypsin deficiency (A1AT) who was referred for lung transplant evaluation and listing. This case study was selected because it is representative of the interdisciplinary approach that is required to care for patients with advanced lung disease in the setting of severe psychosocial concerns, limited support systems, and limited financial resources.

This case was compiled at the end of the patient's transplant evaluation, and after discussion at the Lung Transplant Interdisciplinary Committee meeting where it was unanimously agreed that lung transplantation was the only viable treatment option remaining for this patient.

HISTORY OF PRESENT ILLNESS

34-year-old female with emphysema secondary to 1 (alpha-1) anti-trypsin deficiency (A1AT), diagnosed approximately six years ago. Before her diagnosis, she reports being treated by local primary care physicians for "asthma" since her early 20s. She began seeing a local pulmonary physician at the time of her diagnosis. She has had 10 to 12 hospitalizations for breathing difficulties, the last of which was one year ago. She has required courses of prednisone. Now, she has exertional dyspnea with minimal activities. She requires assistance with many of her activities of daily living: bathing, dressing, household chores, and food preparation. She has more bad days than good days. She has a daily cough, with sputum production of approximately one tablespoonful. She has chest tightness with exertion, but denies any hemoptysis. At the time of this transplant evaluation, she reports activity limitation to walking less than one block and one flight of stairs. The patient had never enrolled in a pulmonary rehabilitation program, though she admitted she had been advised to do so many times in the past. At the time of lung transplant evaluation, the patient reported wearing continuous oxygen at 2 liters per minute flow, as well as receiving Prolastin infusions (3000 mg IVSS) weekly, as antiprotease replacement therapy.

PMH: Pulmonary hypertension, osteoporosis, hypertension, pneumonia, anxiety, depression, h/o ETOH abuse.

PSxH: s/p left hip replacement.

Family hx: She was adopted and does not know her family medical history.

Education: High-school graduate.

Occupation: Teacher's Assistant, disabled x 2 years.

Marital status: Single.

Children: One child.

Housing: Lives in private home with her child and her boyfriend.

Primary support/caregiver: Boyfriend.

Social history: Tobacco 1 PPD x 22 years, quit three years ago; h/o ETOH as teenager, history of outpatient drug rehab, enrolled in Alcoholics Anonymous for two years: to date, without relapse.

Transfusion history: Weekly Prolastin; denies blood transfusions.

REVIEW OF SYSTEMS

The review of systems for GI, GU, neurological, and skin were unremarkable.

HEENT: History of colonization with pseudomonas, varying sensitivities.
Pulmonary: A1AT.
Cardiac: Pulmonary hypertension secondary to A1AT.
Musculoskeletal: Left hip pin placement, left wrist tendon repair; osteoporosis.
Other: Depression/anxiety, extensive substance abuse history. Attends weekly AA meetings and sees a private counselor every two weeks.

Medications: Oxygen 2 liters 24 h/d; Flovent 220 mcg (2) puffs bid, Atrovent (2) puffs qid, albuterol unit dose via nebulizer bid; Xanax 0.25 mg PO bid, Celexa 20 mg PO qd, Remeron 30 mg qhs, Pulmocare dietary supplement 3 cans/day, MVI; Norvasc 2.5 mg PO qd.

Allergies: NKDA.

Infusions: Prolastin 3000 mg IVSS q week.

PHYSICAL EXAM

Ht: 66" Wt: 135 lbs.
Vital signs: HR 104; RR 25; BP 128/76; T 97.6; SaO_2 89% (room air).

General: Well-nourished, well-developed Caucasian female, appears slightly older than stated age.

HEENT: Normocephalic; pupils equal, round, and reactive to light; TMs intact bilateral and without haze or fluid line; nasal turbinates mildly inflamed, clear exudates; pharynx mildly injected with clear exudative postnasal drip.

Pulmonary: Diffuse rhonchi scattered throughout, (+) end-expiratory wheeze with tubular breath sounds Right > Left, markedly diminished bilateral basilar fields.

Cardiac: S_1, S_2; (+) holosystolic Grade III/VI murmur; no heave.

Abdomen: Soft, nontender; palpable liver @ 3 cm: nontender and nonpulsatile; bowel sounds (+) in all four quadrants; no epigastric tenderness.

Musculoskeletal: Markedly diminished strength throughout, decreased hip extensors bilaterally; muscle wasting evident in quadriceps; mild crepitus.

Extremities: No cyanosis; (+) clubbing; (+) mild, nonpitting pedal edema.

Neurological: CN II-XII intact; DTRs +2/4 equal and bilaterally; toes downgoing.

Skin: No lesion or mass; operative scar at left hip, approximately 3" length.

Diagnostics: Performed at time of transplant evaluation.

CXR: Abnormal chest radiograph with evidence of pulmonary nodules and bronchial wall thickening consistent with small airways disease. Hyperinflation of the lungs, increased retrosternal air space and flattening of the hemidiaphragms consistent with obstructive lung disease. The main pulmonary artery segment is mildly enlarged, raising question of the pulmonary arterial hypertension secondary to lung disease.

CT chest (noncontrast): Severe widespread emphysema, and scattered nodular opacities as described, presumably representing infection. No evidence for adenopathy or pleural effusion.

Cardiac catheterization: RV 41 mm Hg/2 mm Hg (4 mm Hg); PA 42 mm Hg/19 mm Hg (29 mm Hg); cardiac output 3.59 L/min.; cardiac index 2.13 L/min/m2.

Pulmonary function tests: FVC predicted = 3.83 Liters; Measured = 1.30 (34% predicted); FEV1 predicted = 3.22 Liters; Measured = 0.30 (9% predicted). Conclusion: There is a severe obstructive ventilatory defect. Residual hyperinflation and gas trapping are present. Respiratory muscle pressures are severely reduced for inspiration (PImax) and mildly reduced for expiration (PEmax), indicating respiratory muscle weakness. However, the severely decreased PImax may be at least partly due to the over-inflated lung volume at which it was measured. The reduction in maximal voluntary ventilation reflects the patient's reduced ventiable volume.

Six-minute walk: Report reads as follows: 6MWT 554 ft on 4 lpm O_2 96%-91%-97%; severely deconditioned; patient reports she is not exercising.

Cardiopulmonary exercise test: The patient has marked ventilatory restrictions to exercise performance. The subject was unable to achieve aerobic threshold and has severe exercise limitations. There is significant oxygen desaturation during exercise suggestive of possible pulmonary limitation to exercise at high workloads. This may in part be because she is experiencing an increase in sputum and cough. There is a component of cardiopulmonary deconditioning. A program of gentle conditioning would help to increase exercise tolerance.

Bone density: Osteoporosis at the total hip and osteopenia at the lumbar spine and normal bone density as measured at the forearm.

Lab review: CBC w/diff, Che12, LFT, lipid panel, CMV, hepatitis A, B, & C, RPR, aspergillus Ab, and HIV 1&2 negative. MMR titers consistent with immunity. HSV 1&2 negative; CMV Positive, Candida Ab Positive.

ABO: O negative, confirmed x 2.

Sputum C&S: Candida albicans; normal commensal flora, negative acid-fast bacilli.

ASSESSMENT/PLAN

1. Severe alpha-1 anti-trypsin deficiency emphysema, phenotype ZZ. Patient receives weekly Prolastin infusions.

Alpha-1 anti-trypsin deficiency (A1AT) is an often missed or late stage diagnosis, with most patients reporting multiple sinopulmonary difficulty with related functional decline (Stoller, 2004; de Serres, 2003). A1AT is a genetic disease characterized by inhibition of the enzyme elastase, which is a proteolytic enzyme. Alpha anti-trypsin (AAT) is a protein produced primarily by the liver, and is found in blood and tissues. Named for its ability to inhibit the action of the protease trypsin, AAT mainly inhibits elastase (specifically inhibiting Human Neutrophil Elastase, or HNE). This HNE is considered an omnivorous protease, which is why patients develop early onset, rapidly progressing "genetic emphysema" (de Serres, 2003). The serum protein deficiency was found on the long arm of human chromosome 14, and has been mapped to chromosome 14q31 – 32.3, called the SERPIN (Serine Proteinase Inhibitor) supergene (de Serres, 2003). Additionally, A1AT has a remarkable sensitivity to environmental factors such as chemical exposures, smoking, and occupational exposures (DeMeo & Silverman, 2004). Smoking remains the single greatest exacerbating agent of A1AT, believed to exert its influence due to the recurrent inflammation of the airways secondary to the smoking process (de Serres, 2003; Wewers, 2004). There are four AAT phenotypes:

1. Normal: Alleles are associated with normal levels of AAT and normal pulmonary function. This allele is referred to as M, normal phenotype MM. Average AAT levels range 110 – 270 mg/dL, depending upon the assay utilized.

2. Deficient: AAT levels 35% below average. This is the Z or S allele, carried by 2 – 3% of the Caucasian population. Classic phenotype is Protease Inhibitor Z (PI*Z), may also include PI*S.

3. Null: No detectable AAT; these patients have the most severe disease, though this is the least common of the A1AT phenotypes.

4. Dysfunctional: Adequate protein production with inadequate function (Stoller, 2004).

Alpha-1 anti-trypsin deficiency is a genetic disease with worldwide prevalence (de Serres, 2002, 2003). Initially believed to be a disease afflicting Caucasians, de Serres (2002) found: "In a total population of 4.4 billion in the 58 countries surveyed, there are at least 116 million carriers and 3.4 million with deficiency allele combinations." This suggests that A1AT "…may be one of the most common serious single-locus genetic diseases in the world" (de Serres, 2003). The implications of this finding are far-reaching: Genetic screening for A1AT is a justified medical endeavor. As the world's population grows, the likelihood of greater co-mingling across races, ethnicities, and borders will lead to even more allele combinations. The potential for creating a new, potentially harmful allele combination exists, and these new mutations will increase phenotype variables. Healthcare providers must include genetic disorders when their patient encounters (for seemingly ordinary complaints) do not conclusively resolve. As providers, we have a fiduciary obligation to act in the best interest of our patients. We must make decisions that implement principles of nonmalfeasance, justice, and beneficence. Quite simply, we must arrive at decisions in a manner of no harm and of intended benefit for our patients (Price, 2000).

Genetic screening will allow great gains. The knowledge allows for early intervention and treatment, and the database of affected individuals will expand with new information about the combination alleles. Additionally, family history alone cannot always be relied upon (Bick et al., 1998) — instances abound where family history is unknown, members are not available, records lost or destroyed, or even, as in our case study, totally unavailable due to circumstances surrounding the privacy of adoption. The information we have accumulated through the present day indicates that A1AT is a disorder we must become more adept at identifying: "Alpha-1 anti-trypsin deficiency is not a rare disease but a disease that is rarely diagnosed" (de Serres, 2003).

Intravenous therapy with pooled human alpha-1 antiprotease is the most popular treatment method. Direct replacement therapy allows for immediate elevation of plasma and lung AAT. *Until recently, Prolastin® was the only available therapy, but with the 2002 Aralast® and 2003 Zemaira® approvals by the Food and Drug Administration, the market availability has improved and some cost-relief was obtained with the addition of competitive products (Rovner & Stoller, 2004). In the event of lung transplantation, replacement therapy should continue, as post-operative inflammation potentially increases elastin breakdown — a hypothesis worthy of consideration given the finding of free elastin in bronchoalveolar lavage (King et al., 1994).*

2. Severe deconditioning/markedly decreased functional tolerance. Patient has been advised to enroll in a cardiopulmonary rehabilitation program.

Cardiopulmonary rehabilitation is a beneficial undertaking for patients with chronic lung disease, which improves overall exercise tolerance and muscle conditioning (Cambach et al., 1999).

3. Osteoporosis, last bone density > two years. Repeat testing today, begin treatment with risedronate (tradename: Actonel) 35 mg PO weekly, Oscal+D one tab PO tid, begin weight-bearing exercises as tolerated in pulmonary rehabilitation program.

When clinical profiles of the once-weekly and once-daily dosing formulations of alendronate and risedronate were evaluated, using hip fracture risk reduction as the primary end point, risedronate was effective at reducing hip fracture vs. placebo (Emkey, 2004). Additionally, when examined over a three-year treatment period and 10-year observation, risedronate proved superior to alendronate and raloxifene: risedronate was less expensive and more effective. Under consideration of current prices and published clinical evidence, risedronate dominates the comparison (Brecht et al., 2004).

4. Pulmonary hypertension, last cardiac catheterization was > three years. Will repeat cardiac testing this week. Treatment, if any, will be determined by arterial pressures.

Pulmonary hypertension is a lethal condition resulting in markedly diminished life expectancy (Mendeloff et al., 2002). Pulmonary hypertension eventually leads to severe distortion of the cardiac geometry with consequent impact on cardiac function (Kasimir et al., 2004). Although prostaglandin infusions have made a significant contribution in disease management, it is not the universal therapy. Lung transplantation (or heart-lung transplantation for those patients with severe, nonretractable right ventricular failure) remains a vital cure for end-stage pulmonary hypertension unresponsive to prostaglandin infusion (Mendeloff et al., 2002).

5. Hypertension, well-controlled on amlodipine (trade name: Norvasc). Will continue current therapy at present time.

Amlodipine is extremely successful in controlling blood pressure in patients with mild hypertension (Kloner et al., 2001). Using amlodipine monotherapy was more efficient than valsartan monotherapy in controlling 24-hour ambulatory BP and morning BP in hypertensive patients (Eguchi et al., 2004).

6. Extensive history of prior ETOH abuse, now in AA without relapse x two years. Patient will remain in AA therapy.

Due to the confidential nature of these meetings, this clinician cannot obtain documented updates. However, patient has agreed to have her sponsor call us on a monthly basis to report attendance and compliance. Additionally, patient will continue outpatient cognitive and behavioral therapy with local counselor, who is a Social Worker. Patient will continue routine follow-up with Transplant Psychiatry and agrees to obtain all psychiatric and narcotics prescriptions from psychiatrist only. Frequent counseling and participation (weekly or more) in Twelve-Step programs have been shown to encourage abstinence (Fiorentine & Hillhouse, 2003). Self-help group participants demonstrated greater "social engagement to maintain...recovery," and data support the assumption that more commonalities than differences exist within successful recoveries from alcohol dependence, independent of help-seeking status (Bischof et al., 2000).

7. Limited social supports, child is a minor and not extensively involved in patient's care. Primary caregiver is boyfriend.

Patient and boyfriend must attend scheduled follow-ups with Transplant Psychiatry and Social Work. They will be required to attend the Lung Transplant Patient Education meetings, and demonstrate understanding when questioned by clinical staff. Ongoing education is a key element to promoting patient awareness and understanding of the post-transplant process. Additionally, increasing a patient's level of knowledge may in turn lead to improved post-operative compliance (Stuart, Abecassis, & Kaufman, 2003).

8. Multiple financial concerns: Patient resides approximately three hours from transplant center, does not own a vehicle, and relies on her boyfriend for transportation to and from medical appointments. Patient receives only Medicaid and does not have additional sources of income. Patient cannot afford travel expenses to and from medical center post-transplant, nor does she have any friends or family residing closer to the medical center to stay with after surgery.

For patients with financial or geographic limitations, a strong support network can be found online with the Alpha-1 Network (Alpha-1 Foundation, 2004). This group offers members a network of guidance, and resources are listed in a central location with links to additional organizations or companies with helpful products. Additionally, their bulletin board is a forum for sharing concerns, fears, and triumphs.

A consult with the Lung Transplant Financial Services Coordinator was obtained for this patient. Under Medicaid guidelines, she has allowable benefits for transportation to medical appointments, though it must be booked no later than 48 hours in advance (New York State Department of Health, 2004).

Patient Assistance Programs (PAP) are offered by pharmaceutical corporations in an attempt to ensure equal access to life-saving medications. This patient's annual income qualifies her for many PAPs, which may allow her greater financial freedom (Gopa et al., 2004).

9. Depression/anxiety. Patient to be evaluated by Transplant Psychiatry, with plan for ongoing evaluation of therapy; patient and family to meet with Transplant Social Worker to assess for integrity and strength of current support systems, and to determine how supports could be improved.

It is imperative for patients, their family, caregivers, and/or partners to receive emotional support. Clinicians as well as ancillary services (ex. Social Work) can assist with referrals to community resources and support networks. Intervention by a psychologist or psychiatrist is warranted for patients suspected for or displaying depressive symptomology. All patients must be screened for depression both pre- and post-testing. Genetic counseling can be obtained, and family members (if available) should attend these sessions. Children of affected patients should be screened for carrier status as well as asymptomatic deficiency allele combinations (Wewers, 2004; Rovner & Stoller, 2004).

10. Severe end-stage lung disease, maximized medical therapy now presenting with increasing frequency of infection and markedly decreased functional tolerance. Lung transplantation remains

the only viable treatment option for this patient; she has been listed with the United Network for Organ Sharing (UNOS) as a double lung transplant candidate.

Early diagnosis and intervention is the pivotal priority measure that health-care providers can do for their A1AT patients. Patients presenting with recurrent pulmonary complaints, bronchiectatic symptomology, and abnormal pulmonary function testing (low-normal or declining) should have AAT levels tested (Needham & Stockley, 2004; Wewers, 2004). This baseline intervention will help direct future care. Once identified, the deficiency should be phenotyped to determine aggressiveness of treatment. More specifically, patients with the Null phenotype require aggressive evaluation for pulmonary disease. Their diagnostic evaluation should include: computerized tomography scans of the thoracic cavity and abdomen, cardiopulmonary exercise testing, laboratory testing to evaluate for liver dysfunction, bleeding diatheses, microbiological abnormalities (i.e., atypical microbes such as mycobacterium, aspergillus, Pneumocystis carinii, etc.), and a physical therapy evaluation. Most important, a full pulmonary function test should be obtained, preferably using National Emphysema Testing Trials (NETT) protocol, which allow for the greatest amount of succinct pulmonary functional status information to be obtained (Cohen & Sahn, 1999; Alpha-1 Anti-trypsin Deficiency Registry Study Group, 1998).

Treatment options for end-stage lung disease were transformed because of lung transplantation, which remains the definitive therapeutic option for end-stage lung disease patients, where medical therapy has been maximized, and no other viable option exists (Arcasoy & Kotloff, 1999).

ADDENDUM

TRANSPLANT COORDINATION

Approximately one year after listing, a suitable donor became available, and I called the patient in for double lung transplantation. I admitted the patient to the transplant floor, and ordered her pre-operative labs, chest X-ray, and medications. Together with the thoracic surgeon, surgical cut times and anesthesia sleep times were reviewed and established; ultimately I communicated these times to our donor team (procurement surgeons) as well as operating room staff.

I obtained a brief history and physical, and documented them in the patient's hospital chart. The following is an excerpt: 35-year-old woman with a history of alpha-1 anti-trypsin deficiency who was admitted this evening for bilateral lung transplant. Her first symptoms of emphysema started about 10 years ago, with mild progressive shortness of breath. She was then told by her PMD of having emphysema after hospitalization about five years ago. She smoked heavily, and had stopped smoking. At the time of transplantation, this patient has been nicotine-free for four years. Prior to quitting, she smoked one pack per day for nearly 20 years. Her last hospitalization was last summer for an exacerbation. At this time, her activities are limited to community ambulation, and she is oxygen dependent around the clock. She uses 2 – 4 liters of oxygen via nasal cannula. She could walk less than one block on the level. She started using oxygen regularly two years ago. She has had use of prednisone in the past. She has osteoporosis, with a history of left hip fracture in the past, and has been on treatment. She also is a recovering alcoholic and has been sober for nearly three years. Additionally, she has an anxiety disorder, for which she sees a local therapist as well as the lung transplant psychiatrist.

This patient underwent double lung transplant, off cardiopulmonary bypass, for alpha-1 anti-trypsin deficiency with severe emphysema, hypoxia, hypercapnia, and pulmonary HTN.

OR course: GEA, double lumen to 8.0 easy intubation. (h/o ETOH abuse w/ resistance to 10 mg of midazolam.)

Operative course notable for bilateral lung transplant with donor CMV+ and infection (treated) with S. Aureus in the right lung. Her ischemic times were 2:51 on the right, 4:15 on the left, and no units PRBC.
Atrial fibrillation x 2, each with reperfusion after transplant of lung, responded well to cardioversion.
Increased PA pressure of 65/27, responded well to nitric oxide.
Bronch @ end of case showed evidence of pulmonary edema, with Hct of 39.
U/O 895, (550 after Lasix 20 mg).
Lactated Ringers 3.5 L/Normal Saline 1 L/Hext 1 L/Cryo 5 u/PRBC 5 u.
Vancomycin 1 g, donor + staph and poss pneumonia.
Zosyn 4.5 g.

Thoracic epidural T 7-8, LOR 6 cm, taped @ 13 cm, bupivacaine 0.125 mg/mL bolus of 5 mL.
RV good filling, LV dry.
Started on dobutamine and Levophed.

POST-OPERATIVE COURSE

Patient transferred to the Cardiothoracic Intensive Care Unit (CTICU) on Levophed at 10 cc.

Vital signs: HR 118 ST BP 63/47 CVP 0 PA 23/11 CO 2

POST-OPERATIVE DAY (POD) #1

Neurological: A&O x 3, on ativan
Pulmonary: Bronch: minimal pulm edema
C/V: Off drips, CO/CI 4.7/2.7
GI: Tolerating oral intake without incident
Renal: Good urine output, Lasix 20 mg q8hr
ID: Vancomycin, Zosyn, tobramycin, ganciclovir (donor +staph, +pulm infiltrates), CMV mismatch Zenapax
Hematologic: Plate 45, CT sanguinous drainage, 2 units FFP, 6 pk platelets given
and PRBC 1 u 11/21
Transplant: Decadron, Prograf, Imuran
Epidural: Bupivacaine 0.25% 6 ml/hr 5 cc bolus

Patient was extubated POD #1.

Transferred to the floor on POD #2.

HOSPITAL COURSE

The patient's course on the floor was notable for gradual decline in O_2 requirement. She had a persistent air leak on the left, which was left on low wall suction (LWS), with hopes to water seal in a few days when leak resolves.

Pain control: Oral analgesia, as per anesthesia pain management team; special consideration given to the patient's substance abuse history.

Current medical issues include: Sternal precautions, post-operative status, deconditioning, rejection management, renal function, pulmonary toilet, and infection control. Skin management includes mobilization, and DVT prophylaxis includes mobilization. Nutritional status is adequate. Currently, the patient is able to ambulate with a rolling walker, and requires moderate assistance with positional changes and personal care.

Medications: Lexapro, Remeron, prednisone, ToBI, tacrolimus, Bactrim, senna, Zosyn, Protonix, nystatin, Lopressor, MgO, Ipatropium, SQ heparin, ganciclovir, Lasix, Colace, Imuran, albuterol, Percocet, lorazepam, Dulcolax, oxygen.

Allergies: NKDA.

Physical exam: Vital signs: BP: 110/70 HR: 90 RR: 20 Temperature: afebrile.
General: Well-developed, well-nourished woman in NAD.
HEENT: Neck supple, no JVD.
Chest: Coarse BS b/l L CT site c/d/i, small air leak.
COR: S_1, S_2, no murmurs, no S_3, no S_4.
ABD: NT/ND, NABS, no HSM.
Extremities: No edema.
Skin: No breakdown. No decubiti.
Psychological status: Mild anxiety.
Laboratory results: CBC: WBC = 14.1; HGB = 10.1; Hct = 31.5; Plts = 146
Chem-7: Na = 134; K = 5.0; Cl = 93; CO_2 = 37; BUN = 37; Cr = 1.4; Gluc = 156
Tacrolimus: 11.5
ABG: pH = 7.46; PCO_2 = 47; O_2 = 128
Coags: PT = 13.2; INR = 0.94; PTT = 30.8
ECG: NSR @ 80 BPM, No acute changes
X-rays: CXR(11/25): L PTx resolving

A/P: 35-year-old female s/p b/l lung transplant for alpha-1 anti-trypsin deficiency.
1) DVT prevention — Continue mobilization and heparin.
2) Decubiti prevention — Continue mobilization. Maintain nutrition.
3) Nutrition — Adequate for now.
4) Bowel/bladder management — Continue bowel regimen, monitor for symptoms of UTI. Remove Foley when possible.
5) Mobility — PT for gait, transfers, and safety. Strengthening and conditioning.
6) Continue to wean O_2 requirement. Thoracic surgery will monitor CT and will d/c when appropriate.
7) S/P transplant — Sternal precautions, wound care. Education about medications and care.
8) HTN — Lopressor.
9) Anxiety/depression — Being followed by psychiatry.
10) Disposition — Inpatient acute rehabilitation.
11) Patient care transferred to inpatient rehabilitation medicine team (attending & resident, PGY3).

References

Alpha-1 Anti-trypsin Deficiency Registry Study Group (1998). *Survival and FEV1 decline in individuals with severe deficiency of alpha-1 anti-trypsin.* American Journal of Respiratory and Critical Care Medicine, 158: 49.

Alpha-1 Foundation. *Alpha-1 Foundation Homepage.* Retrieved Dec. 1, 2004 from: http://www.alphaone.org.

Arcasoy, S.M., Kotloff, R.M. (1999). *Lung transplantation.* New England Journal of Medicine, 340 (14): 1081 – 1091.

Bick, D., Fugger, E.F., Pool, S.H., Hazelrigg, W.B., Yadvish, K.N., Spence, W.C., Maddalena, A., Howard-Peebles, P.N., Schulman, J.D. (1998). *Screening semen donors for hereditary diseases: the Fairfax cryobank experience.* Journal of Reproductive Medicine, 43 (5): 423 – 8.

Bischof, G., Rumpf, H.J., Hapke, U., Meyer, C., John, U. (2000). *Maintenance factors of recovery from alcohol dependence in treated and untreated individuals.* Alcohol Clinical and Experimental Research, 24 (12): 1773 – 7.

Brecht, J.G., Kruse, H.P., Mohrke, W., Oestreich, A., Huppertz, E. (2004). *Health-economic comparison of three recommended drugs for the treatment of osteoporosis.* International Journal of Clinical Pharmacology and Research, 24 (1): 1 – 10.

Cambach, W., Wagenaar, R.C., Koelman, T.W., van Kiempema, T., Kemper, H.C.G. (1999). *The long-term effects of pulmonary rehabilitation in patients with asthma and chronic obstructive pulmonary disease: a research synthesis.* Archives of Physical Medicine and Rehabilitation, 80: 103 – 11.

Cohen, M., Sahn, S.A. (1999). *Bronchiectasis in systemic diseases.* Chest, 116 (4): 1063 – 1074.

de Serres, F.J. (2002). *Worldwide racial and ethnic distribution of alpha-1 anti-trypsin deficiency: summary of an analysis of published genetic epidemiologic surveys.* Chest, 122 (5): 1818 – 1829.

de Serres, F.J. (2003). *Alpha-1 anti-trypsin deficiency is not a rare disease but a disease that is rarely diagnosed.* Retrieved on July 20, 2004 from Environmental Health Perspectives Online. 111 (16): http://ehp.niehs.nih.gov/members/2003/6511/6511.html.

DeMeo, D.L., Silverman, E.K. (2004). *Alpha-1 anti-trypsin deficiency: genetic aspects of alpha-1 anti-trypsin deficiency: phenotypes and genetic modifiers of emphysema risk.* Thorax, 59: 259 – 264.

Eguchi, K., Kario, K., Hoshide, Y., Hoshide, S., Ishikawa, J., Morinari, M., Ishikawa, S., Shimada, K. (2004). *Comparison of valsartan and amlodipine on ambulatory and morning blood pressure in hypertensive patients.* American Journal of Hypertension, 17 (2): 112 – 7.

Emkey, R. (2004). *Alendronate and risedronate for the treatment of postmenopausal osteoporosis: clinical profiles of the once-weekly and once-daily dosing formulations.* Medscape General Medicine, 6 (3): 6. Retrieved Nov. 30, 2004 from: http://www.medscape. com/viewarticle/480498.

Fiorentine, R., Hillhouse, M.P. (2003). *Why extensive participation in treatment and twelve-step programs is associated with the cessation of addictive behaviors: an application of the addicted-self model of recovery.* Journal of Addiction Disease, 22 (1): 35 – 55.

Gopa, G.B., Harris, I.S., Lin, G.A., Moylan, K. (2004). *Washington Manual of Medical Therapeutics,* 31st ed. St. Louis, MO: Lippincott Williams & Wilkins.

Kasimir, M.T., Seebacher, G., Jaksch, P., Winkler, G., Schmid, K., Marta, G.M., Simon, P., Klepetko, W. (2004). *Reverse cardiac remodelling in patients with primary pulmonary hypertension after isolated lung transplantation.* European Journal of Cardiothoracic Surgery, 26 (4): 776 – 81.

King, M.B., Campbell, E.J., Gray, B.H., Hertz, M.I. (1994). *The proteinase-antiproteinase balance in alpha-1 antiproteinase inhibitor-deficient lung transplant recipients.* American Journal of Respiratory and Critical Care Medicine, 149 (4 Pt 1): 966.

Kloner, R.A., Weinberger, M., Pool, J.L., Chrysant, S.G., Prasad, R., Harris, S.M., Zyczynski, T.M., Leidy, N.K., Michelson, E. (2001). *Comparison of candesartan and amlodipine for safety, tolerability and efficacy (CASTLE) study investigators. Comparative effects of candesartan cilexetil and amlodipine in patients with mild systemic hypertension,* American Journal of Cardioliogy, 87 (6): 727 – 31.

Mendeloff, E.N., Meyers, B.F., Sundt, T.M., Guthrie, T.J., Sweet, S.C., de la Moreno, M., Shapiro, S., Balzer, D.T., Trulock, E.P., Lynch, J.P., Pasque, M.K., Cooper, J.D., Huddleston, C.B., Patterson, G.A. (2002). *Lung transplantation for pulmonary vascular disease.* Annals of Thoracic Surgery, 73 (1): 209 – 17.

Needham, M., Stockley, R.A. (2004). *Alpha-1 anti-trypsin deficiency: clinical manifestations and natural history.* Thorax, 59: 441 – 445.

New York State Department of Health. *Medicaid Update Index.* Retrieved Dec. 6, 2004 from: http://www.health.state.ny.us/nysdoh/mancare/omm/medup-index.htm.

Price, D. (2000). *Legal and Ethical Aspects of Organ Transplantation.* Cambridge, MA: Cambridge University Press.

Rovner, M.S., Stoller, J.K. (2004). *Treatment of alpha-1 anti-trypsin deficiency.* Retrieved July 19, 2004, from: http://www.utdol.com/application/topic.asp?file=misclung/6072.

Stoller, J.K. (2004). *Clinical manifestations and natural history of alpha-1 anti-trypsin deficiency.* Retrieved July 17, 2004 from: http://www.utdol.com/application/topic.asp? file=misclung/11739&type=A&selectedTitle=1~28.

Stuart, F.P., Abecassis, M.M., Kaufman, D.B. (2003). *Organ Transplantation,* 2nd ed. Georgetown, TX: Landes Bioscience.

Wewers, M.D. (2004). *Alpha-1 anti-trypsin deficiency: more than a protease imbalance?* Chest, 125 (5): 1607 – 1609.

CASE THREE:
Summary of 14 years of care for a child with Kartegener's syndrome

Joshua was followed by this PNP for 14 years. Joshua was seen multiple times primarily related to his asthma and complications of possible Kartagener's syndrome. Joshua was a developmentally normal child who had situs inversus.

FIRST YEAR OF CARE

Reason for encounter: Health supervision visit for re-evaluation of murmur.

History of present illness: This African-American three-month-old, Joshua, came with his mother, Brenda, for re-evaluation of heart murmur heard for the first time at two months of age. Joshua was thriving and developmentally normal. The PNP and MD decided to see him back in a month to re-evaluate Joshua's murmur since it was louder than expected.

Past medical history: Joshua has an uneventful medical history. No hospitalization. No problems in the first three months of life except for a murmur.

Perinatal history: Joshua was a product of a 40-week intrauterine pregnancy without complication. Child was born to 24-year-old primigravada without any previous miscarriages or abortions. Prenatal care did not start until the sixth month of pregnancy due to lack of health insurance and difficulty getting Medicaid. She did start prenatal vitamins during the fourth month of gestation.

> *While the prevention of neural tube defects with folic acid use was not common knowledge in the 1980s, the use of prenatal vitamins was commonplace. The mother did not have access to prenatal care since she had a low-paying job without health benefits. In 1980, there was no insurance for people who had a low-paying job. Family care programs were not an option for the working poor. The gap in access has been corrected by the state-run program to provide health insurance for the working poor (NJ Family Care, 2005).*

Birth history: Joshua was born at 9 pounds 1 ounce, Ht. 23 inches. He was delivered via NSVD and his Apgars were 9-9.

Neonatal period: Joshua was discharged from the nursery after three days (standard for that period of time). There were no problems in the nursery. Negative VDRL, negative coomb.

Neurodevelopmental: Joshua was developmentally normal and had just started to move from side to side. At this point, Joshua was cooing, smiling, and pleasant. Joshua was looking at his hand, and he already exhibited hand-to-mouth behavior. He moved all four extremities well, had good eye contact, and followed face from side to side.

CURRENT HEALTH STATUS

Sleep: Joshua slept through the night. Joshua took two naps per day. Joshua was easy to put to sleep, rarely crying.

Nutrition: Child was on Similac with iron, taking 5 – 6 ounces per feeding. No cereal or fruit introduction.

Elimination: BM soft, mushy, golden brown, twice to three times a day.

Safety: House has smoke alarm. Joshua sleeps in a crib. No car in use.

Environmental: There was no exposure to household smoke.

Family history: Joshua was the first child for this healthy 24-year-old mother. There was no history of heart disease. The maternal grandmother was 40. The maternal grandfather was never involved with family. Brenda did not know his history and age. The father's family history was not available. Brenda did not talk with the father. As far as she knew, the father was well. They separated shortly after she became pregnant. The paternal family history was unknown.

> *The scenario of having only part of the family history was very common for my practice. Many times, the mother would no longer be talking with the father or any member of the father's family, so being able to do genogram became impossible. It was also common to have young mothers with no idea of their family health history. Family history would evolve over time.*

Medications: Poly-vi-flor .25/1 cc PO od.

Allergies: None.

Social history: Brenda was attending community college part time when she found out she was pregnant. She was a minimum-wage office worker who did filing until she became pregnant. She had no health insurance through her job. In order for her to get health insurance, she had to quit her job and go on welfare. Since her employment history was very spotty, she was able to qualify for welfare benefits and health insurance.

Religious aspects: Brenda attended church services on Sunday.

REVIEW OF SYSTEMS

General: Pleasant, active infant.

Skin: No rashes. Not easily bruisable.

Head: Denied any head injury or falls to ground.

Eyes: Denied any tearing, discharge, and redness.

Ears: No history of otitis. Mom states he responds to sounds.

Nose/sinus: No nose discharge.

Mouth/throat: No medical problems.

Dentition: None.

Neck: Denied wryneck, or difficulty turning head.

Respiratory: No history of wheezing.

Cardiovascular: History of murmur heard at two-month visit. Murmur heard in nursery and told normal newborn murmur.

Gastrointestinal: No vomiting. Normal bowel pattern history. No constipation.

Genitourinary: Denied UTI. Denies blood in urine or difficulty voiding. Denies any discharge or redness of external genitalia.

Musculoskeletal: Denied noticing any difficulty in extremity movement/stiffness.

Neurological: Denied any CNS infection. Denies any seizures or tremors.

Hematologic: Denied history of anemia, or any hematologic disease.

Endocrine: Denied any history of endocrine disease.

PHYSICAL EXAM

Alert, active baby with equal movements who cooed and smiled easily.

VS: RR 40, T 98.6, AR 110, BP 92/52 right arm, BP 102/62 right leg, Weight: 16 pounds 2 ounces (95th percentile), 65 cm (95th percentile), 43 cm (90th percentile).

Skin: Warm and pink, no lesions, bruising.

Head: Scalp without tenderness to palpation, lesions. Normocephalic. Anterior fontanel 2 cm by 2.5 cm. Posterior fontanel closed.

Eyes: Clear red reflex. No sign of strabismus.

Ears: Auricles normally formed and positioned. Canals clear. TMs bilaterally dull normal landmarks. Light reflex dull. No signs of scarring on drum.

Nose: No deviated/perforated septum or intranasal masses/polyps.

Mouth: No lesions present. Lips pink with cracking. Buccal mucosa pink, no tongue-tie or bifid uvula.

Pharynx: Without injection, tongue midline, able to protrude tongue, gag reflex intact.

Dentition: None.

Neck: Trachea midline, thyroid without enlargement. Freely moveable to 180 degrees. Follows objects without pain.

Lymph: No palpable anterior or posterior cervical, supraclavicular, scalene, occipital, axillary, epitrochlear, inguinal, or popliteal lymph nodes palpable.

Chest: No use of accessory muscles.

Lungs: Clear to auscultation anterior. No adventitious sounds.

Heart: S_1 and S_2 normal with regular rhythm II/VI vibratory systolic murmur heard at the lower left sternal border with heart sound heard better on the right side of the chest. Palpation of the apex or PMI was to the left of the nipple line on the right side of the chest. No gallop noted. Femoral pulses equal and regular.

Abdomen: Bowel sounds +, nontender. Liver 1 cm below left costal margins. Spleen tip not palpable.

Genitalia: Normal male, circumcised, both testes palpable and descended. The right testicle hung lower than the left testicle when you held the baby under the arms to the upright position.

Spine: Normal curvature, not tender to palpation.

Musculoskeletal: Full ROM. Negative Allis' sign, negative Barlow and Ortolani maneuvers.

Neurological: Biceps, triceps, brachioradialis reflexes ++ bilaterally.

Extremities: Full ROM.

Based on the above presentation, there were two issues — a murmur and a possible cardiac reversal. The murmur was less concerning since it was vibratory, nonradiating, and localized to the lower sternal border in a thriving infant. The overriding concern was a reversal of the heart and abdominal organs. The differential diagnosis for the latter should include:

1. Situs inversus

Situs inversus is present in .01% of the population (Wilheim & Holbert, 2003). Situs solitus is the usual arrange of organ vessels. Situs inversus is an anatomical arrangement that is the mirror image of situs solitus (Applegate, Goske, Pierce, & Murphy, 1999). The incidence of congenital heart disease with situs inversus is 3 – 5% (Strife, Bisset, & Burrows, 1998).

2. Kartagener's syndrome

Kartagener's syndrome was first described in 1933 (Fogg, 2004). However, it was recognized that anatomically abnormal cilia were not always immobile but could be dysfunctional, dyskinetic, and ineffective, and thus the name was changed to dyskinetic cilia syndrome or primary ciliary dyskinesia (Lillington, 2001). A 1984 review of immobile cilia syndrome points out that cilia have nine microtubules that are joined into a functional unit called the axoneme (Palmblad & Mossberg, 1984). The axoneme constitutes the locomotory machinery of cilia and spermatozoa (Palmblad & Mossberg). Situs inversus with dextrocardia is associated with Kartagener's syndrome 20% of the time (Gutgesell, 1998; Tkebuchava et al., 1996).

Kartagener's syndrome is a subgroup of disorders associated with primary ciliary dyskinesia (Afzelius & Bergstrom, 2004). Primary ciliary dyskinesia is a very rare congenital malformation comprising the classic triad of situs inversus, bronchiectasis, and sinusitis (Tkebuckava et al., 1996). The disease is an autosomal recessive disorder of the microtubules of ciliated cells. The most common cilial abnormality affects the cilia by an absence of the dynein arm which is responsible for ciliary motion (Milisav, 1998). Since the cilia are responsible for clearing the respiratory tract, stagnant mucus can build up and act as a media for the growth of bacteria and chronic infection. Males with Kartagener's syndrome are infertile (Fogg, 2004; Milisav, 1998).

To understand the link between the occurrence of abnormal ciliary function and the abnormal position of the body organs, one needs an understanding of embryology and genetics. When the organs are rotating, there are a variety of proteins including Sonic Hedgehog, Nodal, Lefty, and Pitx-2 on the left side of the body and Activin beta B, Snail, and Fibroblast Growth Factor-8 on the right side which influence normal rotation leading to the left-sided heart and normally positioned organs (Reidy, Sischy, & Barrow, 2000). Abnormal genes and therefore abnormal proteins lead to malposition.

Primary ciliary dyskinesias are characterized by a chronic cough, chronic rhinitis, and chronic sinusitis (Afzelius & Bergstrom). However, at this time, it was believed that this child had just situs inversus since he was an asymptomatic four-month-old.

3. Heterotaxy

Heterotaxy is also known as situs ambiguous. It implies a disordered organ arrangement in chest or abdomen. This is a disorderly arrangement of body organs. This usually occurs from the 28th to the 30th day of gestation. The incidence of congenital heart disease ranges from 50 to 100%. There is a predominance of males with the syndrome (Applegate, Goske, Pierce, & Murphy, 1999).

- *Polysplenia (left atrial isomerism): This syndrome is highly associated with congenital heart disease (Shannon, 2003). In this syndrome, both lungs have two lobes and branches of the bronchi given off below the point where the pulmonary artery crosses the bronchus. The main bronchus passes inferior to the ipsilateral main pulmonary artery on each side. In this syndrome there is a bi-lobed lung with midline liver and multiple spleens which are located along the greater curvature of the stomach, which can be anywhere in the abdominal cavity (Applegate, Goske, Pierce, & Murphy, 1999). Malrotation, transverse liver, and genitourinary abnormalities are associated with polysplenia heterotaxy syndromes (Shannon).*

- *Asplenia (right atrial isomerism): This syndrome is associated with congenital heart disease. Both lungs have three lobes and a main bronchus that is superior to the ipsilateral main pulmonary artery on each side. There is a midline liver and an absent spleen with variable location of the stomach. This syndrome is associated with congenital heart disease, intestinal malrotation, and asplenia (Shannon, 2003a). The infant can present with distress and cyanosis in the newborn period with an associated cyanotic defect such as total anomalous pulmonary venous return, common atrioventricular canal, univentricular heart, or transposition of the great vessels (Applegate, Goske, Pierce, & Murphy, 1999).*

4. Space occupying lesion

Bronchial tumors, bronchogenic cysts, and sequestrations are rare in infancy, but could cause mediastinal shift and shifting of the heart sounds (Laberge, Puligandla, & Flageole, 2005).

5. Congenital lobar emphysema

This usually presents with severe respiratory distress in infancy but can be delayed in 5% (Laberge, Puligandla, & Flageole, 2005). Congenital lobar emphysema affects the left and middle lobe, but the left upper lobe is the most common site. Due to overdistention, there can be atelectasis of the ipsilateral normal lung, and the mediastinum becomes shifted to the contralateral side with impaired function. This would be seen on chest X-ray. Asymptomatic congenital lobar emphysema may regress spontaneously so the patient can be observed (Laberge, Puligandla, & Flageole).

6. Congenital cystic adenomatoid formation (CCAF)

This is a rare congenital lung malformation (Vaughn & Zimmerman, 2002). These children can present with acute respiratory distress, recurrent lung infections, hemoptysis, dyspnea, and failure to thrive. There can be a mediastinal shift causing shifting of the heart sounds with decreased breath sounds on the affected side (Laberge, Puligandla, & Flageole, 2005). The chest X-ray shows a mass with air-filled cysts. The major mortality results from pulmonary compromise, but children can present later in childhood (Vaughn & Zimmerman).

The main differential for the heart murmur at the lower left sternal border included:

1. Vibratory (Still's) murmur

The most common innocent murmur is a vibratory systolic murmur (Still's murmur) which is most common between 2 and 6 years of age but can occur as early as infancy (Bernstein, 2004). The murmur has a twangy sound, and origins of this murmur may arise from the vibration of pulmonary valves during systole (Pelech, 2004).

2. Ventricular septal defect

A ventricular septal defect (VSD) can also present with a murmur at the lower left sternal border and is usually a loud, long, and rough murmur (McNamara, 1990; Pelech, 2004). The size of the VSD is not directly related to the intensity of the murmur. If the VSD is loud, there may be less pressure difference between the two ventricles and therefore the intensity of the murmur may be less (Pelech). The exam of a child with a VSD depends on the size of the defect, pulmonary blood flow, and pulmonary pressure (Bernstein, 2004). Very small defects with small left-to-right shunt flow can present with a soft, high-pitched murmur (Pelech). The infant with a small VSD is asymptomatic (Bernstein), and the murmur is usually picked up during a routine exam. If a murmur is loud and long, it can obscure the second heart sound (McNamara).

3. Coarctation of the aorta

Coarctation of the aorta is another acyanotic lesion which can be asymptomatic. The classic sign of coarctation of the aorta is decreased femoral pulses in comparison to the upper extremities as well as differences in blood pressure (Bernstein, 2004). In a normal person the systolic blood pressure in the legs is 10 – 20 mm Hg higher in the legs (Bernstein). A short systolic murmur may be heard in the 3rd to 4th intercostal space (Bernstein). In this child, the leg BP was greater than 10 mm Hg than the arm BP.

4. Tricuspid regurgitation

An isolated tricuspid regurgitation is uncommon in childhood unless accompanied by other abnormalities (Pelech, 2004). It is frequently associated with right ventricular dysfunction as well as Ebstein anomaly of the tricuspid valve which can present with cyanosis (Bernstein, 2004). There may also be an accompanied atrial septal defect. The murmur is usually holosystolic and low pitched (Pelech).

5. Mitral valve prolapse

This is the result of abnormal mitral valves and is usually not recognized until adolescence or adulthood (Bernstein, 2004). The apical murmur is systolic but is frequently accompanied by a click.

6. Transposition of the great arteries

Transposition of the great arteries is a cyanotic lesion which usually presents in the first days of life with hypoxemia and tachypnea (Bernstein, 2004). The second heart sound is usually single and loud with a soft systolic ejection murmur at the mid-left sternal border. If there is a transposition of the great arteries with a large accompanying VSD, the cyanosis may be mild and go undiagnosed in some infants for a few months (Bernstein). However, the murmur is usually loud and accompanied by a thrill (Pelech, 2004). In an l-transposition of the great arteries (corrected transposition), the signs and symptoms are variable. If the pulmonary outflow is not obstructed, the signs are similar to a VSD (Bernstein, 2004).

ASSESSMENT	PLAN
3-month-old with heart murmur and questionable situs inversus	1. Consult with attending physician 2. Chest X-ray, a-p & lateral now 3. Explain about the clinical findings and the need to seek cardiology referral to the mother 4. Cardiology referral 5. Be present when mom goes for cardiac appointment since she needs help to understand the abnormality

Chest X-ray: To confirm the exam findings, I put a paper clip covered by heavy bandages on the left shoulder and did the chest X-ray. The repeat film clearly showed a heart on the right side, a liver on the left side, a right-sided arch, and a reversal of the gastric bubble. Actually, Joshua had a total reversal or situs inversus. The mother was given a thorough explanation of the meaning of the findings. Since there is a 3 – 5% incidence of congenital heart disease observed in situs inversus with dextrocardia (Gutgesell, 1998), Joshua was referred for a cardiology appointment the next day. The most common kind of congenital heart disease with situs inversus is transposition of the great vessel.

The following day, Brenda brought Joshua for his cardiology appointment. I was in the room when the cardiologist arrived. After an examination, EKG review, and echocardiogram, it was determined that Joshua had a structurally normal heart, although it was reversed. The cardiologist told the mother, "This problem could have been missed his whole life. It is hard to find this anomaly." The child was asymptomatic, so he was followed carefully. There were no signs of intestinal malrotation. Lillington (2001) writes that usual course is recurrent upper respiratory infections in infancy or early childhood, which respond well to antibiotic therapy. Eventually, as they grow into adolescence, the chronic sinusitis, otitis media, and recurrent lower respiratory tract infections develop. In retrospect, the patient received what he needed, which was excellent follow-up until he was symptomatic.

Knowledge deficit of well-child care introduction	1. Review feeding with mom 2. Continue formula and no cereal 3. Safety measures: child will roll over 4. Importance of talking with infant 5. Discuss the normal immunization schedule 6. Review sleep pattern & stool pattern 7. Poly-vi-flor .25 mg/1 cc (at that time vitamins were started at the 2-month visit). Today, these vitamins would be started at the 6-month visit.

This mother needed the education and support. Health supervision visits were scheduled every month for the first six months. Young, high-risk mothers received education and support, and developed a relationship with the provider. Normal well-child teaching could be reinforced and problems were dealt with as they arose. The recommendations for health supervision visits with breastfeeding mother have changed so that those infants are seen at 3 – 5 days of life, 2 – 3 weeks of life (Section on Breastfeeding, 2005), and then follow the schedule of 2 months, 4 months, 6 months, 9 months, and one year. However, in 1980, well-child visits were monthly for the first six months, then every two months for the next six months. Thus, new mothers had nine scheduled visits during the first year of life, giving ample opportunity to educate, support, and get to know the family.

ASSESSMENT	PLAN
Knowledge deficit of situs inversus	1. Discuss what this means in terms of anatomy 2. Discuss why this would be important for health-care providers to know 3. To prevent misdiagnosis that results from failure to recognize reversed anatomy, it is important to inform all health providers of the reversal. For example, Joshua would have left lower quadrant pain as a presentation of appendicitis or left upper quadrant pain in cholecystitis.

The mother listened very carefully to the explanation of the disease process and what this would mean. She was also interested in what the cardiologist had stated about Joshua being able to go through his whole life without anyone picking it up. For many years, she never disclosed his problem when he presented for care to the ED. On several occasions, Brenda was told that this practice of withholding his underlying diagnosis was dangerous, and in case of a cardiac arrest, could pose a life-threatening problem. I suggested that she buy a medic alert bracelet. However, over the first eight years, she would never voluntarily tell health-care professionals about his anomaly. I thought she was embarrassed at not having a perfect child. When I queried her about this, she told me she liked to see if someone would pick it up. While education continued throughout these first eight years, ultimately it was the mother's decision to inform other health professionals.

Over the next eight years, Joshua had annual episodes of wheezing. Despite these episodes, Joshua continued to grow on the 90th to 95th percentile. Joshua's development was normal. By the time he was eight, his wheezing and coughing episodes increased to three to four episodes per year, associated with sinusitis.

YEAR 8 OF CARE

Joshua was admitted to a PICU with compartment syndrome. He had hurt his right lower leg and developed severe swelling. He underwent a fasciotomy to relieve the compartment syndrome. I did not know about the admission until after his discharge.

Compartment syndrome occurs when the tissue pressure in the leg is higher than the perfusion through the blood vessel (Sherk & Black, 2000). It is a medical emergency and can follow vascular trauma to the leg. Any injury including vigorous exercise can cause this problem. The compartment syndrome follows the path of the injury, and within the compartment the blood supply becomes increasingly compromised.

As the intracompartmental pressure rises, the perfusion pressure increases. Eventually the intracompartmental pressure rises so that it overwhelms the ability of the body to autoregulate and injury develops. Tissue perfusion equals the capillary perfusion pressure minus the intravascular pressure. When the tissues become hypoxic, vasoactive substances such as histamine and serotonin are released, increasing capillary permeability. This further increases pressure by fluid leaks into the tissue. Nerve conduction slows and anaerobic metabolism occurs, causing the pH to fall. At this point, muscles start to develop necrosis and myoglobin is released. If this cycle is not stopped before the blood supply is cut off, loss of limb can occur (Crowther & McCance, 2004). Pain with passive movement is the most common early manifestation. Sensory nerve conduction slows before motor conduction slows. The treatment of choice is a fasciotomy (King, King, & Coates, 2005).

Reidy, Sischy, & Barrow (2000) reviewed key points regarding special consideration when delivering anesthesia to patients with Kartegener's syndrome. The anesthesiologist must do a meticulous assessment of the cardiopulmonary system as well as use less irritating anesthetic agents.

Three days after discharge, the chief resident told me Joshua was admitted for compartment syndrome. A discussion of the case revealed that the situs inversus was not documented during the hospitalization. The next day, Brenda appeared for a follow-up hospital visit. I was concerned that she had failed to tell the doctors about Joshua's situs inversus. I re-educated her and she agreed to tell the doctors about his problem from that day forward.

YEAR 10 OF CARE

Reason for encounter: Asthma and yellow nasal discharge. Last visit was six months earlier for a well-child check-up.

History of present illness: This 10-year-old presented with a one-week history of persistent nasal discharge with the new onset of acute wheezing not responding to albuterol. Joshua had a persistent fever to 103 for three days, a mild frontal headache, and copious yellow mucus mixed with blood. Brenda reported using albuterol, normal saline, and inhaled steroids without relief of wheezing.

Past medical history: Over the past six months, he has been seen three times in the ED with wheezing. He had responded well to oral steroids, albuterol, and inhaled steroids. The mother had not been able to come for follow-up because she was going to school during the day when the clinic was open.

Joshua was symptomatic with shortness of breath at least two times a week over the past two months. The mother reported almost daily use of triamcinolone acetonide. The mother reported that his shortness of breath was interfering with his ability to play basketball. He was taken out of games due to obvious shortness of breath. Over the past two years, he had been treated for sinusitis on two separate occasions.

Neurodevelopmental: Joshua is in fourth grade and is a B student. His main problem was math and he received special help for his math problems.

CURRENT HEALTH STATUS

Sleep: Joshua slept on an eight-year-old mattress and a three-year-old pillow. Joshua reported that roaches crawled on him, disrupting his sleep. The mother reported that the present apartment had so many roaches that they were in the mattresses.

Nutrition: Joshua had an excellent appetite. His diet was low in fruits and vegetables. His calcium intake was inadequate, only drinking one small glass of milk a day and a daily cheese. The mother admitted that there is no grocery store nearby and so she had limited access to fresh fruit.

Elimination: One formed stool a day. Denies any constipation.

Safety: Apartment has smoke alarm. There were rats in the apartment, which the mother dispersed by acquiring two female cats.

Medications: Albuterol, Azmacort one puff bid prescribed. However, the mom uses one puff od.

Allergies: None

SOCIAL HISTORY

Brenda returned to school part-time. The apartment was not infested with roaches until four months earlier when new tenants moved in. The new tenants were dirty by the mother's history. She knew that Joshua needed a new mattress, but she could not afford it with the limited welfare fund. The family was struggling financially since the rent for the apartment was over 70% of the family income. Brenda took out a loan to go to school. Joshua had a baby sister, Janice, who was four years old and healthy. Joshua's father occasionally helped the family financially. There was no exposure to household smoke. There was no wood stove or wood-burning fireplace.

REVIEW OF SYSTEMS

General: Pleasant child who smiles easily.

Skin: No rashes. Not easily bruisable.

Head: Denied any head injury or falling to ground.

Eyes: Denied any tearing, discharge, and redness.

Ears: History of four episodes of otitis media.

Nose/sinus: Two episodes of sinusitis over the past two years.

Mouth/throat: No medical problem.

Dentition: One dental cavity in repair.

Neck: Denied wryneck, or difficulty turning head.

Respiratory: Asthma usually well controlled with inhaled steroids and albuterol.

Cardiovascular: Situs inversus. Innocent murmur.

Gastrointestinal: No vomiting. Normal bowel pattern. No constipation. No symptoms of reflux.

Genitourinary: Denied UTI. Denied blood in urine, or difficulty voiding. Denied any discharge or redness of external genitalia.

Musculoskeletal: Denied noticing any difficulty in extremity movement/stiffness.

Neurological: Denied any CNS infection. Denies any seizures or tremors.

Hematologic: Denied history of anemia, or any hematologic disease.

Endocrine: Denied any history of endocrine disease.

PHYSICAL EXAM

Alert, interactive, answers questions, pleasant.

VS: RR 28, T 102, AR 118, Weight: 100 pounds (90 – 95th percentile), 60 inches (90 – 95th percentile), BP 100/70

Skin: Warm and pink, no lesions, bruising.

Head: Scalp without tenderness to palpation, lesions. Normocephalic.

Eyes: Clear red reflex. No sign of strabismus.

Ears: Auricles normally formed and positioned. Canals clear. TMs bilaterally dull normal landmarks. Light reflex dull. No signs of scarring on drum.

Nose: No deviated/perforated septum or intranasal masses/polyps. Red mucosa with thick green purulent nasal discharge. Positive pain on pressure over the forehead as well as fullness and pain when bending head over.

Mouth: No lesions present. Lips pink with cracking. Buccal mucosa pink, no tongue-tie or bifid uvula.

Pharynx: Without injection, tongue midline, able to protrude tongue, gag reflex intact.

Dentition: None.

Neck: Trachea midline, thyroid without enlargement. Freely moveable to 180 degrees. Follows objects without pain.

Lymph: One cm cervical adenopathy freely moveable with enlargement of the tonsillar nodes at 1.5 cm. No palpable posterior cervical, supraclavicular, scalene, occipital, axillary, epitrochlear, inguinal, or popliteal lymph nodes palpable.

Chest: No use of accessory muscles, but inspiratory and expiratory wheezing bilaterally.

Lungs: Clear to auscultation anterior. No adventitious sounds.

Heart: S_1, S_2 normal splitting. Regular rhythm. II/VI vibratory systolic murmur heard at the lower left sternal border with heart sound heard better on the right side of the chest. PMI to the left of the nipple line on the right side of the chest. No gallop. Normal femoral pulses.

Abdomen: Bowel sounds +, nontender. No hepatomegaly.

Genitalita: Tanner II testicular volume. Normal male, circumcised, both testes palpable and descended. The right testicle hung lower than the left testicle.

Spine: Normal curvature, not tender to palpation.

Musculoskeletal: Full ROM.

Neurological: Biceps, triceps, brachioradialis reflexes ++ bilaterally.

Extremities: Full ROM.

ASSESSMENT	PLAN
1. Frontal sinusitis	1. Amoxicillin 500 mg PO tid for 10 days and normal saline nose drops qid 2. Explore environmental triggers 3. RAST testing

The frontal sinuses appear at age 7 to 8 and are not fully developed until the end of adolescence (Subcommittee on Management of Sinusitis and Committee on Quality Improvement, 2001). These same guidelines point out that acute severe sinusitis will present with a significant fever of 102 or greater with purulent nasal discharge for three to four days in a child who looks ill (Subcommittee on Management of Sinusitis and Committee on Quality Improvement). Joshua certainly met this 2001 criteria, and he was appropriately managed.

Amoxicillin at 40 mg/kg/day was the drug of choice in 1990. Pneumococcal resistance was not as significant a problem. A pubmed review showed out of the 235 pages of reference, over 200 pages are from 1980 forward. Pneumococcal resistance was present in the 1980s, but the problem grew during the 1990s. Augmentin was not, and is still not a first-line agent (Subcommittee on Management of Sinusitis and Committee on Quality Improvement, 2001). The 2001 guidelines for treatment of sinusitis would recommend the use of high-dose amoxil at 90 mg/kg. This was unnecessary in 1990. However, it would be important to note that aggressive use of antibiotics with a child with Kartagener's syndrome would be acceptable practice (Reidy, Sischy, & Barrow, 2000; Lillington, 2001). As far as the use of normal saline, this may help to liquefy secretions and prevent crust formation as well as act as a mild vasoconstrictor of blood flow (Subcommittee on Management of Sinusitis and Committee on Quality Improvement).

| 2. Acute asthma | 1. Start treatment with albuterol and give oral corticosteroid at 2 mg/kg
2. Re-evaluate after albuterol treatment
3. Look for triggers in the environment as a source
4. Medication at discharge
  • Albuterol via nebulizer qid for two weeks
  • Aerobid 250 mcg per puff bid for two weeks
  • Prednisone 60 mg in 20 mg doses tid for five days
5. Follow-up for asthma in two days (as listed below) and in two weeks
6. Use of peak flow meter to establish personal best and monitor asthma (see #5 below) |

1. Asthma is the most common pediatric chronic disease, affecting 7% of all children. African-American children have the highest rates (National Asthma Education and Prevention Program, 2002). It is a chronic inflammatory disease of the airways which is characterized by complete or partial reversible airway obstruction, increased mucus production, and airway edema (Laskey, 2003; National Asthma Education and Prevention Program). Genetics and environment play an influential role in the development of the phenotypic presentation, with urban patients with low income and exposure to cigarette smoke having an increased rate of asthma (Elward, Pollart, & Kline, 2002).

2. The child improved after a treatment with albuterol and oral corticosteroids. The wheezing was markedly less and the child was comfortable. New treatments for asthma available today that would have been excellent choices for Joshua include leukotriene inhibitors (Lasley, 2003).

3. Common asthma triggers include sinusitis and upper respiratory infections; indoor and outdoor allergens; food; aerobic exercise; irritants such as smoke, air pollution from dust and vapors; strong emotions; medications such as aspirin or beta blockers; gastroesophageal reflux disease; sulfites; and occupational exposures to allergenic or irritant substances.

4. The decision was made to significantly increase the inhaled steroids given the symptoms over the past three months. It was also important to get the environmental controls in place before the child was weaned to a lower dose of inhaled steroids. While the 1991 guidelines on asthma had not yet been issued, the use of inhaled steroids in my practice had been in place for about three years. Evidence-based practice was not a term at the time. However, there were weekly grand rounds as well as a weekly journal club that kept our practice current.

ASSESSMENT	PLAN

3. Environmental hazards	1. RAST testing for cockroach allergies, cat dander, dust, mold
	2. Advocacy for new mattress and pillow case
	    a. Called charitable agency social worker and explained situation
	    b. Write letter of support
	    c. Obtain an allergen-proof mattress covering and new pillow until new mattress can be obtained
	    d. Get funds for mother to buy roach "bomb"
	3. Recommend environmental controls
	    a. Vacuum mattress and floors as often as possible
	    b. Remove all stuffed animals from room
	    c. Keep child's bedroom as dust-proof as possible
	    d. In the spring, open the windows as often as possible
	    e. Keep food stored in refrigerator or in sealed containers
	    f. Change sheets as often as possible
	    g. Teach mother about using boric acid to prevent further roach infestation
	4. Follow-up in two days at the last appointment to maximize the mother's time in school

1. Cockroach excrement is a well-known allergen. RAST testing was done instead of a referral to an allergist since Brenda had significant difficulty making day appointments. Brenda did not want allergy shots and decided she would try environmental control once the RAST testing results came back. However, since the roaches were interfering with Joshua's sleep, I did want her to institute environmental controls to help her alleviate the roach situation. The RAST testing came back with +4 allergies to dust and cockroaches, but no allergies to mold. This enabled us to do targeted environmental controls.

2. A local charity had limited funds for special requests. In this case, I typed a letter of medical necessity and contacted the appropriate persons to arrange for a new mattress to be delivered. The mother called up Joshua's father for the funds to buy the "bomb" for the roaches. Unfortunately, in a poor community, resources were used up quickly.

3 – 4. The mother came for a follow-up for re-evaluation of the child's asthma, reinforcement of medication and environmental controls, and to see when Joshua could have a new mattress. Within one week, his asthma was under control; the "bomb" had significantly reduced the cockroach population; boric acid was put in the apartment; the new mattress was delivered; and the mother had successfully developed a plan for cleaning.

ASSESSMENT	PLAN
4. Situs inversus, Kartagener's syndrome	1. Pediatric pulmonologist consult for evaluation and pulmonary function tests 2. ENT consult 3. Explain reason for nasal biopsy to mom 4. Explain to mother need to follow up with pulmonologist every six months for continued monitoring of pulmonary function testing

1. The child with situs inversus can have pulmonary problems. Joshua's asthma would be classified as mild persistent in 2005. One of the criteria for referral to pulmonology was noncompliance. At times the "specialist aura" resulted in improvement in compliance. In making the referral, I was also concerned that the child could have bronchiectasis and Kartagener's syndrome. The pulmonologist was excited about seeing a child with Joshua's history. He felt that the child had Kartagener's syndrome and agreed with the ENT referral for a nasal biopsy to rule out immobile cilia syndrome. Immobile cilia syndrome has been renamed immobile ciliary dyskinesia.

2. The pulmonologist talked to the ENT about the way to do the biopsy. Lillington (2001) states that to demonstrate the typical ciliary abnormalities using electron microscopy, the specimens must be obtained and handled properly. However, if ciliary malorientation is the only manifestation, the diagnosis can be difficult (Lillington, 2001). Impaired mucociliary clearance can also be assessed by measuring the nasal taste transit time (saccharin test). This test has a high sensitivity but a low specificity with false positive in asthma, bronchiectasis, chronic bronchitis, CF, and acute respiratory infections (Lillington, 2001). Another method to look for cilial dyskinesia is looking for abnormal wave forms of ciliary beat frequency by scintigraphic methods.

3. Brenda agreed to the biopsy. The biopsy was nonconfirmatory and the pulmonologist wanted it repeated, but the mother refused. He felt that this child had Kartagener's syndrome although the diagnosis was not confirmed via a nasal biopsy of the cilia. Patients with Kartagener's syndrome have a normal life expectancy if their bronchiectasis is treated vigorously (Lillington, 2001).

5. Activity intolerance due to recurrent wheezing	1. Teach the mother about the need to limit activity while the child is wheezing 2. Reinforce the use of the peak flow meter 3. Get personal best so that child can monitor his lung function 4. Discuss need to give inhaler rescue medication such as albuterol if peak flow is low or child is asymptomatic 5. Stress the need for preventive medication

Brenda became very compliant with treatment since she could see the improvement in Joshua's activity tolerance. She initially was compliant with using the peak flow meter, but when he was better stopped using it. While the 1991 guidelines and the 1999 guidelines suggested the peak flow meter for monitoring asthma, the 2002 guidelines did allow either peak flow meter or symptom monitoring as a way of judging asthma severity (National Asthma Education and Prevention Program, 1991, 1999, 2002).

ASSESSMENT	PLAN
6. Sleep pattern disturbance	1. Better management of asthma as outlined above 2. Get a new mattress and pillow for the child as discussed above 3. Establish a bedtime regime of story and bath. Get medication before bedtime 4. Change sheets on a daily basis until new mattress is acquired

Richard Ferber (1995) discusses the difference in sleeplessness in different ages of children. In the school-age child, he feels that education of the parent is most important, and he stresses the need for consistency and firmness within a well-established bedtime ritual. Ferber, a sleep expert, pointed out the importance of consistency in nighttime sleep regimes. In Joshua's case, it was important to get the environmental issues solved, and to get the asthma under control. A bedtime regime was established and, by the two-week visit, the child was able to sleep through the night again.

ADDENDUM

After 14 years, Joshua was referred to another provider. His mother graduated from college, found a good job, and obtained private insurance. The pulmonologist continued to follow Joshua and reported his sinusitis became more chronic by mid-adolescence, convincing him that Joshua had Kartegener's syndrome. I was happy the family's quality of life had improved and Brenda was able to provide for her family.

References

Afzelius, B., Bergstrom, S. (2004). *Primary ciliary dyskinesia (immobile-cilia syndrome).* UpToDate Online, 2005: 13.1. Retrieved Mar. 13, 2005, from UpToDate database.

Applegate, K.E., Goske, M., Pierce, G., Murphy, D. (1999). *Situs revisited: imaging of the heterotaxy syndrome.* Radiographics, 19, 837 – 852.

Bernstein, D. (2004). *The cardiovascular system.* In R.E. Behrman, R.M. Kliegman, & H.B. Jenson (Eds.), Nelson Textbook of Pediatrics (pp. 1475 – 1598). Philadelphia, PA: W.B. Saunders Company.

Crowther, C.L., McCance, K.L. (2004). *Alterations of musculoskeletal function.* In S.E. Huether & K.L. McCance (Eds.), Understanding Pathophysiology (pp. 1071 – 1116). St. Louis, MO: Mosby & Co.

Elward, K.S., Pollart, S., Kline, K. (2004). *Asthma & allergies.* Retrieved on Mar. 12, 2005 at http://www.aafp.org/x28296.xml.

Ferber, R. (1995). *Sleeplessness in children.* In R. Ferber & M. Kryer (Eds.), Principles and Practice of Sleep Medicine in the Child (pp. 79 – 91). Philadelphia, PA: W.B. Saunders Company.

Fogg, E. (2004). *Diagnostic challenges from your case files: Kartegener's syndrome.* Journal of the American Academy of Physicians Assistants, 17, 52 – 55.

Gutgesell, H.P. (1998). *Cardiac malposition and heterotaxy.* In A.G. Garson, D.J. Fisher, & S.R. Neish (Eds.), Science and Practice of Pediatric Cardiology, Vol. 2 (2nd ed., pp. 1539 – 1561). Philadelphia, PA: Williams & Wilkins.

King, B.R., King, C., Coates, W.C. (2005). *Critical procedures.* In M. Gausche-Hill, S. Fuchs, & L. Yamamoto, (Eds.), The Pediatric Emergency Medicine Resource (pp. 752 – 754). Sudbury, MA: Jones and Bartlett Publishers.

Laberge, J.M., Puligandla, P., Flageole, H. (2005). *Asymptomatic congenital lung malformations.* Seminars in Pediatric Surgery, 14 (1): 16 – 33.

Lasley, M.V. (2003). *New treatments for asthma.* Pediatrics in Review, 24 (7): 222 – 234.

Lillington, G.A. (2001). *Dyskinetic cilia and Kartagener's syndrome.* Clinical Reviews in Allergy and Immunology, 21, 65 – 69.

McNamara, D.G. (1990). *Value and limitations of auscultation in the management of congenital heart disease.* Pediatric Clinics of North America, 37 (1): 93 – 114.

Milisav, I. (1998). *Dynein and dynein-related genes.* Cell Motility and the Cytoskeleton, 39 (4): 261 – 274.

National Asthma Education and Prevention Program (2002). *NAEPP Expert Panel Report Guidelines for the Diagnosis and Management of Asthma — Update on Selected Topics 2002* (NIH Publication No. 97 – 4051, pp. 1 – 280). Washington, DC: National Institutes of Health; National Heart, Lung, and Blood Institute.

NJ Family Care (2005). Retrieved on Mar. 11, 2005 from http://www.njfamilycare.org/.

Palmblad, J., Mossberg, B. (1984). *Ultrastructural, cellular, and clinical features of immotile-cilia syndrome.* Annual Reviews, 35, 481 – 491.

Pelech, A.N. (2004). *Heart sounds and murmurs.* In R.M. Kliegman, L.A. Greenbaum, & P.S. Lye (Eds.), Practical Strategies in Pediatric Diagnosis and Therapy (pp. 178 – 210). Philadelphia, PA: W.B. Saunders Company.

Reidy, J., Sischy, S., Barrow, V. (2000). *Anaesthesia for Kartagener's syndrome.* British Journal of Anaesthesia, 85 (6): 919 – 921.

Section on Breastfeeding (2005). *Breastfeeding and the use of human milk.* Pediatrics, 15 (2): 496 – 507.

Shannon, K. (2003). *Heterotaxy, polysplenia.* Retrieved Mar. 10, 2005. Available at http://www.emedicine.com/ped/topic2514.htm.

Shannon, K. (2003a). *Heterotaxy, asplenia.* Retrieved Mar. 10, 2005. Available at http://www.emedicine.com/ped/topic2513.htm.

Sherk, H., Black, J. (2000). *Orthopedic emergencies.* In Textbook of Pediatric Emergency Medicine, 4th ed. (pp. 1396 – 1402). Baltimore, MA: Williams & Wilkins.

Strife, J.L., Bisset, G.S., Burrows, P.E. (1998). *Cardiovascular system.* In: D.R. Kirks & N.T. Griscom (Eds.), Practical Pediatric Imaging: Diagnostic Radiology of Infants and Children, 3rd ed., 546 – 50. Philadelphia: Lippincott-Raven.

Subcommittee on Management of Sinusitis and Committee on Quality Improvement (2001). *Clinical practice guideline: management of sinusitis.* Pediatrics, 108 (3): 798 – 808.

Tkebuchava, T., Niederhauser, U., Weder, W., von Segesser, L.K., Bauersfeld, U., Felix, H., et al. (1996). *Kartagener's syndrome: clinical presentation and cardiosurgical aspects.* Annals of Thoracic Surgery, 62, 1474 – 1979.

United States Environmental Protection Agency (2004). *Asthma home environment checklist.* Retrieved on Nov. 12, 2004. Accessed at http://www.epa.gov/asthma/pdfs/home_environment_checklist.pdf.

Vaughn, D.J., Zimmerman, J. (2002). *Congenital cystic adenomatoid formation.* Retrieved on Apr. 2, 2005. Accessed at http://www.emedicine.com/ped/topic534.htm.

Wilheim, A., Holbert, J.M. (2003). *Situs inversus.* Retrieved on Mar. 15, 2005 at http://www.emedicine.com/radio/topic639.htm.

A 57-year-old woman with end-stage liver disease secondary to primary biliary cirrhosis referred for liver transplantation

PRE-TRANSPLANTATION INITIAL CONSULTATION

Initial visit with hepatologist

Patient Jane Smith presented to our center for a hepatology consultation on day 1. The patient was referred to our center by her community gastroenterologist for liver transplantation. Jane was a 57-year-old female and had end-stage liver disease (ESLD) secondary to primary biliary cirrhosis (PBC). The hepatologist performed a new patient consultation and then referred the patient to me, the nurse practitioner (NP), for a future consultation visit to begin a transplant evaluation. At the time of the hepatology consultation, and prior to meeting with me, the following standard transplant evaluation tests were ordered: abdominal ultrasound with Doppler, CT of the abdomen, EGD, stress test, ABG, PPD, bone density scan, mammogram, psychiatric consultation, social work consultation, pulmonary consultation, cardiology consultation, surgical consultation, MRI of the brain, carotid and transcranial Dopplers, neurological consultation, CXR, colonoscopy, and routine transplant laboratory testing. The patient started to obtain these tests and was given an appointment to see me in consultation two months later. The patient was instructed to see her endocrinologist for management of hypothyroidism.

Initial NP consultation was commenced on week 6 as part of the transplant evaluation process.

HPI: Jane was diagnosed with PBC 12 years ago after having abnormal liver function tests (LFTs) and a biopsy consistent with this diagnosis and was previously treated with Actigall. She reports that her complications of ESLD included mild encephalopathy exhibited by poor short-term memory and fatigue (despite the use of lactulose), and bilateral lower extremity edema (BLLEE).

PMH: PBC confirmed by liver biopsy, pulmonary sarcoidosis, hypothyroidism, atrial fibrillation (a-fib), childhood rheumatic fever, with mitral valve prolapse and immune thrombocytopenic purpura (ITP). There were no prior records to review, and all PMH was per patient report. She reports being asymptomatic from a pulmonary perspective until five years ago. The patient over her lifetime reports a history of frequent colds with cough. The patient underwent a workup for her dyspnea on exertion five years ago and was diagnosed with "sarcoidosis" by transbronchial biopsy, which revealed noncaseating granulomas. Pulmonary function studies dated three years prior to her visit with our office revealed a post-bronchodilator FVC of 2.35 liters, a post-bronchodilator FEV1 of 1.15 liters, and FEV1/FVC of 49%; a post-bronchodilator total lung capacity of 5.07 liters (89% predicted) and a DLCO of 14.

PSH: Mediastinoscopy which led to the diagnosis of pulmonary sarcoidosis, splenectomy (secondary to ITP), tonsillectomy.

Meds: Lactulose 2 tbsp tid, Actigall 300 mg tid, Coumadin 1 mg Sat, Sun, Mon, and Wed, Tenormin 25 mg bid, calcium 600 mg bid, combivent inhaler prn, Advair discus inhaler 500/50 bid, prednisone 20 mg qd for pulmonary exacerbation (last dose was 20 mg bid), Lanoxin 0.25 mg qd, Demadex

10 mg qd, quinine sulfate 325 mg qhs prn for muscle cramping, hydroxyzine 25 mg prn for pruritus. The patient denied any herbal supplements.

Allergies: PCN.

Family history: Mother deceased (80 years old) from unknown etiology. Father deceased secondary to coronary artery disease (80 years old). The patient has one sister who has Graves' disease.

Social history: Jane had worked full time as a teacher and was on disability leave. She is single and has no children. She denies any tattoos. She had a 40-pack/year smoking history. She quit 12 years ago. Her other occupational and environmental history is unremarkable. She has no documented beryllium exposure. She previously drank one unit of alcohol a few times per week. She stopped alcohol use when she was diagnosed with liver disease. She denies any history of drug use and lives with five cats.

ROS: The patient reports an intentional 30-pound weight loss over the last year, wears glasses, and has dental prosthetics. She otherwise reports good dental health. She has dyspnea on exertion (DOE) which has improved while on the prednisone. She reports easy bruisability and poor short-term memory. She is able, however, to manage her medications and care for herself without assistance. She also reports occasional dizziness, having had one fall leading to head trauma which was insignificant and didn't require any intervention. She specifically denies fever, chest pain, nausea, vomiting, diarrhea, genitourinary complaints, or depression. All other ROS was unremarkable.

> *Easy bruisability is a common symptom in cirrhotic patients. Patients with portal hypertension often have hypersplenism resulting in thrombocytopenia and are often coagulopathic due to impaired hepatic synthesis of coagulation factors. In addition, Jane is on Coumadin therapy, increasing her risk for coagulopathy. Additionally, prednisone therapy causes many side effects including bruising (Katzung, 1998). Hepatic encephalopathy is graded from 0 – 4. Grade 1 encephalopathy is often exhibited by forgetfulness (Green, 2004).*

PE: Ht. 5' 4", Wt. 170 lbs., afebrile with BP of 90/50. HR 88 and irregularly irregular. She appeared well with a steady gait and was alert and oriented to person, place, and time. She was lucid and her speech was normal without slurring. She was able to provide her medical history without assistance.

> *Cirrhotics are often hypotensive. The circulatory system is affected during cirrhosis due to its pathophysiological, clinical, and therapeutic relationships with the liver. Cardiovascular and circulatory changes are seen in the late stages of cirrhosis and involve subclinical latent cardiomyopathy with hyperdynamic circulation. However, this is clinically seen by increased cardiac output and decreased peripheral resistance (Merkel, 1993).*

Her oropharynx was benign. She had dental prosthetics, no cervical lymphadenopathy, and was anicteric. Her lungs revealed finely coarse breath sounds throughout all fields. Her cardiac exam revealed S_1, S_2, with an irregular rhythm, and a II/VI holosystolic ejection murmur (SEM) heard best at the second intercostal space left of the sternum. Jugular venous distention was not assessed.

> *Chronic mitral regurgitation can be caused by rheumatic heart disease or other etiologies. It can be diagnosed by characteristic physical findings including an apical holosystolic murmur (Green, 2004). Grade 2 murmurs are quiet but heard immediately upon placing the stethoscope on the chest (Bates, 1995).*

Her abdomen was soft, nondistended, and nontender, with bowel sounds and mild ascites exhibited by a fluid wave. Her skin was notable for multiple excoriations that she had self-inflicted secondary to pruritus. There were no signs of infection of these lesions. Psychologically and neurologically she was within normal limits. She had bilateral lower extremity edema (BLLEE) approximately 3+ up to her knees. Neurologically she was grossly intact. A full neurological exam was deferred, but there was no asterixis. Breast and rectal exams were deferred as they were done by the patient's referring physician and gynecologist.

> *Portal hypertension complicates cirrhosis and presents with ascites (Green, 2004). Testing for fluid wave is done by pressing on the midline of the abdomen and tapping on one flank sharply with fingertips. An impulse on the opposite flank suggests ascites. However, this test is often negative until ascites is marked, and can be positive in patients without ascites, making it lacking in sensitivity or specificity (Bates, 1995). Patients with PBC often present with symptoms of pruritus (Feldman, 2002). Patients with cirrhosis and portal hypertension often have abnormal extracellular fluid volume regulation, resulting in accumulation of fluid as ascites, edema, or pleural effusion (Cardenas, 2004).*

Labs: glucose 76, BUN 55, creatinine 1.4, Na 127, AST 66, ALT 69, TB 3.3, AP 184, Alb 2.7, K 4.6, INR 3.5, WBC 7.2, Hgb 9.6, Hct 32.3, PLT 321, AFP 3.7.

DIAGNOSTIC TEST RESULTS

At the time of this consultation, I reviewed the following test results ordered by the hepatologist as part of the transplant evaluation:

The EGD report was reviewed and revealed grade 1 esophageal varices without recent hemorrhage. There was a hiatal hernia with mild erosive gastritis.

> *Gastroesophageal varices occur in up to 60% of patients with cirrhosis, and 30% of those experience variceal hemorrhage within two years of the diagnosis of varices. Variceal size is an important risk factor for variceal bleeding. Grade 1 varices are considered small, without luminal prolapse (Feldman, 2002). Identification of varices allows the clinician to prophylax against bleeding episodes with pharmacologic therapy. Several drugs can be used in the treatment of portal hypertension induced varices. These recommended include beta blockers, long-acting nitrates, vasopressin, nitroglycerin, terlipressin, and somatostatin or octreotide (Feldman, 2002).*

CXR revealed a calcified lung nodule in the right middle lung lobe and cardiac enlargement.

Colonoscopy three years ago revealed benign adenomatous polyps. This was done to rule out any colon cancer that could proliferate at the time of transplant due to immunosuppression.

> *Extra-hepatic carcinoma is a contraindication for transplantation. For transplant candidates, curative therapy needs to have been performed, and a two-year period without recurrence is sufficient for most nonhepatic malignancies. However, for breast cancer, colon cancer, and malignant melanoma, longer periods of recurrence-free survival are desirable (Feldman, 2002).*

EKG was done to rule out any new cardiac arrhythmias. It revealed stable atrial fibrillation in a controlled rate.

MRI of the brain was done as the patient had revealed to the hepatologist that she had a history of syncopal episodes. It revealed T1 shortening in the basal ganglia bilaterally. The report commented that this was presumably related to hepatic disease and microvascular ischemic changes.

The CT of the abdomen, which was done to rule out hepatocellular carcinoma, which is more common in cirrhotics, revealed that there was no hepatic mass, confirmed splenectomy, and identified renal calculi.

> *Chronic cholestatic liver disease may be complicated by hepatobiliary malignancy. Early detection is of utmost importance in evaluating the candidate for transplantation (Jones, 1998). The gold standard for surveillance for hepatocellular carcinoma is undefined. However, in an analysis of these studies, the use of ultrasound in this setting was rated as weak evidence. In a study prospectively comparing ultrasound and computed tomography (CT) in a screening program, the sensitivity of CT (88%) was significantly higher than US (59%) (Bolondi, 2003). Alpha-fetoprotein (AFP) levels less than 20 ng/mL have less than 50% sensitivity for a diagnosis of HCC, but values greater than 200 ng/mL may heavily correlate with HCC. In addition, HCC is frequently detected when there is a significant rise of AFP even when the presence of mass on imaging is not found (Bolondi, 2003).*

Abdominal ultrasound was performed to verify hepatic vessel patency and rule out any biliary dilatation or stricturing. It revealed an enlarged, echogenic liver, with patent vessels and no biliary dilatation.

> *Color Doppler sonography is useful in observing abnormalities in blood flow, which are often seen in both diffuse and focal disease processes of the liver as well as in biliary abnormalities. Because the hepatic vessels are of large caliber and have significant flow, they are easily examined by ultrasound. Vascular invasion often occurs with hepatomas, and color Doppler is very useful in detecting involvement of the portal vein, hepatic vein, and inferior vena cava (Shapiro, 1998).*

An ABG was performed on room air, and revealed Ph 7.48, CO_2 44, PO_2 86, HCO_3 33, O_2 Sat 98%. ABG 100% oxygen revealed Ph 7.50, CO_2 43, O_2 638, HCO_3 33, O_2 Sat 99%. Her PPD was neg. This was done to rule out prior exposure to TB that could be reactivated post-transplant with immuno-suppression. An anergy panel was not done.

Pulmonary function tests revealed mild obstructive and restrictive airway disease. These revealed a post-bronchodilator FVC of 2.62 liters (76% predicted), a post-bronchodilator FEV1 of 1.56 liters (56% predicted), and a FEV1/FVC of 60%. Lung volumes reveal a TLC of 4.29 liters (76% predicted), a normal RV/TLC ratio, and DLCO 14.8 mL/mm Hg/min (65% predicted).

> *In attempt to rule out hepatopulmonary syndrome (HPS), and due to the patient's smoking history and history of sarcoidosis, a pulmonary evaluation was necessary and included pulmonary function testing to rule out restrictive or obstructive lung disease, or signs of HPS. An ABG was ordered to rule out hypoxemia and to assure that the patient could be oxygenated at 100% FiO_2 at the time of the transplant.*

> *Hepatopulmonary syndrome consists of hypoxemia, cirrhosis, and intrapulmonary vascular dilatation, without other pulmonary disease. The dilation of pulmonary pre-capillary vessels impairs diffusion-perfusion and causes unequal ventilation-perfusion. The diagnosis is made based on PaO_2 measurements on room air and 100% oxygen (Muller, 1999). In a prospective study of 111 patients with cirrhosis, a contrast echocardiogram, arterial blood gas, and pulmonary function testing were done to detect pulmonary vasodilation. 24% had HPS, and their mortality was significantly higher than the patients without HPS. The presence of HPS worsens the prognosis of patients with cirrhosis (Schenk, 2003).*

> *The PPD was ordered to rule out TB exposure. Mycobacterium tuberculosis causes active tuberculosis in only a small percentage of infected persons. Typically, it is latent, although*

immunosuppression can cause reactivation of a latent M. tuberculosis infection (Scanga, 1999).

Bubble echocardiogram was performed to rule out hepatopulmonary syndrome, to verify normal wall motion, and to rule out any signs of pulmonary hypertension. It revealed normal left ventricular (LV) size and normal ejection fraction. There was moderate mitral valve (MV) stenosis and no wall motion abnormalities. Her left atrium (LA) and right atrium (RA) were moderately dilated and there was mitral regurgitation (MR) and tricuspid regurgitation (TR) with an elevated gradient across the MV, indicating moderate mitral stenosis. There was a right-to-left cardiac shunt, indicating a possible patent foramen ovale. Additionally, the right atrial pressure measurement of 10 mm Hg calculates to a peak systolic pressure of 56 mm Hg (nl <40). There was moderate right atrial dilatation (with normal systolic function).

These findings were a concern for pulmonary hypertension. However, the accuracy of these echocardiographic findings being suggestive of pulmonary hypertension was unclear given the patient's underlying lung disease. A right heart catheterization was performed at a later date to accurately measure her PA pressures and formally evaluate her for pulmonary hypertension. A cardiac consultation was ordered which occurred at a later date.

Dobutamine stress test was performed and revealed an ejection fraction (EF) of 75% and no evidence of ischemia or coronary artery disease (CAD).

A cardiac evaluation with pharmacological stress test was performed to rule out exercise-induced ischemia. A bubble echocardiogram was done to rule out signs of pulmonary hypertension, wall motion abnormalities, or other pathology, especially given the patient's history of rheumatic fever.

The pre-transplant cardiac condition of patients is important in determining their peri-operative and post-transplant outcome after being exposed to the stresses of liver transplantation. Minor cardiac events may influence post-operative morbidity, and immunosuppressive therapy may have short-term effects with adverse effects on long-term cardiac risk. It is suggested that a Dobutamine stress test be performed in patients who have the presence of a clinical predictor for coronary artery disease, and that a two-dimensional and contrast echocardiogram are recommended to assess left ventricular function and estimate pulmonary artery pressure, and exclude intrapulmonary shunting (Therapondos, 2004).

Psychiatric consultation revealed adequate social support, euthymic mood, and appropriate affect. Her Axis I diagnosis was grade 1 hepatic encephalopathy; Axis II was deferred; Axis III was PBC with pulmonary sarcoidosis, atrial fibrillation, and hypothyroidism; Axis IV was moderate stress due to her recent retirement. She was deemed to have good coping skills, and there were no contraindications to transplantation. The psychiatrist recommended that she complete a health-care proxy and that she attend the transplant education workshops.

Social work evaluation was conducted, the patient was educated at that time about transplantation, and her insurance plan was verified. There were no contraindications for transplantation identified.

A psychosocial evaluation was implemented to include a consultation with the psychiatrist and social worker. The psychiatrist evaluation was requested to assess for appropriate coping mechanisms, or any potential for psychiatric imbalance post-transplant while on prednisone. The social worker was consulted to evaluate the patient's insurance status, home situation, and social support available to care for her.

The psychosocial factors of transplant candidates are important during the evaluation for listing patients (Twillman, 1993) and are widely used by transplant programs in determining candidacy for transplantation (Levenson, 1993). Patients post-transplant are typically given prednisone as center protocol as part of the immunosuppression protocol, which was the plan for Jane. In a study of 32 patients receiving bursts of prednisone, the patients were evaluated for mania and depression using the Hamilton Rating Scale for Depression, the Young Mania Scale, the Brief Psychiatric Rating Scale, and the Internal State Scale. They were measured before, during, and after corticosteroid use. There was a statistically significant change in mood during brief courses of corticosteroids, at modest doses, and the symptoms were primarily manic (Brown, 2002).

Carotid Dopplers revealed less than 40% stenosis bilaterally, and transcranial Dopplers were normal as well. It is the Center protocol to obtain carotid Dopplers on all patients over 60 or in patients who are symptomatic. Since Jane had a history of dizziness in the past leading to falls, the hepatologist had ordered a carotid Doppler to rule out an etiology such as carotid artery stenosis.

The carotid arteries are evaluated using a duplex scanner. Plaques, calcification, ulcers, or narrowing are identified and correlated with clinical symptoms. It can be used perioperatively to detect intravascular lesions (Doherty, 1997).

Mammogram revealed a new left breast calcification. The radiologist recommended that it be repeated for clarification. It was repeated, and a suspicious breast lesion was confirmed. A needle biopsy was recommended by the radiologist. The radiologist also recommended a follow-up mammogram in six months if the biopsy was negative.

Extra-hepatic carcinoma is a contraindication for transplantation. For transplant candidates, curative therapy needs to have been performed, and a two-year period without recurrence is sufficient for most nonhepatic malignancies. However, for breast cancer, colon cancer, and malignant melanoma, longer periods of recurrence-free survival are desirable (Feldman, 2002). Fine needle biopsies are a reliable and accurate technique for the diagnosis of breast lesions, with sensitivity in diagnosis neoplasm ranging from 90 – 98% (Doherty, 1997).

Consultation with the pulmonologist was conducted to determine her candidacy for transplantation.

This was necessary due to her diagnosis of pulmonary sarcoidosis, requiring prednisone therapy, a lung nodule noted on a prior chest CT done locally, which could have been a neoplasm, and mildly abnormal PFTs.

The pulmonologist felt that the patient had moderate obstructive and mild restrictive ventilatory defect on PFTs without hypoxemia and without intrapulmonary shunting. She commented that the lung function and diffusion capacity (DLCO) was stable for three years. Of concern was the pulmonary lesion, as the concern for cancer was present, which would exclude Jane as a transplant candidate, since extra-hepatic malignancy is a contraindication to transplantation, as described earlier. The pulmonologist recommended a biopsy of the lung lesion, given her pre-existing history of tobacco use, putting her at risk for primary lung cancer.

Bone density scan revealed osteopenia.

Osteoporosis and osteopenia can occur in patients with cholestatic liver disease. Bone mineral density should be done in all patients at the time of diagnosis of cholestatic liver disease (Green, 2004).

Hematology consult was not ordered, as the patient had already undergone splenectomy. It would have been warranted, however, to confirm that ITP was indeed her diagnosis and to verify that nothing else was present and missed by prior providers.

IMPRESSION (at the time of my initial consultation)

Jane was a 57-year-old female with PBC who was a Childs C cirrhotic with mild decompensation undergoing a transplant evaluation. The complications of ESLD included mild encephalopathy (*exhibited by fatigue and short-term memory loss*), edema, easy bruisability, and ascites.

> *The Child-Turcotte-Pugh classification is used to systematically score severity of disease among patients with end-stage liver disease (Brown, 2002). It has three classes: Childs A, B, and C. This scoring system was supported by a 15-year study of 620 patients with chronic liver disease (Lucey, 1998). Points are awarded for the grade of encephalopathy, amount of ascites, serum levels of total bilirubin, albumin, and INR. Patients with 7 – 10 points are a Childs class C, and are considered to have decompensated cirrhosis. Previously, these patients were considered to have met minimal listing criteria for transplantation with the United Network for Organ Sharing (UNOS).*

> *Jane has grade 2 encephalopathy, as evidenced by ongoing fatigue and forgetfulness in the setting of cirrhosis. The grading system for hepatic encephalopathy ranges from 0 – 4 with 0 being normal and 4 representing coma (Green, 2004). Blood that bypasses the liver is not detoxified and the blood levels of toxins increase (Butterworth, 2003). This awards her 2 Childs points. She has ascites on exam, so she is awarded 2 points. Her total bilirubin, albumin, and INR all together award her 6 points, giving her a total of 10 points, making her a Childs C cirrhotic. This Childs class exhibits the sickest cirrhotic patient.*

PLAN

The treatment of choice for decompensated PBC with impaired synthetic function is liver transplantation. I asked the patient to follow up with the additional testing and consultations needed (some already ordered prior to this visit by the hepatologist) for her to be listed for transplantation. I also asked that she obtain a Pap smear and follow up with a breast surgeon locally for breast lesion noted on the mammogram.

> *The best therapeutic alternative for patients who have end-stage PBC is liver transplantation (Feldman, 2002). Extra-hepatic carcinoma is a contraindication for transplantation. For transplant candidates, curative therapy needs to have been performed, and a two-year period without recurrence is sufficient for most nonhepatic malignancies. However, for breast cancer, colon cancer, and malignant melanoma, longer periods of recurrence-free survival are desirable (Feldman, 2002). The American College of Obstetricians and Gynecologists recommend that annual screening for cervical cancer be conducted in females under age 30. Women over age 30 who have had three consecutive test results negative for abnormality can extend screening to two or three years. However, it is still recommended that women obtain annual examinations (Ressel, 2003). Fine needle biopsies are a reliable and accurate technique for the diagnosis of breast lesions, with sensitivity in diagnosis neoplasm ranging from 90 – 98% (Doherty, 1997).*

I increased her calcium to tid with vitamin D, as she already had osteopenia, and was at increased risk for osteoporosis as she had PBC and ongoing prednisone use.

> *Osteopenic bone disease with its predisposition to spontaneous fractures is common in patients with chronic cholestatic liver diseases such as PBC. Treatment includes supple-*

mental calcium and vitamin D (Feldman, 2002). Glucocorticoid-induced bone loss is dose- and duration-related, develops rapidly (within months of therapy), and leads to an increased risk of fractures (McIlwain, 2003).

I recommended that an upper endoscopy (EGD) be repeated in one year to re-evaluate for any progression of esophageal varices and whether or not she needed prophylaxis with beta blockade for variceal bleeding.

Gastroesophageal varices occur in up to 60% of patients with cirrhosis, and 30% of those experience variceal hemorrhage within two years of the diagnosis of varices. Variceal size is an important risk factor for variceal bleeding. Grade 1 varices are considered small, without luminal prolapse (Feldman, 2002). Identification of varices allows the clinician to prophylax against bleeding episodes with pharmacologic therapy. Medication use for treating esophageal varices was explained earlier as described by Feldman in 2002.

Of note, prior to the next patient encounter, I checked the iron studies, which were normal. I received the Pap smear report by mail and it was negative for malignancy. Lastly, the patient was seen by a breast surgeon locally, and a biopsy of the breast lesion was performed and was negative for malignancy.

CONTINUATION OF TRANSPLANT EVALUATION PROCESS

On week 10, the patient had a cardiology consultation (previously ordered by the hepatologist for clearance for transplantation), in light of her history of rheumatic fever, subsequent mitral stenosis, and concern for pulmonary hypertension given her moderately dilated cardiac chambers. The cardiologist performed a right and left cardiac catheterization. She had an RA pressure of 20, RV 57/8, pulmonary artery (PA) 56/25, and pulmonary capillary wedge pressure (PCWP) 28 with cardiac output (CO) 4.5. Her cardiac index (CI) was 2.3.

The left cardiac catheterization revealed 30% stenosis of the proximal right coronary artery (RCA) and 50% stenosis of the left anterior descending artery (LAD). The cardiologist recommended that no treatment was necessary. At the time of the catheterization, the cardiologist felt that Jane was fluid overloaded and likely did not have true pulmonary hypertension. Therefore, the cardiologist recommended that she undergo aggressive diuresis and have a repeat right heart catheterization in order to optimize her cardiac status before reassessing her pulmonary hypertension. A trans-esophageal echocardiogram (TEE) was suggested to evaluate the degree of mitral stenosis and MR.

I presented the patient's case, including all test results and consultation recommendations, at the liver transplant multidisciplinary conference (surgeons, hepatologists, psychiatrists, social worker, financial coordinator, NPs, residents, fellows, medical students), and the plan for repeat catheterization after diuresis with TEE was agreed to. It was felt that this could be best handled if the patient were admitted to the hospital for close observation. The surgeon felt that a neurological consult should be performed given the findings on her brain MRI, and the history of syncopal episodes reported by the patient.

PRE-TRANSPLANT INPATIENT ADMISSION

The patient was admitted to the hospital by the cardiologist and was managed by the cardiologist. I rounded on the patient daily. On week 12 a TEE was performed and revealed left ventricular hypertrophy (LVH) with hypokinesis, a thickened MV with stenosis, and moderate MR. There was trace aortic insufficiency and moderate TR. There were no shunts seen and there were no masses or thrombi. The pulmonary artery was dilated and there was mild atherosclerotic disease of the thoracic aorta.

She was successfully diuresed, and after a 21-pound fluid weight loss, her ascites and edema had resolved. The Coumadin was held to prevent any bleeding, and she underwent repeat right cardiac catheterization.

> *According to the American College of Cardiology, the American Heart Association, and the European Society of Cardiology, it is the consensus that patients with atrial fibrillation, who do not have mechanical valves, can have anticoagulation held for up to one week for procedures that carry a risk of bleeding (Fuster, 2001). The guidelines for patients with atrial fibrillation can be generalized to patients with co-existing valvular disease (Singer, 2004). However, Fuster, 2001 describes that patients with rheumatic mitral valvular disease fall into Class I for anticoagulation, and recommends that these patients should be anticoagulated with a target INR of 2 – 3 (Fuster, 2001). Therefore, it may have been beneficial to administer heparin to Jane, which is shorter acting, until the day of the procedure. The liver transplant team followed the recommendations of the consulting cardiologist.*

The diuresis was successful, and revealed a reduction and improvement in her hemodynamic pressures. Her RA pressure was 5, RV 29/2, PAP 26/7, PCWP 11, CO 4.4, CI 2.4. It was recommended by the cardiologist that we avoid any fluid overload in Jane, and maintain her in a dry/euvolemic state. I educated the patient to monitor daily weights, aiming to keep her weight at approximately 150 pounds (which was weight at time of catheterization). The cardiologist suggested using a beta-blocker to avoid tachycardia, which she may not have tolerated peri-operatively. She was cleared for liver transplantation from a cardiac perspective.

> *Beta-blockers can be used to avoid tachycardia-induced drops in cardiac output. Jane would also need to have antibiotic prophylaxis to prevent bacterial endocarditis related to her valvular disease.*

The neurological consultation recommended by the multidisciplinary team was performed while the patient was in the hospital, and the patient was cleared for transplantation by the neurologist. He felt that the findings on brain MRI were insignificant.

During the hospitalization for the above cardiac workup, Jane sustained a fall and complained of subsequent back pain. A lumbosacral spine film was negative for fracture; however there was loss in height of L3-L4. She continued to complain of back pain, in the setting of recently having had a cardiac catheterization, therefore a retroperitoneal bleed was of concern. She underwent CT of the abdomen, which was negative for retroperitoneal bleed.

> *Retroperitoneal bleeding is a rare but serious complication after cardiac catheterization. A retrospective review of 9585 femoral artery catheterizations over five years was conducted. The investigators identified and evaluated all of the patients with retroperitoneal hemorrhage. Retroperitoneal hematoma developed in 0.5% of patients. Statistically significant predictors of this complication included being a female sex, low platelet count, and excessive anticoagulation. There were several signs and symptoms that were noted, including severe back and lower quadrant pain in 64% of patients with retroperitoneal hematoma (Kent, 1994).*

One week later, while the patient was still an inpatient, I presented the patient's case again at our multidisciplinary conference. I presented the following concerns: Jane's cardiac status, including MV stenosis and pulmonary hypertension when fluid overloaded, and cleared by cardiologist; the patient's stable pulmonary nodule; and the patient's debilitation secondary to back pain was discussed. The team was concerned about her ability to tolerate transplantation with her cardiac status given the frequent fluid shifts that typically occur during transplantation, but were confident in the clearance by the cardiologist. They were also concerned about a possible pulmonary malignancy. The plan was that the patient would have a follow-up consultation with the pulmonologist.

DECISION TO DISCHARGE PATIENT TO LONG-TERM REHABILITATION CENTER

The team felt that she was too debilitated to undergo transplantation, so I suggested to the team that she undergo physical rehabilitation in a long-term care facility for her back pain, as she was bed-bound. All were in agreement that if she could rehabilitate, then she could be considered for transplantation.

I initiated a repeat pulmonary consult. The patient underwent repeat pulmonary consultation while still an inpatient, on week 13. A repeat CT of the chest had been done a month earlier as an outpatient, and revealed that the pulmonary lesion had reduced in size. This encouraging finding led the pulmonologist to believe that the lesion was likely to be inflammatory, and concern for malignancy was low; therefore, the previously planned biopsy of the lesion was deferred. She was cleared for transplantation from a pulmonary standpoint.

Jane was discharged from the hospital into an inpatient rehabilitation center with help from the social worker who obtained placement/insurance clearance.

I arranged an outpatient visit with the rehabilitation center. I arranged for the patient to leave the long-term care facility and attend her clinic visit with me via ambulette transportation. The patient reported ongoing back pain to me, despite receiving care in the inpatient rehabilitation center. I ordered an MRI of the lumbo-sacral spine, which revealed a bilateral sacral fracture, and an MRI of the pelvis revealed a compression deformity in L3 with a bulge of the L2-3 disc space. I felt that the patient should remain in the long-term rehabilitation facility, optimizing her candidacy for transplantation. After two months, she gained strength, was ambulatory, and was strong enough to undergo transplantation. VNS services were instituted to do home assessments of the patient and educate her further.

> A retrospective review of 21 cases of severe back pain of various causes was conducted. Patients with back pain were evaluated with MRI, in addition to conventional modes such as regular X-rays, CT scans, and radionuclide studies. There was a characteristic pattern on MRI of the patient's lesion and signal intensity that helped delineate the etiology of back pain. In conclusion, it was noted that the MRI was particularly suited to use in the differential diagnosis of nonspecific back pain (Abram, 1988). However, the order in which one would begin the diagnostic workup is typically based on clinical information, as starting with an MRI is a costly first choice for a radiological diagnostic evaluation.

The patient's case was again presented at the multidisciplinary conference, and all were in agreement that she was an appropriate risk for transplantation. I listed Jane for transplantation that day.

ON THE TRANSPLANTATION WAITING LIST

I saw the patient in follow-up. She reported being advised by her local physician to take in more oral fluids despite our instructions to limit volume intake with a goal to maintain her weight at 150 pounds for her cardiac status. The patient was afebrile, denied pedal edema, but had abdominal ascites which was ongoing. On exam, I noted a decubitus ulcer on her buttocks that had occurred during her stay in the hospital and in the long-term care facility. The visiting nurse was managing it at home, and it was healing (currently at stage 2). Her exam revealed bilateral pulmonary crackles halfway up the lung fields. I planned for the patient to continue to maintain diuresis. The patient was counseled for 40 minutes on diet and sodium restriction to prevent edema, and encouragement was provided for protein intake in small amounts in order to avoid encephalopathy.

> *An excess of nitrogen worsens hepatic encephalopathy. Restriction of dietary protein at the time of encephalopathy with subsequent increments to assess tolerance is a "classic cornerstone of therapy." However, it may result in malnutrition and aggravate the prognosis. According to the practice guidelines for hepatic encephalopathy, protein can be withdrawn during acute episodes and then increased according to tolerance, while using pharmacologic measures (Blei, 2001). Jane was being treated with lactulose as a pharmacologic measure. I recommended protein in small amounts in order to assess tolerance to protein intake. If tolerated, the amount could be increased accordingly in order to prevent malnutrition.*

The patient had routine laboratory testing at the time of the visit. Labs were stable and the results were sent to her local doctor (per her request) for Coumadin management. I ordered a hospital bed with an air pressure mattress, to promote wound healing of the decubitus ulcer and prevent additional ulcers. I wrote a letter of medical necessity (LOMN) to the insurance company to support the need. They determined that the need was justified, and the bed and mattress were delivered.

> *The amount of anticoagulation for atrial fibrillation involves a balance between preventing ischemic stroke and avoiding hemorrhage. Maximum protection against ischemic stroke is achieved with an international normalization ratio (INR) of 2 to 3, and an INR range of 1.6 to 2.5 is considered ineffective at preventing stroke (Fuster, 2001), especially in light of her coexisting mitral stenosis.*

TRANSPLANTATION

On week 17 the patient was called into the hospital from home by the surgeon for orthotopic liver transplantation. After being NPO and obtaining pre-operative testing by the transplant fellow, including laboratory testing, CXR, and EKG, the patient was transplanted. A hepatectomy with choledocholedochostomy liver transplantation was performed, and the patient was transferred to the surgical intensive care unit (SICU). The patient received a cytomegalovirus (CMV) antibody positive donor, which put her at high risk for CMV infection, as she was CMV antibody negative at the time of transplantation. The patient also received a donor liver that was hepatitis B core antibody positive. According to the operative report, the estimated blood loss was difficult to estimate. However, she received: Plasmalyte 2000 mL, Hextend 1000 mL, albumin 1000 mL, cell-saver blood 5 units, packed red blood cells 6 units, fresh frozen plasma 13 units, platelets 6 units.

> *Receipt of a hepatitis B core antibody positive donor liver means that the donor had been exposed to hepatitis B in the past, but did not currently have active infection. The significance of this for Jane is that she will require lifetime suppressive HBV therapy with lamivudine, in order to prevent de-novo hepatitis B. In a retrospective study, 12 patients received liver transplants from hepatitis B core antibody positive donors over three years. All patients receive hepatitis B immune globulin for seven days post-transplant and also received lamivudine. All recipients were hepatitis B negative pre-transplant. None of the recipients have become infected with hepatitis B with a follow-up of 38 months. The investigators concluded that the peri-operative use of hepatitis B immune globulin used with long-term lamivudine can prevent hepatitis B infection in recipients of grafts from hepatitis B core antibody positive donors (Holt, 2002).*

The hepatectomy pathology report of Jane's native liver revealed cirrhosis, with chronic cholestasis and bile duct paucity, consistent with late PBC.

POST-TRANSPLANTATION

Inpatient management/Surgical ICU

Jane's intraoperative course was smooth, without complications, and she was transferred to the SICU intubated. The SICU team managed the patient until she was transferred to the transplant floor. I rounded on the patient daily. The SICU resident and team wrote all orders. While in the SICU, she was weaned from the ventilator and extubated. On post-operative day 1 (POD #1), Jane had a new troponin leak, with a peak of 23 ng/mL (normal 0 – 0.4 ng/mL) and electrocardiogram (EKG) findings consistent with a new septal infarct. An echocardiogram was ordered and confirmed that the heart motion was normal, making a new myocardial infarction less likely. The troponin levels decreased daily until normal on POD #4.

> *Approximately 75% of patients with acute coronary syndromes have abnormal EKGs. In patients with no EKG changes, a rise in cardiac isoenzymes including CK-MB or troponin is usually definitive. However, in this patient without significant coronary artery disease, a normal echocardiogram made the diagnosis less likely. Troponin levels typically increase 3 – 12 hours after the onset of myocardial infarction and peak at 24 – 48 hours. Then the troponin levels are expected to return to baseline within 5 – 14 days (Green, 2004). Troponin I marker levels begin to increase within 4 – 6 hours after acute myocardial infarction, and peak between 10 and 24 hours. It returns to normal between approximately 10 and 15 days, with 95% specificity and at least 98% sensitivity (Wallach, 1996).*

She was followed as an inpatient by the cardiologist with echocardiogram and EKGs. She had normal LV function and no cardiac wall motion abnormalities. She had ongoing mitral stenosis and mitral regurgitation, which were pre-existing. Her follow-up EKGs were unchanged and returned to baseline.

She continued to receive antibiotic prophylaxis with Levaquin due to her MS, central line in place (risk for infection seeding the valve), and history of rheumatic fever. Levaquin was used instead of gentamicin or vancomycin, as these are typically avoided post-transplantation for preservation of renal function in light of coexisting nephrotoxic drugs. A routine post-transplant abdominal ultrasound was ordered to verify patency of hepatic vessels, which was normal.

> *Prophylaxis with antibiotics is recommended for patients who have cardiac valvular disease and are planning to undergo procedures that can cause bacteremia (Taubert, 1998).*

> *The ultrasound was done to rule out any hepatic artery or vein thrombosis, which is a common complication immediately post-transplant. Vascular problems are a major cause of graft failure after liver transplantation, and include thrombosis, stenosis, pseudoaneurysm, and rupture. Doppler ultrasound is the initial modality of choice for screening for vascular complications. It is highly sensitive and specific (Norman, 2001).*

On POD #3, Jane was tolerating clear fluids without vomiting. Her vital signs remained stable and liver function was improving daily. Her pain was managed with morphine sulfate IM for pain, as needed. Lasix, a loop diuretic, was used to correct the fluid overload sustained by IV fluids given intraoperatively. The nurse obtained finger blood glucose measurements every six hours, since the medications, specifically prednisone, frequently result in hyperglycemia. Bilateral Venodyne compression boots were used on bilateral lower extremities to prevent deep vein thrombosis (DVT) due to immobility. She was transferred to the floor.

DVT prophylaxis should include mechanical prophylaxis with graded compression stockings and pneumatic compression devices, which are almost as effective as low-dose subcutaneous heparin administration (Doherty, 1997).

INPATIENT FLOOR MANAGEMENT

That same week, I called her local referring physician and provided an update on her status. I continued to round on the patient. The residents and physician assistants wrote the orders for the patient. On POD #5, thyroid function tests were ordered as the patient was on Synthroid, and Prograf was started to prevent rejection. The patient was treated with ganciclovir for CMV prophylaxis; she received a CMV positive donor, and she was CMV negative, making her high risk for contracting CMV infection.

When the donor is CMV positive, and the recipient is CMV negative, the risk of CMV infection post-transplant is approximately 60 – 70% (Norman, 2001).

On POD #7, the patient had a normal bowel movement and felt stronger daily. She had mild incisional pain controlled with Percocet. On POD #11, the patient complained of constipation, and a Dulcolax laxative suppository was ordered for Jane, with an effective result. She denied pain, so the narcotics were discontinued, *which would help with the constipation.*

Bisacodyl stimulates colonic peristalsis. Medications such as opiates, and metabolic diseases such as hypothyroidism, may contribute to constipation. Additionally, lack of exercise and prolonged immobilization can lead to constipation (Green, 2004).

She had an episode of uncontrolled atrial fibrillation with a heart rate of 130 beats per minute during the night. The resident consulted with the cardiologist who decided to increase the frequency of the beta-blocker to every six hours to maintain a normal heart rate. The patient was asymptomatic during the episode. She reported feeling better daily. I was aware of the daily management of the tacrolimus (Prograf) level with daily dosage changes to keep the level approx. 10 – 12 during the immediate post-operative period.

Tacrolimus (Jane is on the brand Prograf) is a macrolide antibiotic that works as a calcineurin inhibitor, which prevents rejection post-transplant. Tacrolimus dosing is based on trough blood levels (recommended at 5 – 15 ng/mL) (Green, 2004).

The ganciclovir was converted to PO valganciclovir, per center protocol. It was planned that the patient would continue this for three months post-transplant to prevent CMV infection.

ACUTE INPATIENT REHABILITATION

On week 18, the patient was transferred to the acute rehabilitation center for her deconditioning with continued cardiology follow-up. Her EKGs continued to be unchanged and the patient had a successful rehabilitation in the rehab facility. Her liver function had normalized. At the time of discharge from the facility, the patient was discharged to home with the following community resources: visiting nurse services (VNS), physical therapy, and occupational therapy several times per week at home.

DISCHARGE PLANNING

I educated the patient and family caregiver for two hours, while an inpatient, on medication purposes and side effects. She was also educated with verbal and written information about the post-transplant care at home including foods, exercise, and driving instructions. I gave her a follow-up appointment with me in the transplant outpatient office. She was educated to have her Coumadin managed weekly by her outpatient regular physician. I clarified orders with VNS. I ordered the patient's medications through a mail-order pharmacy that participated with the patient's insurance. This was clarified by the social worker. The social worker worked with the financial coordinator to explain to the patient her required and expected co-payments for each drug. She was able to afford the co-payments for these medications, and this was evaluated pre-transplant by the financial coordinator. I consulted with the Doctor of Pharmacy for the transplant center and reviewed the medications for drug interactions. Although the medications required specific administration guidelines, there were no medication interactions that would not be avoided with proper administration of the drugs. Medications were delivered to me, and I brought them to the patient's bedside for review. We practiced filling her pill-box that would be used at home, and the patient demonstrated this accurately.

> *The one-on-one education that I provided with the patient was aimed at explaining the indications for each drug, and to teach her how to identify the medications, learn possible side effects, and help prevent errors during at-home administration.*

The medications at the time of discharge from the acute rehab on week 19 included:

- Prograf 7 mg PO bid (*anti-rejection immunosuppression*)
- Cellcept 1 g PO bid (*anti-rejection immunosuppression*)
- Prednisone 15 mg PO qd (*steroid anti-rejection immunosuppression*)
- Lamivudine 100 mg PO qd (*hepatitis B prophylaxis as pt received HBV core Ab pos liver*)
- Valganciclovir 900 mg PO qd (*CMV prophylaxis as pt received CMV Ab pos liver*)
- Nystatin susp. Swish and Swallow 5 cc qid (*antifungal for thrush prophylaxis since immunosuppressed*)
- Digoxin 0.125 mg PO qd (*for control of atrial fibrillation*)
- Materna MVI 1 tab PO qd (*vitamin supplement until eating normally*)
- Bactrim 1 tab PO Mon/Wed/Fri (*for pneumocystis carinii pneumonia prophylaxis since immunosuppressed*)
- Oscal-D 500 mg PO tid (*supplement to prevent worsening osteoporosis secondary to steroid use*)
- Protonix 40 mg PO bid (*proton pump inhibitor to prevent duodenal ulcers common from Cellcept*)
- Actigall 300 mg PO tid (*to improve bile flow post-transplant*)
- Synthroid 50 mcg PO qd (*thyroid hormone to treat hypothyroidism*)
- Colace 100 mg PO tid (*stool softener to prevent straining post-operatively*)
- Coumadin 1.5 mg PO qd (*blood thinner for thrombosis prophylaxis since pt has a-fib; ordered by cardiologist*)
- Metoprolol 25 mg PO q6 (*beta blocker to control heart rate with a-fib; ordered by cardiologist*)
- Epogen 40,000 u sq q week (Saturdays) (*growth factor for anemia of chronic disease*)
- Vitamin D q Thursday (*a supplement to help calcium get absorbed to prevent worsening of osteoporosis*)
- Fosamax 70 mcg PO q Mon (*biphosphonate used to treat osteoporosis*)
- Advair Diskus 100/50 bid (*inhaler for asthma; ordered by pulmonologist*)
- *Combivent* 2 puffs q6 prn (*inhaler for asthma; ordered by pulmonologist*)
- Florinef 1 mg PO qd (*used to treat hyperkalemia induced by Prograf; common side effect of Prograf*)
- TEDS Hose to be worn during the day on lower extremities (*compression stockings to prevent worsened pedal edema*)

Laboratory results upon discharge were stable and included: INR 2.58, sodium 142, potassium 5.5, BUN 28, creatinine 1.2, Prograf trough level 11.4, WBC 5.7, Hgb 8.0, Hct 27.7.

OUTPATIENT MANAGEMENT

On week 20, I made a follow-up phone call to the patient at home to assess her progress. The patient complained of weight gain of approximately 10 pounds over the last week. The patient was advised to reduce her fluid and sodium intake and would be re-evaluated in the office that week. She complained of a productive cough of white sputum and that her Advair Diskus was a different, lower, dose than she took pre-transplant. I clarified these orders with the pulmonologist and called them into the pharmacy. She requested additional teaching for her Procrit injections, which I planned for her next visit.

> *Iso-osmolar extracellular fluid overload was suspected with the patient's history, and symptoms such as shortness of breath, weight gain, and dyspnea. If a cardiac component is suspected, it is managed by the "three D's," to include diuretics, digitalis, and diet. The patient was already on digitalis, and once evaluated could be placed on diuretic therapy. A diet low in sodium reduces fluid volume since less sodium is available for water retention (Monahan, 1998).*

That same week Jane had a follow-up visit with me. The patient was evaluated for her weight gain and for other routine post-operative issues. The patient reported feeling well with the exception of the cough. Her vital signs were stable. On physical exam she had bilateral pulmonary rhonchi. Her weight was stable and her atrial fibrillation was in control, at a normal rate. She had 2+ BLLEE with TEDS hose on. At the time of the visit, lab testing was done to check her renal function before starting her on diuretic therapy.

> *The risk of acute renal insufficiency exists with the use of combination nephrotoxic agents such as the immunosuppressive agents and Lasix combined. Post-operative acute renal failure is a complication resulting in high mortality. Patients may be at risk for this problem because of an underlying medical problem, nature of surgery, nephrotoxin exposure (Prograf, furosemide, valganciclovir), or a combination of factors (Reddy, 2002).*

The differential diagnosis for the bilateral edema in Jane included a side effect of Florinef therapy, right heart failure, or thyroid dysfunction. I checked the computer for the result of the TSH, which had been sent on the day of Jane's discharge, approximately one week prior. It was elevated at 51.23. Since the TSH was elevated, I increased her Synthroid dose to 125 mcg qd. A repeat TSH was sent, as this was the only TSH value in the system. Since this was a surprising level, I wanted to repeat the test to verify that it was indeed 51.23, and that it wasn't a false reading. Additionally, I wanted to see if the level was rising or falling, as a trend had not yet been established.

> *The etiologies for edema include heart failure, pericarditis or restrictive cardiomyopathy, nephrotic syndrome, hypoproteinemia, cirrhosis, drug side effects, pregnancy, chronic venous insufficiency, lymphedema, myxedema, and idiopathic edema (Cho, 2002). Given Jane's history of cardiac abnormality and a-fib, hypothyroidism, and use of Florinef, these were the most likely causes for her edema. A 24-hour urine may have been helpful to rule out nephrotic syndrome, although this was not done. Florinef is a synthetic corticosteroid and has potent salt-retaining activity (Katzung, 1998), which could subsequently lead to edema.*

> *In suspected primary hypothyroidism, plasma TSH is the best initial diagnostic test. A markedly elevated value (>20) confirms the diagnosis. The goal of therapy is to maintain TSH within normal range (0.35 – 6.20) using therapy with levothyroxine. The usual dose is 100 – 125 mcg qd and most patients require between 35 – 150 mcg qd (Green, 2004).*

The patient was started on Lasix at 20 mg qd for edema. I stopped the Florinef (used to reverse her inpatient hyperkalemia), as this can cause edema. The Lasix being started should stabilize her potassium, allowing it to remain normal without the Florinef.

> *A loop diuretic such as Lasix was the chosen agent as it is not potassium sparing, and patients post-transplant who are on immunosuppressive agents are at risk for hyper-kalemia. Loop diuretics usually have the most effect for diuresis (Cho, 2002).*

> *Florinef is a synthetic corticosteroid and has potent salt-retaining activity (Katzung, 1998), which could subsequently lead to edema.*

The differential diagnosis for the productive cough included typical or atypical pneumonia, CMV pneumonitis, pulmonary sarcoidosis exacerbation, viral syndrome, or other opportunistic infection. A CMV DNA PCR was sent to rule out CMV pneumonitis.

> *CMV can affect a broad range of organs. Progressive CMV can cause leukopenia, thrombo-cytopenia, pneumonia, gastrointestinal ulceration, hepatitis, and other syndromes. The most valuable diagnostic test for diagnosing CMV infection is with a serum CMV DNA, by polymerase chain reaction (PCR) (Norman, 2001).*

I ordered a stat chest X-ray to rule out pneumonia or other etiology for the productive cough, and prescribed empiric treatment for pneumonia with Levaquin (a fluoroquinolone) 500 mg qd for 14 days pending the results of the chest X-ray.

> *Fluoroquinolones are extremely well-tolerated, broad-spectrum agents. They are effective in infections of soft tissues, bones, joints, intra-abdominal infections, and respiratory infections, including infections resistant to multiple drugs (Katzung, 1998).*

A sputum specimen was sent for culture, and was subsequently (four days later) deemed negative. She had a rash under the breast area that appeared red, excoriated, and fungal in origin. Nystatin powder was prescribed. Laboratory tests revealed that her INR was stable at 2.7.

> *Nystatin is useful in the topical therapy of Candida albicans infections. The recommended dosage for topical preparations of nystatin in treating intertriginous candidiasis is application bid-tid (Katzung, 1998). The amount of anticoagulation for atrial fibrillation was described earlier (Fuster, 2001).*

Her liver function tests were normal. Her Hgb rose to 8.6 with Procrit. Her FK level was therapeutic at 9, and her creatinine had come down to 1.1.

> *Tacrolimus (Jane is on the brand Prograf) is a macrolide antibiotic used to prevent rejection post-transplant. Tacrolimus dosing is based on trough blood levels (recommended at 5 – 15 ng/mL) (Green, 2004).*

I re-educated the patient and family for 20 minutes on subcutaneous injection administration of Procrit. At the end of the visit, I consulted with the cardiologist over the telephone, as given her cardiac history, the possibility for heart failure leading to edema existed. The patient had a cardiology consultation the same day. The cardiologist paged me after the consult, and verbalized agreement with the medication changes. She did not feel that the patient had heart failure, based on an echocardiogram done in the cardiologist's office.

> *Traditionally, in right heart failure increased venous pressure due to cardiac dysfunction increases capillary pressure, resulting in extravasation of fluid which inadequately gets returned to the vascular space, causing edema (Cho, 2002). In left heart failure, patients will present with pulmonary findings suggestive of pulmonary edema.*

The CXR results were received later in the day, and revealed atelectasis, prominent pulmonary vasculature, a reduction in pleural effusions, and no pneumonia. The Levaquin was continued for prophylaxis given her clinical findings, and risk for infection secondary to immunosuppression. The above information was communicated to the referring physician via a faxed letter.

Two days later the patient called and complained of continued nonproductive cough and worsening pedal edema. I increased her Lasix dose to 40 mg qd. Patient was referred to see the pulmonologist because of her ongoing cough and possibility of exacerbation of sarcoidosis, which was a diagnosis she carried from pre-transplant. The possibility of fluid overload and pulmonary edema existed. I communicated via telephone with the pulmonologist at that time about her referral. The pulmonologist agreed to see the patient. She called me after the consult. She felt that ongoing diuresis and prophylactic Levaquin were appropriate, and that if the condition did not improve, Jane would need a fiberoptic bronchoscopy for evaluation of an atypical infection.

The patient had a follow-up visit with me on week 21. At that time the patient had worsening BLLEE, despite reporting a stable weight and a higher dose of Lasix. Her cough was nonproductive. The patient was afebrile and more fatigued, with weakness and mild SOB. However, she was not in acute distress. The patient's vital signs were stable, but on physical exam she had severe bilateral pulmonary rales with inspiratory and expiratory wheezes bilaterally. She had 4+ BLLEE extending to the sacrum with pitting. I increased her Lasix to 60 mg qd, and the Florinef was still held. It was apparent that she had myxedema from hypothyroidism resulting in pulmonary edema and a related low cardiac output resulting in systemic fluid overload, despite the echocardiogram findings and the chest X-ray results.

> *Myxedema is a condition of peripheral edema resulting from hyperthyroidism and hypothyroidism. It occurs more frequently in hypothyroidism than hyperthyroidism (Cho, 2002). It is well-known that hyperthyroidism causes a hyperdynamic cardiac state, leading to high cardiac output and low systemic vascular resistance, which is associated with a fast heart rate and better left ventricular function; hypothyroidism is characterized by the opposite changes (low cardiac output, bradycardia, and poor left ventricular function) (Fazio, 2004).*

I increased her Synthroid dose to 200 mcg qd. I instructed the patient to see her endocrinologist that week for a stat consultation so that a specialist could manage her hypothyroidism. I also educated the patient and family on when to call our office if symptoms were exacerbated, and she was also educated on the proper timing of her Synthroid.

> *Thyroid hormone should be taken 30 minutes before meals, to maximize absorption, as fiber can inhibit absorption (Green, 2004).*

I discussed the possibility of an inpatient hospital admission in person with the hepatologist and over the phone with the pulmonologist. She was given an immediate appointment the same day with the pulmonologist for ongoing shortness of breath and cough. She found the patient to be dyspneic, edematous, and fatigued with an O_2 saturation of 94%. On exam, she had pulmonary edema. She too recommended that the patient continue the Levaquin and agreed with the Synthroid increase. The patient was sent by the pulmonologist for a stat CT of the chest on the day of the visit and repeat PFTs. The CT of the chest revealed no new pathology. There was no evidence of pneumonia or sarcoidosis that had advanced. The PFTs were worse than pre-transplant, and revealed that her FEV1 was low at 24% of predicted and her DLCO was only 37% of predicted. The room air ABG revealed her to be hypoxemic with a PO_2 of 60 and an O_2 sat of only 90%. The patient's a-fib was still controlled.

The decision for admission was deferred by the pulmonologist. Since the patient was at high risk for infections due to her immunosuppressed state, the pulmonologist also recommended that the patient undergo fiberoptic bronchoscopy to rule out any opportunistic infectious pathogens. The patient was given a one-week follow-up appointment with the hepatologist. Of note, her incision was healing well and her decubitus ulcer was healing. I had notified the hepatologist of the events that had happened that day.

> *Pulmonary infection is the most common tissue-invasive infection observed in organ transplant recipients. Early diagnosis justifies the use of invasive diagnostic techniques which provides fast identification of pathogens (Norman, 2001).*

Jane underwent fiberoptic bronchoscopy with the pulmonologist. According to the pulmonologist's verbal report, there were mucous plugs that were removed, and the patient was started on Mucomyst inhaler therapy for ventilatory treatments to loosen her pulmonary secretions. There were no other treatments at that time, and cultures from the bronchoscopy were followed up and revealed pulmonary alveolar macrophages, indicating that there was an inflammatory response occurring of unknown etiology. The cultures were negative for PCP, aspergillus, or CMV. However, the cultures did reveal that the patient had respiratory syncytial virus (RSV), and the pulmonologist felt that no treatment was necessary, except for supportive therapy with Mucomyst and inhalers.

> *Treatment of RSV is primarily supportive, aimed at relieving symptoms. This includes suctioning of secretions (done during bronchoscopy), humidified oxygen, and anti-bronchospastic agents (Mucomyst breaks up secretions, and the inhalers prevent bronchospasm) (Kasper, 2005).*

I ordered an echocardiogram to further rule out any heart failure. The patient was seen in follow-up on week 22 by the hepatologist. No changes were made.

> *"Echocardiography is a noninvasive ultrasound procedure used to evaluate the structure and function of the heart" (Pagana, 1994). The diagnosis of heart failure can be confirmed with echocardiography, radionuclide ventriculography, or cardiac catheterization with left ventriculography (Green, 2004). However, patients with valvular disease may have pulmonary congestion despite normal echocardiographic findings.*

The results were stable and unchanged from the last echo, refuting heart failure as the cause of her edema. It was still felt that the pulmonary edema was related to her myxedema secondary to hypothyroidism. The cardiologist concluded this during a phone consultation with me.

The patient had an outpatient visit on week 23 with me, and disability forms were filled out. Jane was doing much better, however she complained of a new fever of 99.5. Her weight had steadily decreased with the use of diuretics and with management of the myxedema (hypothyroidism). She felt well, was eating and sleeping well. Her vital signs were stable, and her cough had improved markedly. Her medications at that time included Prograf 7 mg bid, Cellcept 1 g bid, Prednisone 10 mg qd, Septra SS TIW, Valcyte 900 mg qd, Protonix 40 mg bid, Nystatin Swish and Swallow 5 cc qid, Synthroid 200 mcg qd, Digoxin 0.125 mg qd, metoprolol 25 mg qd, Materna qd, Actigall 300 mg tid, Neurontin 300 mg qd, Epivir 100 mg qd, Colace 100 mg bid, Oscal 500 mg tid, Coumadin 2 mg qd, Advair discus 500/50 bid, Combivent bid prn, Fosamax 70 mg q week, Vitamin D q week, Procrit 40,000 u sq q week, Lasix 40 mg qd, hydrocodone 5/500 prn, nystatin powder to breast area bid, MgOx 400 mg tid, Albuterol nebulizer q6 hrs, Mucomyst nebulizers 10% bid.

Laboratory tests revealed an INR of 1.25, which was sub-therapeutic. Hgb 8.8, Hct 30, Plt 320,000, Na 143, K 4.2, Cr 0.9, glucose 78. LFTs were normal, TSH had declined to 28.9, and the FK level was stable at 7.3. At the time of the visit, it was thought that her hypothyroidism was improving. I referred Jane to her local physician for Coumadin adjustment and asked her to return to our office in one week for a follow-up visit with me and for laboratory testing. She had a follow-up scheduled with the pulmonologist and cardiologist as well. I made no medication changes at the time of the visit. Due to the patient's low-grade fever, I ordered urine and blood cultures. These were sent with the intent of ruling out a urinary tract infection, or bacteremia, and were subsequently negative.

In a randomized clinical trial of 103 patients with mitral stenosis and atrial fibrillation, it was concluded that anticoagulation with a target INR of 2 was considered effective and safe in high-risk patients with atrial fibrillation and mitral stenosis (Pengo, 2003).

One week later (week 24) the patient underwent routine laboratory testing. Her INR was still sub-therapeutic at 1.67, and the labs were faxed to her local physician for management. Her TSH had come down to 22, and the patient's dose was unchanged. Her LFTs were stable, and she was advised to continue her current dosing of immunosuppression without changes.

A follow-up visit one week later with me revealed that the patient was two months post-transplant and was doing much better. Her fevers spontaneously resolved, she was afebrile at the visit, had increased energy, and her cough was much less severe. Her weight had dropped to 130 lbs. and her Lasix was discontinued. I called the pulmonologist to see if she wanted to see the patient, as a courtesy. She was appreciative, and joined me during the visit. Jane's vital signs were stable, but she still complained of continued mild dyspnea on exertion and a cough on deep inspiration. On auscultation she had rhonchi that cleared with cough. Her HR was irregular with a-fib but was controlled in rate. The fungal infection under her breasts had resolved and her incision had healed. The decubitus ulcer was well-healed. The patient's and family's questions were answered. I provided counseling for approximately 35 minutes. The pulmonologist educated the patient on pulmonary inhaler use. Cardiopulmonary rehabilitation as an outpatient was recommended by the pulmonologist to maximize her endurance. Laboratory tests were done and I reviewed the results that day, and then sent them via fax, per the patient's request, to her local MD for management of Coumadin. Her renal function and liver function were normal. The Actigall was discontinued.

Actigall has been used in cholestatic disorders of the liver and biliary tree. Although the mechanism is not known, it is postulated that it reverses intracellular accumulation of toxic bile acids, resulting in improvement in hepatic enzyme levels and hepatic histology (Katzung, 1998).

She was asked to follow up in two weeks in our office for a visit with me and for laboratory testing in one week. I updated the referring physician via a faxed letter, which I dictated.

I conducted the follow-up visit two weeks later, and the patient was feeling well and remained afebrile. Her lungs were clear to auscultation at the visit and there was no edema on exam. Her vital signs were stable and her weight was stable. Jane requested to see a dentist, so dental prophylaxis was provided with clindamycin according to the American Heart Association guidelines, as she is PCN allergic. There were no other medication changes made.

The American Heart Association's latest guidelines for prevention of bacterial endocarditis in patients with mitral valve prolapse were revised in 1998. Prophylaxes with antibiotics are recommended for patients who have cardiac valvular disease and are planning to undergo procedures that can cause bacteremia. Such procedures include oral and dental procedures. For these procedures, a single dose of amoxicillin is recommended. In patients who are penicillin allergic, clindamycin is recommended (Taubert, 1998).

The patient followed up with the pulmonologist, who adjusted her inhalers and ordered repeat PFTs for three weeks later with a follow-up visit with the pulmonologist. I reviewed Jane's laboratory tests that week, which revealed stable liver function tests. Her Prograf level was elevated at 12.8, so her evening dose was reduced. Her creatinine rose to 1.3, which was likely a result of her elevated FK level.

> *Prograf is nephrotoxic, so an elevated Prograf level in the setting of a rising creatinine may indicate Prograf-induced nephrotoxicity.*

Her TSH had continued to decline to a level of 7.5 (toward normal). Her INR was stable at 2.56, which was therapeutic, indicating she was on the correct dose of Coumadin. Laboratory results were faxed to her local physician.

> *The amount of anticoagulation for maximum protection against ischemic stroke was described earlier (Fuster, 2001).*

One week later, at week 25 (8 weeks post-transplant), the patient called the office in the late afternoon, and spoke with me. She complained of severe abdominal pain. Upon questioning, she reported that she had diffuse cramping in the lower abdomen, which was unrelenting, continuous, and unassociated with movement. Nothing relieved the pain. It had worsened over the course of four days. She also reported a fever of 101.5, which had spontaneously resolved the day prior. She denied nausea and vomiting, constipation, and diarrhea. She denied bleeding. Due to the severity and escalation of the pain, and the late timing in the day, she was referred to the emergency room (ER). I called the ER attending to alert him of her expected arrival. Her history and current condition were relayed by phone to the ER attending. Suggestion of abdominal imaging (abdominal X-ray to rule out small bowel obstruction, abdominal CT to rule out fluid collection or other etiology) was relayed to the attending physician in the ER. I also suggested a workup for gynecologic etiology, and the need for pain management was relayed. She was admitted to the hospital from the ER, and managed by the liver transplant team. I did not manage the patient during this admission, but rounded on her daily. Abdominal X-ray, abdominal CT, and pelvic transvaginal ultrasound ordered by the resident, and were normal. Jane was treated with oral narcotics for pain, and had relief. She was discharged from the hospital on week 30 with abdominal pain of unknown etiology. Of note, her CMV DNA PCR was negative.

As an outpatient, the patient continued to report abdominal pain to me. I spoke with the hepatologist, as previous workup was negative, but the patient had ongoing pain. She recommended an upper endoscopy (EGD) and colonoscopy to rule out a digestive component. Later that week, these were performed by the hepatologist; both were negative.

> *The EGD could survey the esophagus, stomach, and duodenum for ulcerations or inflammation/gastritis including gastrointestinal CMV. The colonoscopy could reveal colitis or diverticulitis.*

She had continued abdominal pain. On week 31 (just over three months post-transplant) she underwent hepatic MRV, ordered by the hepatologist, to verify patency of the hepatic vessels, as a vessel blockage could cause pain. This too, was negative. Jane had a follow-up visit with the hepatologist, who reviewed the negative workup with the patient. The hepatologist discontinued the Cellcept, as it is known to have GI side effects. The hepatologist discontinued the Procrit, as she was no longer anemic. Her Synthroid was decreased to 175 mcg by the hepatologist, as her TSH had gone into a mildly hyperthyroid state. PFTs were repeated and they were normal.

> *Cellcept is associated with serious side effects related to the gastrointestinal tract. These include gastrointestinal hemorrhage and perforations, ulceration, diarrhea, constipation, nausea, dyspepsia, vomiting, esophagitis, flatulence, gastritis, gastroenteritis, GI moniliasis, ileus, and rectal disorders (Spratto, 2001).*

Laboratory tests were performed on week 32 and revealed a normal TSH at 2.4 and a normal digoxin level. Her transaminases were elevated in the 40s. Her INR was 2.2 and therapeutic. Her Valcyte for CMV prophylaxis was discontinued per office protocol since she was three months post-transplant. Her abdominal pain had resolved. I reviewed the labs with the hepatologist with regard to the elevated LFTs, and to discuss the possibility of a liver biopsy to rule out rejection. The hepatologist chose to defer the biopsy.

The patient had her labs repeated one week later and still had elevated LFTs. She had presumed rejection since her Cellcept had been recently discontinued, which resulted in a rise in liver function tests. The decision was made to avoid liver biopsy, which is invasive, if possible. In lieu of the Cellcept, which was stopped due to abdominal pain, the hepatologist started Jane on Imuran 50 mg qd with a prednisone taper starting at 40 mg bid. The hepatologist and I made this decision together.

> *Removal of an immunosuppressive agent could lead to an increase in the immune system's activity, resulting in graft rejection. Acute cellular rejection that occurs after three months post-transplant is typically related to inadequate or fluctuating levels of immunosuppressive medications or illness (Norman, 2001). Imuran helps in maintaining renal allografts and may be of value in other tissues (Katzung, 1998). Treatment for acute rejection typically consists of intravenous methylprednisolone therapy (Norman, 2001).*

One week later her laboratory tests were checked and had improved. She complained of vomiting once. Imuran has been documented to be a known risk of pancreatitis, so I added an amylase and lipase to the blood test that week.

> *Medications are a cause of acute pancreatitis. Over 55 drugs have been blamed for cases of pancreatitis. There are several immunosuppressant drugs that cause acute pancreatitis, one of which is azathioprine (Jane is on the brand name Imuran). Ninety percent of patients with acute pancreatitis present with nausea and vomiting. Laboratory tests used to diagnose pancreatitis include pancreatic enzymes, including amylase and lipase, with lipase being the more specific test. Both serum amylase and lipase have a sensitivity of between 85% and 100% (Feldman, 2002).*

Jane's TSH was normal as well as her INR. Laboratory tests revealed a normal amylase and lipase, refuting the idea of pancreatitis. According to the patient, her vomiting resolved spontaneously.

On week 36, the patient complained of 101.5 fever for three days. I decided to admit the patient. I arranged the admission with the transplant team, communicated with the resident, and recommended that Jane undergo an extensive workup for fever of unknown etiology, including chest X-ray, ultrasound of abdomen, urine and blood cultures, echocardiogram to rule out endocarditis, and serum testing for CMV DNA. All previous CMV DNA had been negative to date.

> *A chest X-ray was done to rule out a pulmonary etiology such as pneumonia, and an ultrasound of the abdomen was performed to rule out a biliary stricture leading to cholangitis, and to rule out any fluid collections that could have become abscesses leading to fever. Blood cultures were obtained to rule out bacteremia, and the urine cultures were done to rule out a urinary tract infection. Due to the mitral valve abnormalities that Jane has, endocarditis was one of the differential diagnoses. Lastly, the CMV culture was necessary to rule out CMV infection, which often presents in post-transplant patients with a fever. Additionally, when transplanted, Jane was CMV antibody negative but received a CMV positive organ, making her high risk for CMV infection (Norman, 2001).*

Once admitted, the echocardiogram verified vegetation on her aortic leaflet, which led to the suspicion of endocarditis. The residents initiated treatment with IV antibiotics for endocarditis. Blood cultures were sent (and were subsequently all negative). A cardiac consultation was requested by the resident and conducted. The cardiologist read the echocardiogram and felt that the strands seen on the echo were not suggestive of endocarditis. Subsequently, I received the result of the CMV DNA PCR, and it was positive for active CMV infection, which can cause abdominal pain and fever. The interventional radiologist placed a peripherally inserted central catheter (PICC line). Jane was discharged to home with VNS services for home infusion of ganciclovir for two weeks.

> *CMV can cause hepatitis, fever, leukopenia, thrombocytopenia, and other events. (Norman, 2001). The diagnosis is made by liver biopsy or by detecting viral DNA (Norman, 2001). Treatment requires intravenous ganciclovir for two or four weeks until clearance of the virus. (Norman, 2001). Most patients requiring four to eight weeks of intravenous therapy, especially in the home care setting, should have a PICC line placed (Doherty, 1997).*

I ordered repeat CMV cultures in the outpatient clinic two weeks after the IV ganciclovir was started, and they were negative. Although I typically remove the PICC lines in the office, I requested that the surgeon remove Jane's PICC line, as the patient was on Coumadin therapy, which posed a risk for bleeding, especially if the tip had migrated or adhered to the vessel wall. The patient was converted to PO Valcyte 900 mg qd for three months per office protocol for CMV infection.

At the time of this written case study, the patient's liver function had stabilized, her INR was therapeutic, and she was euthyroid. Clinically, her fever and abdominal pain resolved. Jane is scheduled for weekly laboratory testing, and her prednisone will be tapered per protocol. I will see Jane in the office for routine follow-up.

References

Abram, S., Tedeschi, A.A., Partain, C.L., Blumenkopf, B. (1988). *Differential diagnosis of severe back pain using MRI.* Southern Medical Journal, 81 (12): 1487 – 1492.

Bates, B. (1995). *A Guide to Physical Examination and History Taking* (6th ed.). Philadelphia: J.B. Lippincott Company.

Blei, A., Cordoba, J., and The Practice Parameters Committee of the American College of Gastroenterology (2001). *Practice guidelines: hepatic encephalopathy.* American Journal of Gastroenterology, 96 (7): 1968 – 1976.

Bolondi, L. (2003). *Screening for hepatocellular carcinoma in cirrhosis.* Journal of Hepatology, 39 (6): 1076 – 1084.

Brown, E., Suppes, T., Khan, D.A., Carmody, T.J. (2002). *Mood changes during prednisone bursts in outpatients with asthma.* Journal of Clinical Psychopharmacology, 22 (1): 55 – 61.

Brown, R.J., Kumar, K.S., Russo, M.W., Kinkhabwala, M., Rudow, D.L., Harren, P., Lobritto, S., Emond, J.C. (2002). *Model for end-stage liver disease and Child-Turcotte-Pugh score as predictors of pretransplantation disease severity, post-transplantation outcome, and resource utilization in United Network for Organ Sharing status 2A patients.* Liver Transplantation, 8 (3): 278 – 284.

Butterworth, R. (2003). *Hepatic encephalopathy.* Alcohol Research and Health, 27 (3): 240 – 246.

Cardenas, A., Kelleher, T., Chopra, S. (2004). *Review article: hepatic hydrothorax.* Alimentary Pharmacology & Therapeutics, 20 (3): 271 – 279.

Cho, S., Atwood, E. (2002). *Peripheral edema.* The American Journal of Medicine, 113 (7): 580 – 586.

Doherty, G., Baumann, D.S., Creswell, L.L., Goss, J.A., Lairmore, T.C. (Eds.) (1997). The Washington Manual of Surgery. New York: Little, Brown, and Company.

Fazio, S., Palmieri, E.A., Lombardi, G., Biondi, B. (2004). *Effects of thyroid hormone on the cardiovascular system.* Recent Progress in Hormone Research, 59, 31 – 50.

Feldman, M., Friedman, L.S., Sleisenger, M.H. (2002). *Gastrointestinal and Liver Disease Pathophysiology, Diagnosis, Management* (7th ed. Vol. 2). New York: Saunders.

Fuster, V., Ryden, L.E., Asinger, R.W., Cannom, D.S., Crinjns, H.J., Frye, R.L., Halperin, J.L., Kay, G.N., Klein, W.W., Levy, S., McNamara, R.L., Prystowsky, E.N., Wann, L.S., Wyse, D.G., Gibbons, R.J., Antman, E.M., Alpert, J.S., Faxon, D., Fuster, V., Gregoratos, G., Hiratzka, L.F., Jacobs, A.K., Russell, R.O., Smith, S.C., Klein, W.W., Alonso-Garcia, A., Blomstrom-Lundqvist, C., Debacker, G., Flather, M., Hradec, J., Oto, A., Parkhomenko, A., Silber, S., Torbicki, A., American College of Cardiology/American Heart Association/ European Society of Cardiology Board (2001). *ACC/AHA/ESC guidelines for the management of patients with atrial fibrillation: executive summary*. Journal of the American College of Cardiology, 38 (4): 1231 – 1266.

Green, G., Harris, I.S., Lin, G.A., Moylan, K.C. (Eds.) (2004). *The Washington Manual of Medical Therapeutics* (31st ed.). New York: Lippincott Williams & Wilkins.

Holt, D., Thomas, R., Van Thiel, D., Brems, J.J. (2002). *Use of hepatitis B core antibody-positive donors in orthotopic liver transplantation*. Archives of Surgery, 137 (5): 572 – 575.

Jones, B., Gores, G.J. (1998). *Hepatobiliary malignancy*. Clinics of Liver Disease, 2 (2): 437 – 449.

Kasper, D., Fauci, A.S., Longo, D.L., Braunwald, E., Hauser, S.L., Jameson, J.L. (Eds.) (2005). Harrison's Principles of Internal Medicine (16th ed. Vol. 1). New York: McGraw-Hill.

Katzung, B. (1998). *Basic & Clinical Pharmacology* (7th ed.). Stamford: Appleton & Lange.

Kent, K., Moscucci, M., Mansour, K.A., DiMattia, S., Gallagher, S., Kuntz, R., Skillman, J.J. (1994). *Retroperitoneal hematoma after cardiac catheterization: prevalence, risk factors, and optimal management*. Journal of Vascular Surgery, 20 (6): 905 – 910.

Levenson, J., Olbrisch, M.E. (1993). *Psychosocial evaluation of organ transplant candidates: a comparative survey of process, criteria, and outcomes in heart, liver, and kidney transplantation*. Psychosomatics, 34 (4): 314 – 323.

Lucey, M., Brown, K.A., Everson, G.T., Fung, J.J., Gish, R., Keefe, E.B., Kneteman, N.M., Lake, J.R., Martin, P., Rakela, J., Shiffman, M.L., So, S., Wiesner, R.H. (1998). *Minimal criteria for placement of adults on the liver transplant waiting list: a report of a national conference organized by the American Society of Transplant Physicians and the American Association for the Study of Liver Diseases*. Transplantation, 66 (7): 956 – 962.

McIlwain, H. (2003). *Glucocorticoid-induced osteoporosis: pathogenesis, diagnosis, and management*. Preventive Medicine, 36 (2): 243 – 249.

Merkel, G., Sacerdoti, D., Angeli, P. (1993). *Cardiac involvement in liver cirrhosis*. Annali italiani di medicina interna, 8 (4): 244 – 247.

Monahan, F., Neighbors, M. (1998). *Medical-Surgical Nursing: Foundations for Clinical Practice* (2nd ed.). Philadelphia: W.B. Saunders Company.

Muller, C., Schenk, P. (1999). *Hepatopulmonary syndrome*. Wien Klin Wochenschr, 111 (9): 339 – 347.

Norman, D., Turka, L.A. (Eds.) (2001). *Primer on Transplantation* (2nd ed.). Mt. Laurel, NJ: American Society of Transplantation.

Pagana, K., Pagana, T.J. (1994). *Diagnostic Testing & Nursing Implications* (4th ed.). Philadelphia: Mosby.

Pengo, V., Barber, F., Biasiolo, A., Pegoraro, C., Noventa, F., Iliceto, S. (2003). *Prevention of thromboembolism in patients with mitral stenosis and associated atrial fibrillation: effectiveness of low intensity (INR target 2) oral anticoagulant treatment*. Thrombosis Haemostasis, 89 (4): 760 – 764.

Reddy, V. (2002). *Prevention of postoperative acute renal failure*. Journal of Postgraduate Medicine, 48 (1): 64 – 70.

Ressel, G. (2003). *ACOG releases guidelines on cervical cytology screening*. American Family Physician, 68 (10): 2081, 2084.

Scanga, C., Mohan, V.P., Joseph, H., Yu, K., Chan, J., Flynn, J.L. (1999). *Reactivation of latent tuberculosis variations on the Cornell Murine model*. Infection and Immunity, 67 (9): 4531 – 4538.

Schenk, P., Schoniger-Hekele, M., Fuhrmann, V., Madl, C., Silberhumer, G., Muller, C. (2003). *Prognostic significance of the hepatopulmonary syndrome in patients with cirrhosis*. Gastroenterology, 125 (4): 1042 – 1052.

Shapiro, R., Stancato-Pasik, A., Glajchen, N., Zalasin, S. (1998). *Color Doppler applications in hepatic imaging.* Clinical Imaging, 22, 272 – 279.

Singer, D., Albers, G.W., Dalen, J.E., Go, A.S., Halperin, J.L., Manning, W.J. (2004). *Antithrombotic therapy in atrial fibrillation: the Seventh ACCP Conference on antithrombotic and thrombolytic therapy.* Chest, 126 (Suppl 3): 429S – 456S.

Spratto, G., Woods, A.L. (2001). *PDR Nurse's Drug Handbook* (2001 ed.). Albany, NY: Delmar Publishers and Medical Economics Company.

Taubert, K., Dajani, A.S. (1998). *Preventing bacterial endocarditis: American Heart Association guidelines.* American Family Physician, 57 (3): 457 – 468.

Therapondos, G. (2004). *Cardiac morbidity and mortality related to orthotopic liver transplantation.* Liver Transplantation, 10 (12): 1441 – 1453.

Twillman, R., Manetto, C., Wellisch, D.K., Wolcott, D.L. (1993). *The transplant evaluation rating scale: a revision of the psychosocial levels system for evaluating organ transplant candidates.* Psychosomatics, 34 (2): 144 – 153.

Wallach, J. (1996). *Cardiovascular diseases.* Interpretation of Diagnostic Tests (6th ed., p. 117). New York: Little, Brown, and Company.

CASE FIVE:

Postpartum care for a 30-year-old woman whose newborn sustained significant anoxic brain damage with multi-organ system injury secondary to severe asphyxia due to cord compression

NARRATIVE CASE STUDY

Reason for encounter(s): Postpartum for emergency cesarean section; newborn with severe asphyxia; long-term palliative care plan for newborn; infant's death and process of mother's grieving.

SUMMARY OF ANTENATAL CARE AND LABOR/DELIVERY

Adjoa is a 30-year-old G1P1 African-American woman who came to the birthing center with her partner, Sallah, for prenatal care and birthing. Adjoa is a fashion model by profession and Sallah an actor. Adjoa was very verbal and committed to a concept of natural childbirth. She registered for prenatal care at 8 weeks' gestation and had a normal, healthy pregnancy. She was very excited about the birthing process and presented a detailed birth plan, including squatting positions. Her prenatal course was uneventful. At 40 weeks I discussed with them the management plan for post-dates care, to prepare them for fetal non-stress testing (NST), and biophysical profiles to ensure the well-being of the baby and placenta, with preparation for an induction at 42 weeks if no spontaneous labor had occurred (Varney, 2004).

Management of post-dates

At 40 weeks/5 days, I ordered an NST and a modified biophysical profile to test for adequacy of amniotic fluid. On the NST strip, there was minimal baseline variability and occasional decelerations noted with fetal movement. I advised Adjoa and her partner that she needed to be evaluated on the L&D Unit of our back-up hospital. I consulted with the attending on L&D, who agreed he would evaluate the status of the fetus, and I gave Adjoa a written consult. I also informed my team midwife, as she would cover my caseload while I was away.

Adjoa and Sallah did go to the hospital as advised. The NST was nonreassuring and the sonogram showed oligohydramnios. The attending physician advised cautious induction of labor with the possibility of cesarian section if the fetus did not tolerate labor. Adjoa signed herself out of the hospital against medical advice, telling the attending physician (according to the chart documentation) that she believed her baby was healthy and she planned to have a natural childbirth. Two days later she appeared at the birthing center stating she believed she was in early labor. The CNM present did a fetal monitoring strip which showed late decelerations to 60 BPM with slow recovery. An ambulance was called. At the hospital an emergency cesarian section was performed, with a classical incision (involves the upper contractile uterine segment [corpus/fundus]) (Varney, 2004). Baby girl delivered with nuccal cord x 3; pediatrics were present and initiated resuscitation and intubation of the baby in the DR; baby's Apgars were 0, 1 (for heart rate at 5 minutes, 2 (for heart rate and color at 10 minutes). The baby was transferred to the NICU with endotracheal intubation. Ventilator connected, umbilical artery catheterization performed, IV glucose given in NICU as per protocol. Baby's Wt.: 7 lb. 4 oz.

PAST HEALTH HISTORY

AP hx: My practice x 12 visits; healthy course. Total weight gain 25 lbs. Attended private childbirth classes with partner.

GYN/sexual hx: No previous pregnancies. Menses 13 x 28 x 4-5 d. No hx STIs. HIV negative with current pregnancy as per NY mandate for counseling and testing.

States hx sexual relations beginning age 17, all male, four partners. With current partner in monogamous relationship x one year. States satisfaction with relationship.

States no hx abnormal Paps. Certain LMP with pregnancy.

Medical hx: Denies diabetes, hypertension, heart disease, kidney disease, neurologic problems, psychiatric problems, hepatitis, thyroid dysfunction, trauma/violence, blood transfusion, surgery.

Allergies: None.

Family hx: Mother and father alive and well. Father with HTN on medications x two years. Maternal GM with breast CA, age 74. Two siblings, ages 28 & 25; no health problems. Her siblings do not have children.

Social/cultural hx: Adjoa lives with partner x 10 months (they have been together one year). She states this was a planned pregnancy for her, though Sallah was less certain he wanted a child as he travels a great deal with his work. Adjoa began work as a fashion model at age 18; she finished college. They live in a renovated house and have a busy social life in the art world. She expresses pride in her "African-ness" and has researched birthing practices. She denies smoking, alcohol, or drugs. She took prenatal vitamins from a health store because "they didn't contain any preservatives." She denies use of other herbal medications. A massage therapist came to her home for weekly sessions during the pregnancy. She states she eats "carefully" because it is very important that her body return to its previous size after delivery so that she can continue her modeling work. She expresses extreme happiness with the pregnancy. She states she is financially secure.

Genetic hx: Client and her partner verbalize understanding of the following conditions and deny family hx of: neural tube defects, thalassemia, Down syndrome, sickle cell disease or trait, hemophilia, cystic fibrosis.

Prenatal labs:

Blood type: O positive, antibody screen negative
Hematocrit: 34.5 (at 36 weeks)
Platelets: Normal
Gct: 118 (at 28 weeks)
PPD: 00mm
HbsAg: Negative
VDRL: Negative (at 36 weeks)
Gonorrhea, chlamydia, group beta strep: neg (at 36 weeks as per protocol); HIV negative
Triple screen: wnl
Ultrasound: At 18.5 weeks: nl fetal anatomy, placenta anterior, amniotic fluid index nl; at 40.5 weeks: markedly reduced amniotic fluid, oligohydramnios

Visit PP day 3: OB unit in hospital

(First visit post my return from off-call)

Current health status

S: "I cannot believe I had to have a c-section. And now my belly will have a terrible scar. Have you seen my daughter? She is just beautiful, looking just like her father."

Patient alone in room. States she has been having many visitors and many celebrations about the birth of her daughter. States Sallah visits her daily but has work obligations and can only spend a few hours.

States baby is in NICU on a respirator. "She is a fighter."

States she believes her baby will be all right but wants me to speak with the head of the NICU to learn more.

States her breasts are full with milk and she is starting to pump to save the milk for when the baby can feed.

States she is ambulating now; takes Tylenol #3 for pain relief when needed. States on regular diet as of today.

Review of systems

General state of health: Denies fever, chills.

Skin: Denies disease, pruritus, rash, lesions.

HEENT: Denies head injury, dizziness, eye problems, sores in mouth, dysphagia, sore throat, swollen glands. (+) dental care yearly.

Breasts: Denies hx breast CA, pain, lumps. Performs SBE. + enlargement, + tenderness, + breastmilk from nipples.

Respiratory: Denies cough, wheezing, shortness of breath, pain on breathing.

Cardiovascular: Denies chest pain, palpitations, fatigue, edema.

Peripheral vascular: Denies pain or numbness in extremities, ulcers, varicose veins.

GI: Denies nausea, vomiting. No hx constipation. No bowel movement since cesarian section x three days.

Urinary: + frequency since surgery; denies dysuria, urgency.

Genitalia: Denies vaginal itching, odor. + moderate bleeding.

Musculoskeletal: Denies joint pain, stiffness, back pain, limited range of motion.

Hematologic: Denies bleeding problems, excessive bruising.

Endocrine: Denies hx polydipsia, polyphagia, polyuria.

Psychiatric: Denies hx depression, anxiety, or mood change in past.

PHYSICAL EXAM

B/P 114/72; P 80; T 98.8

Ht. 5' 6"; Wt. 135 (Wt. at last AP visit 145)

Thyroid: No enlargement, no masses.

Lymph nodes: No tenderness, enlargement.

Heart: RR S_1, S_2 without murmurs.

Lungs: Without use of accessory muscles, without adventitious sounds.

Breasts: Enlarged, tender, prominent nipples, + colostrum.

Extremities: Reflexes +2, - Homan's.

Abdomen: Dressing removed, vertical incision + staples, nonreddened, without drainage. + BS.

GYN: Fundus 3 FB below umbilicus, firm, nontender; pad: + lochia, rubra, moderate, - odor.

Labs: Hct. a.m. 32.4, WBC 8.0

A: Post-cesarian section Day 3
  - Incision healing without s&s of infection.
  - At risk for altered emotional status due to birth experience.
  - At risk for altered emotional status due to unknown status of baby.
  - In need of family and social service support.

P: Regular diet; Colace 100 mg qd. Anticipate tolerance of solid foods with bowel movement.
  - Ambulate as desired.
  - Discharge in a.m. post staple removal if without elevated temperature.
  - I will visit and consult with Perinatal Attending in NICU to learn status of baby.

Referrals:
  - Lactation consultant visit to support pumping breast milk in anticipation of giving breast milk to baby.
  - Social services to evaluate emotional adaptation to traumatic birth experience.

INTERVAL NOTE:
CONSULTATION WITH PERINATOLOGIST (Same day)

In NICU. Baby is on respirator. No spontaneous respiratory effort. Hypotonic muscle tone. Unresponsive to stimuli.

Perinatologist informs me that baby had severe anoxic episode, probably caused by the nuccal cord x 3 and reduced amniotic fluid. Concern that prolonged ischemia is leading to brain tissue necrosis.

Hypoxic-Ischemic Encephalopathy (HIE).

> *Significant anoxic brain damage with multi-organ system injury secondary to severe asphyxia due to cord compression (Wu, 2004).*

Prognosis very guarded for quality of life.

Plan is to order CT scan for a.m. to assess for cerebral hemorrhage; continue baby on respirator with IV fluids.

I discuss Adjoa's emotional status with MD. There is a distinct discrepancy between Adjoa's description of the baby's status and the perinatologist's evaluation. I discuss her state of denial with the MD.

> *Denial is an initial response to the grieving process (McGrath, 2003).*

We agree to a joint consultation with Adjoa and Sallah on the status of the baby in the a.m., post CT scan and prior to Adjoa's discharge.

> *As the nurse-midwife, I have responsibility for both the physiological needs as well as the psychosocial needs in supporting this family in crisis (Best, 1993).*

VISIT 2: PP DAY 4 NICU

Team meeting attended by perinatologist, head nurse of NICU, Adjoa, Sallah, social worker, and me.

MD explains to Adjoa and Sallah that their baby is very sick. Baby continues on a respirator, has minimal spontaneous muscle movements in limbs, no spontaneous respiratory effort at present, no response to stimuli. He explains that a CT scan done that morning showed no acute cerebral bleed, + diffuse edema of the brain tissue. He explained that the prolonged anoxic insult to the baby's brain led to edema and the beginning stages of necrosis of the brain tissue. This is a process that cannot be stopped and will lead to encephalomalacia with the eventual formation of cystic material. He could not anticipate if the baby would have any ability to function independently of the respirator, nor to what extent organ damage would be manifested.

> *In severe cases of HIE, clinical manifestations are coma, flaccid tone, suppressed brainstem function, seizures, and increased intracranial pressure (Perlman, 1989).*

He informed them of this news gently and respectfully.

> *Sharing information with the family helps avoid feelings of isolation and abandonment, and begins the development of partnerships between providers of end-of-life care for babies and the parents (Sahler, 2000).*

He concluded that they would assess on a day-by-day basis the baby's status.

Adjoa was attentive and appeared to be grappling with the information. She asked if the baby would live. I repeated the information and said it was going to be a waiting period to see at what point the necrosis stopped. She would need to mobilize her resources to be with the baby. She would also need to take the time to let her body heal from the cesarian section. We agreed that she would continue to pump the breast milk in the event the baby could be fed. She seemed relieved at that. Sallah said that he had felt uneasy that she had signed herself out of the hospital last week and had an ominous feeling. There appeared to be tension between the couple.

DISCHARGE SUMMARY: POST-OP DAY 4

S: "I tried so hard to believe that the baby would be okay. I want her to live so badly." Very weepy. Sallah trying to comfort Adjoa.

States she does not want to go home and leave her baby. Expresses feeling of isolation and fear for her baby.

Adaptation to parenthood has been referred to as a developmental or maturational stressor. The birth of a less-than-perfect baby creates an additional situational or accidental stressor. When these events happen simultaneously, resulting pressure can overwhelm a person's usual coping mechanisms (McGrath, 2003).

Verbalizes that she understands what happened to her baby at the time of birth. States she feels like a failure to deliver her baby in the way she wanted.

Acknowledgement of failure to deliver as hoped is an important psychological task in working through the feelings of guilt and failure (Best, 1993).

Expresses wanting to know how it will turn out for the baby. States she is relieved she can keep breast pumping as she knows her baby will need the milk when she can feed. I encourage her, as it establishes an interaction with the infant's care that is positive.

Sallah is mostly silent during the discharge process. I ask him what he is feeling, and he says he is angry, though he cannot clarify exactly what he is angry about.

It is critical to allow parents the freedom to express negative ideas without being judged. These arise from fear and frustration over inability to control their infant's circumstances (Best, 1993).

He states he will be in and out of the apartment as he has to travel for his job.

Adjoa tolerating nl diet, + BM, ambulating without assistance, using Tylenol 500 mg 2 tabs prn for pain relief.

O: B/P 120/70, P 74, T 98.6

Heart S_1, S_2 without murmurs

Lungs without adventitious sounds

Breasts engorged, tender, nonreddened

Abdomen: nontender, fundus 4FB, + BS. Staples removed by me, incision site nonreddened, closed, no signs of infection

Lochia moderate, rubra, nonmalodorous

Extremities (-) Homan's

Labs: (a.m.) Hct 34.2; WBC 8.5

A: Normal physiological recovery from classical cesarian section

Breast engorgement

Stress r/t very ill newborn with prognosis guarded

At risk for postpartum depression

At risk for stress on relationship with partner

In need of family and social service support

P: I instructed Adjoa in care of incision (cleaning with peroxide, exposure to air, daily showers). No heavy lifting, rest when possible. No sexual relations x six weeks for healing process r/t classical cesarian section. I discussed need to consider what form of contraception they would want initiated at six weeks.

I informed Adjoa that when/if she should decide to have another pregnancy, she would need to have an operative delivery due to the classical vertical incision.

Classical incision is an absolute contraindication to vaginal birth after cesarian section (Varney, 2004).

I instructed Adjoa to take warm showers and massage her breasts to relieve the engorgement. I reviewed ways to rent a breast pump to save milk. At this point I agreed with Adjoa that this gave her a concrete action in the event the baby would be allowed NG tube feedings and allowed her to claim her motherhood in a very difficult situation. I instructed her to monitor for elevated temperature or signs of redness on the breasts as indications of possible mastitis.

I discussed ways to obtain family support. I discussed that this was a time of not knowing the baby's prognosis; the baby could die or the baby could live with extremely impaired functioning. I acknowledged the extreme stress and worked to develop a plan for support. Adjoa thought her sister could stay with her in the apartment, especially while Sallah traveled. I suggested that social services could refer them to a family counselor with expertise in this area and she was relieved to have the referral. Sallah spoke little and appeared detached from the discussion.

In working through the intense feelings of overwhelming shock, helplessness, and denial, parents move also to feelings of resentment and anger. They may avoid emotional involvement with the infant as a way to protect themselves from the pain of possible loss (McGrath, 2003).

I listened to them. I acknowledged the pain of their situation. I talked about the process of grieving for a very sick baby who might not live. I discussed how people go through stages of grief, shock, denial, anger, guilt and shame, and acceptance (Best, 1993). I also told them that this happened individually, that each person grieved differently and at different paces. I thought this might apply to the two of them as they presented with different emotions.

I discussed her adaptation to the intensive care environment. Adjoa stated that she was getting to know the nurses and routines and they were teaching her how to give care to the baby. I encouraged her engagement with her infant to begin to know her baby.

Milstein (2003) contends that encouraging families to engage with their sick and/or dying infants helps detoxify the experience and make it meaningful to the parents.

I urged her and her partner to attend family support sessions run by the NICU to find a community to help them.

I arranged for a one-week appointment at my center with Adjoa to check her progress on recovery and discuss her needs and coping abilities. I also told her that I would be available to consult with the perinatologist as to the baby's status whenever she requested. I made a referral via social services for a family therapist. Adjoa was relieved that I was committed to being part of the team as she grappled with the baby's health status.

VISIT 5: POSTPARTUM WEEK 1 (Office visit)

S: "I am seeing my baby every day. She is showing some signs of breathing. They are trying to wean her off the respirator. This is good news. I am pumping my breasts — they are less sore. My sister is moving in with me for a while. Sallah seems so busy working. I have an appointment for the therapist you suggested. This is so unreal, what is happening to my life!"

Adjoa tells me this and then bursts into tears. She says that Sallah is on the road a lot and while loving when he is home, she feels he is distancing himself. She says she repeats over and over in her mind her decision to sign herself out of the hospital, and tells me that she believed she was doing the right thing. She tells me she is frightened and sad and feels very out of control. She is getting support from her sister and says she feels happiest when she is pumping her breasts because she hopes it will help her baby.

O: B/P 116/72, P 68, T 98.2

    U/A negative for albumen, glucose, ketones

    Breasts full, not engorged, nontender

    Fundus 4 FB below umbilicus

    Incision healing well; steri-strips removed

    Lochia scant

A: Progress in healing from surgery

    Attempting to cope with grief, guilt over baby's status

    At risk of change in relationship with partner

    At risk for emotional lability re: baby's status

    In need of therapeutic support

P: I advised Adjoa that her body was healing well, given the challenging situation she was experiencing. I gave her praise for her courage to be there for her baby. I reviewed nutrition, rest, and the importance of accepting support from her sister.

I supported her seeking therapeutic help for increasing her mechanisms of coping. I praised Adjoa's bonding efforts with the baby. I offered referral for couples' counseling. I offered to meet with her and Sallah if that would be of use.

I consulted with the perinatologist while Adjoa was in my office. He reported that he had informed Adjoa that in response to the baby's signs of respiratory effort yesterday, they had extubated the baby today and the baby was breathing spontaneously. Muscle tone remained hypotonic, with no sucking effort. The baby was to be started on NG tube feedings, and the breast milk would be given to the baby if tolerated. His management plan was cautious observation with a repeat CT scan in the next week to determine the amount of necrosis. Dependent on those findings, he would develop a management plan and options for Adjoa.

As I discussed these findings with Adjoa, she expressed being grateful that her breast milk might be of use. This act seemed to ground her through this time.

I discussed the possible feelings of guilt she might be experiencing and the importance of her agreement to start therapy in working this through.

> *According to Kennell and Klaus (1982), nursing responsibilities include: a. helping mother re-conceptualize image of 'ideal' infant to image of her acutely ill infant; b. helping mother deal with feelings of guilt; c. helping parents develop affectionate ties with infant; d. assisting parents to gain confidence in participating in caretaking tasks; e. assisting parents in support for transition to home care following discharge.*

I said I would be available for consultation with the perinatologist as the situation became clearer regarding the baby's status. I also reminded Adjoa that she could call my answering service if she needed to talk.

We scheduled a return visit for three weeks.

Interval note: Postpartum week 4

Consultation in hospital with Adjoa, perinatologist, head nurse of NICU, social worker, and myself regarding: baby's status. Sallah declined attendance due to work schedule. Perinatologist informed us that the baby had spontaneous respirations. However, there was evidence of multiple organ system dysfunction. The baby was unable to suck or move her limbs spontaneously; she was unresponsive to stimuli. She was feeding via an NG tube. He praised Adjoa for providing breast milk as this would help the baby's immune system. He told us that the baby had HIE with minimal cerebral functioning. He said the baby could live like this for an undetermined amount of time. When Adjoa asked what that meant, he said possibly months, though he did not really know. With a chronically ill baby being fed by NG tube, many other problems could potentially arise:

a. The depressed immune system could make the baby susceptible to infectious processes.

b. The NG tube kept the esophageal/gastric junction open, creating the possibility for aspiration and pneumonia.

c. The hypotonia would eventually turn to a contracted state; the baby would need physical therapy to maximize integrity of the muscles and skin.

d. With the baby unable to move spontaneously, the skin was at risk for breaking down, which could lead to infection.

He concluded that a long-term placement for palliative care was needed for the baby. He told Adjoa that she had two primary options:

a. Palliative care for the baby by placement in a long-term facility, which would care for the baby for the duration of her life.

b. Palliative care for the baby at home, with supportive services including specialized pediatric health attendants and physical therapists, with outpatient pediatric care. He cautioned that this option was a challenging one, as it was a full-time occupation, both emotionally and physically.

I stated that there was no judgment in whatever option Adjoa decided; this was her decision and a complicated one. I asked that she take time to talk this over with her family, including Sallah, as well as the social worker who could give more content as to what was involved in the options.

Adjoa appeared very stoic during the meeting. She said that she had held out hope that her baby would get better. She also said that this was her baby and she planned to take her baby home; for her there were no other options.

The perinatologist suggested that no decision had to be made for a week. I suggested that during this time Adjoa could spend time in the NICU and learn in greater detail what care would be needed for the baby. She could also meet with her family and her therapist to understand implications of her decision. I also suggested that she explore long-term residential facilities to become more familiar with that option. In this way she would make the decision with more thought and preparation. I also stated that if she decided to take the baby home for long-term palliative care, she could re-evaluate the situation if it became too difficult.

A: Newborn with severe anoxia leading to HIE in need of long-term palliative care

Mother in process of grief and acceptance; considering options for placement

Social service support needed

Therapeutic support needed

P: I facilitated a schedule for Adjoa to be present in the NICU when the nursing staff could instruct her in care for the baby, including management of the NG tube and feedings and skin care. This would include time with the physical therapist. The NICU nursing staff discharge team developed a plan which enabled Adjoa to assume responsibilities as she became proficient.

> *Family-centered care is based on two principles: enabling and empowering. These are more challenging when the parents are faced with a critically ill newborn. Whether a family attains growth from a positive resolution of this crisis or splinters because of a mal-adaptation depends on quality of support provided by the nursing staff (McGrath, 2003).*

This approach increased her skills as well as her confidence and attachment to the baby.

I scheduled an appointment with social services to again discuss palliative care and placement options. I gathered a list of online resources for Adjoa if she wanted to pursue more information. These included Children's Hospice International (*www.chionline.org*) and Footprints Program (*www.footprintsatglennon.org*) (Sudia-Robinson, 2003).

Social services agreed to coordinate obtaining services at home (home health aide, physical therapist).

I discussed with Adjoa the importance of giving herself permission to look at both options fully. I asked her about the involvement of Sallah; she confided that he had called her from another city and essentially told her that he did not plan to return at present. He admitted that he could not accept what had happened to the baby and needed space to "get his life together." When I explored how Adjoa felt about this additional loss, she told me that she was the one who had primarily wanted the pregnancy, so perhaps she was better off alone with the baby to give her full attention to learning how to care and love her baby. I told her I respected her courage and strength in an unimaginably difficult time.

We agreed to a visit in one week at the clinic, to include her postpartum care and discuss her decision.

VISIT 6: POSTPARTUM 5+ WEEKS (Office visit)

S: "I am bringing my baby home tomorrow. I have given it a lot of thought and I need to do this. My sister will stay with me for the next month at least. I am sad; I want my baby home, even if she is very sick."

States Sallah returned last week and took his things from the apartment. States she may be angry at him later for leaving, but right now her energy is just focused on her baby.

States she did think a lot about her options; she went online with the social worker and looked at placement sites for long-term care for the baby in the area. She verbalized that she understands what they offer, and that she could visit and be involved with the baby. However, she does not feel she needs this now.

States she has worked with the NICU discharge nurse to coordinate services for her baby to decrease fragmentation of care. She has arranged for specialized pediatric home care services who will come daily to her house to help with the baby; she also has interviewed two physical therapists and will schedule visits at home to see how they handle the baby. She has discussed and planned with the discharge nurse for physician services, nursing services, rehabilitative services, social work services, and nutritional support for the baby.

> *Determination of the services needed, their frequency and duration, and specific supplies and equipment requirements are critical to the discharge plan by the nursing staff (Therrien, 1993).*

States that she has family and financial support for this period of time in her life and her baby's needs.

She is continuing to pump her breasts; she feels this will help the baby's immune system.

She states she has learned a lot from the nurses at the hospital on managing feedings and skin care.

She states she is not interested in contraception at present as she does not anticipate becoming sexually active at present.

She inquired as to when she could start exercising, particularly her abdominal muscles.

She states she is seeing the therapist weekly and will continue, as this is helping her accept what is happening.

States that she is tired and has little appetite.

O: BP 116/70; P 68; T 98.4
U/a neg x 3
Wt. 125
Heart RR without murmurs
Lungs without adventitious sounds
Breasts soft, without masses, lactating. SBE reviewed
Abdomen nontender, + BS. Vertical incision well-healed. +2 diastasis recti
Extremities (-) Homan's, (-) varicosities
GYN: Vulva nl
Vagina pink, rugated
Cx closed, (-) d/c
Uterus nl size, A/V
Adnexa nonpalpable bilaterally
Good Kegels

A: Uterine involution completed.
At risk for exhaustion physically and emotionally from adaptation to chronically ill baby at home.
At risk for postpartum depression r/t baby's status and separation from partner.
At risk for isolation.
At risk for fragmentation of care.

P: Contraception discussed and options reviewed when Adjoa has a sexual relationship.
I instructed that she could begin moderate exercises, particularly abdominal, to strengthen abdominal muscle wall.
I ordered CBC to evaluate for anemia.
I prescribed multivitamins qd. I encouraged eating high-protein foods to meet increased energy needs.

I discussed my support as Adjoa initiated her new life with long-term palliative care for her baby at home. I initiated discussion of how she felt about the birth experience to assess her emotional coping with her decisions. She informed me that she had looked at this with her therapist, and though she felt great guilt at her decisions, she was working to accept them. She felt she had become much more stable and looked forward to having the baby home as her opportunity to mother this child. I explored that she have realistic goals about the challenges of meeting the needs of a baby with constant care. I wanted to reinforce that this was not a test of her ability to mother and that she could revisit options for placement if she changed her views. As she was clear about her decision, other than reminding her of the options, I supported her in her decision.

> *The American Academy of Pediatrics (2000) issued guidelines for the care of children with life-threatening and terminal conditions. The principles it has established for palliative care are: 1) respect for the dignity of parents and children; 2) access to competent and compassionate palliative care; 3) support for the caregivers; 4) improved professional and social support for pediatric palliative care; and 5) continued improvement of pediatric palliative care through research and education (AAP, 2000).*

I reviewed that she had supportive services in home to help. She had a schedule of pediatric visits at the back-up hospital, as well as adequate home support. I encouraged her work with the NICU discharge team to maximize coordination of care with the multidisciplinary team that has been assembled.

> *Discharge planning ensures that families have a plan for continuity of care as they transfer from acute care in a hospital setting to care in their community (Therrien, 1993).*

I supported her advocacy for her baby's care as an important step in gaining confidence in her ability to give care to her baby.

I suggested that I could do a home visit in a few weeks if that would be something she desired. She was grateful for my support and told me she would call.

I reminded her of her need for her annual Pap in three months.

HOME VISIT (Baby now 8 weeks old)

S: "We are doing okay, I think. I barely have a moment to think for myself, because the care for the baby takes all my time. I am getting good support from my sister and from the health-care people that work with me. In a strange way, I am learning new things about myself."

States she is eating (though not a lot) and does sleep at night. She goes out once a week alone to see the therapist. Otherwise she is with the baby around the clock.

States she has started having a few close women friends visit at home, and this helps her spirits. She has also started exercising at home as she still worries that she will not be able to return to modeling at some future point. She states she is okay financially for now. She said that Sallah visited the house last week for a few hours to see the baby. She does not imagine she will resume a relationship with him.

She states that she continues to pump her breasts, though not as often as it is too tiring. The baby gets two feeds/day via NG tube of breast milk.

I watched her feed the baby, exercise her limbs, coo and kiss her. I am able to hold the baby for a while; her muscle tone is becoming contracted.

When I leave, I tell Adjoa that she is courageous and impressive. She seems to have worked through her denial and guilt and at present has evidenced acceptance of her baby's quality of life. She has a sense of pride in her ability to find ways to love and care for her baby.

TELEPHONE CALL (Six + months after baby's birth)

I receive a call at work from Adjoa's sister. She tells me that the baby developed pneumonia three days ago, was taken to the ER, and admitted. The baby died yesterday in the hospital. She says that Adjoa wanted me to know and informs me of the funeral, to be held later this week. I thank her and ask when I can call Adjoa. She says that her sister is grieving and also very strong. She also says that in her own way her sister had been preparing for the baby's death while she learned to love her.

I talk with Adjoa later that day by phone. We cry together on the phone. She tells me that she knows she gave her baby the best care she could, and now the baby is at peace. She states she has lots of family support and would welcome my presence at the funeral. I ask her if she has called the therapist for support, and she states she plans to do that later that day.

VISIT 8 (Telephone call)

S: "I appreciate your calling me. I am sad but I also feel okay. I am going to go to visit family for a few weeks, and then I need to think about work and going on with my life."

States she has had help from her family rearranging the house and putting the baby's things away. She has visited the grave site several times and has a morning ritual prayer for the baby. States she cries often but also is able to imagine the future again. States eating and sleeping adequately.

A: Grieving appropriately.

P: As we talk, I assess that Adjoa is working through her grief appropriately. In fact, she has been doing this since the baby's birth. Her decision, in this case, to provide long-term palliative care at home, allowed her to claim an experience, mothering, that she needed in order to come to some acceptance of her decisions before the birth.

> There is growing recognition from the National Association of Neonatal Nurses, the Association of Pediatric Oncology Nurses, and the Society of Pediatric Nurses of the need for neonatal and pediatric palliative care. They have adapted the Last Acts Precepts (www.lastacts.org) for neonatal and pediatric patients (Kavanaugh, 2003).

I told Adjoa that the process of grieving is unique and varies in expression, duration, and meaning. She would probably experience it in different ways over the course of her life. I urged her to seek support whenever she needed.

> Kavanaugh (2003) stresses that bereaved families need to hear that grief is individualized; grief is a process; and family members should not hesitate to seek assistance with their grief, even years after the child's death.

I also gave her feedback that I thought she was in the stage of reorganization, or integrating her loss into her life, as she had done so much work on both holding on and letting go of her baby. I also informed her that investigators have found that women may exhibit grief behaviors for years following the death of a child (Walsh, 2001).

I shared with her that I have also learned a great deal about respecting a patient's ability to make decisions and live with them, after receiving education about the impact of these decisions. I have learned about courage and the ability to greatly alter one's life when challenges demand this.

I reminded her that I am available for her well-woman care as well as grieving support as needed.

> Walsh (2001) writes that the woman's health-care provider continues to be a primary supportive resource for the woman and that continued assessments through the year following

the birth provide support for the woman and provide the opportunity for referrals that may be necessary when grieving is not progressing in a healthy way.

References

American Academy of Pediatrics (2000). *Palliative care for children.* Pediatrics, 106 (2): 351 – 357.

Best, M. (1993). *The family in crisis.* In P. Beachy & J. Deacon (Eds.), Core Curriculum for Neonatal Intensive Care Nursing. Philadephia: W.B. Saunders Company, 537 – 548.

Contro, N., et al. (2004). *Hospital staff and family perspectives regarding quality of pediatric palliative care.* Pediatrics, 114 (5): 1248 – 52.

Flavin, N. (2001). *Perinatal asphyxia: a clinical review, including research with brain hypothermia.* Neonatal Network, 20 (3): 31 – 40.

Kavanaugh, K., Wheeler, S. (2003). *When a baby dies: caring for bereaved families.* In C. Kenner & J. Lott (Eds.), Comprehensive Neonatal Nursing (3rd ed.). New York: Saunders, 108 – 126.

Kavanaugh, K., Paton, J. (2001). *Communicating with parents who experience a perinatal loss.* Illness, Crisis, and Loss, 9, 369 – 380.

Kennell, J.H., Klaus, M.H. (1982). *Parent-Infant Bonding* (2nd ed.). St. Louis: C.V. Mosby.

Kubler-Ross, E. (1969). *On Death and Dying.* New York: Macmillan.

Liben, S. (1996). *Pediatric palliative medicine: obstacles to overcome.* Journal of Palliative Care, 12 (3): 24 – 28.

McGrath, J. (2003). *Family-centered care.* In C. Kenner & J. Lott (Eds.), Comprehensive Neonatal Nursing (3rd ed.). New York: Saunders, 89 – 107.

McGrath, J. (2001). *Building relationships with families in the NICU: exploring the guarded alliance.* Journal of Perinatal and Neonatal Nursing, 15 (4): 1 – 10.

McHugh, M. (2004). *Recognition and immediate care of sick newborns.* In Varney's Midwifery (4th ed.). Boston: Jones and Bartlett Publishers, 1029 – 1040.

Milstein, J. (2003). *Detoxifying death in the neonate: in search of meaningfulness at the end of life.* Journal of Perinatology, 23 (4): 333 – 6.

National Hospice and Palliative Care Organization (NHPCO) (2000). *Compendium of Pediatric Palliative Care.* New Orleans: NHPCO.

Perlman, J. (1989). *Systemic abnormalities in term infants following perinatal asphyxia: relevance to long-term neurologic outcome.* Clinical Perinatology, 16: 475 – 484.

Rushton, C.H. (2000). *Pediatric palliative care: coming of age.* Innovations in End-of-Life Care, 2 (2) (Online journal).

Sahler, O., et al. (2000). *Medical education about end-of-life care in the pediatric setting: principles, challenges, and opportunities.* Pediatrics, 105 (3 Pt 1): 575 – 84.

Stephenson, J. (2000). *Palliative and hospice care needed for children with life-threatening conditions.* Journal of the American Medical Association, 284 (19): 2437 – 2438.

Sudia-Robinson, T. (2003). *Hospice and palliative care.* In C. Kenner & J. Lott (Eds). Comprehensive Neonatal Nursing (3rd ed.). New York: Saunders, 127 – 131.

Therrien, L. (1993). *Discharge planning for the high-risk neonate.* In P. Beachy & J. Deacon (Eds.), Core Curriculum for Neonatal Intensive Care Nursing. Philadelphia: W.B. Saunders Company, 565 – 572.

Varney, H., et al. (2004). *Varney's Midwifery* (4th ed.). Boston: Jones and Bartlett Publishers.

Walsh, L. (2001). *Midwifery Community-Based Care During the Childbearing Year.* Philadelphia: W.B. Saunders Company, 480 – 486.

Wu, Y. (2004). *Etiology and pathogenesis of neonatal encephalopathy.* Retrieved in 2004 from http://www.uptodate.com.

Medication management decisions for two adults with Parkinson's disease

The care provided for two patients with Parkinson's disease is reviewed in this case study to examine the application of limited information regarding potential adverse medication effects in the clinical decision-making process.

CONTEXT OF THE DISCUSSION

In 2002, a case review in Mayo Clinic Proceedings reported three patients with severe, unexplained tricuspid regurgitation who were treated with pergolide for Parkinson's disease (PD) (Pritchet, 2002). Histologic examination of the patients' surgically excised valves revealed surface fibroproliferative lesions with preserved underlying valve architecture. Similar findings had been described in carcinoid syndrome (Simula, 2002; Robiolio, 1995), methysergide (Bana, 1974), ergotamine (Redfield, 1992; Hauck, 1990), fenfluramine, and dexfenfluramine valvular heart disease (Connolly, 1997). None of the patients had been treated with these medications and carcinoid heart valve disease was excluded. The authors suggested that there might be an association between pergolide and fibrotic valvular heart disease (FVHD) (Pritchett, 2002).

Pergolide, an ergot derivative dopamine agonist, was approved for the treatment of PD in 1989 (Mizuno, 1995). The most common side effects of pergolide are dyskinesias, hallucinations, somnolence, insomnia, nausea, constipation, diarrhea, and dyspepsia (Waters, 2002). Retroperitoneal, pericardial, and pleural fibrosis are very rare adverse events (Jimenez-Jimenez, 1995; Pfitzenmeyer, 1996; Shaunak, 1999; Ling, 2004; Mondal, 2000).

After reading the article, I searched Medline and did not find previous reports of pergolide associated valvular heart disease (PAVHD). The literature described FVHD as a complication of ergotamine, fenfluramine, and dexfenfluramine (Weissman, 1998; Redfield, 1992) and hypothesized that these medications caused FVHD through serotonin-mediated abnormal fibrogenesis by the 5-HT2B receptors expressed in heart valve fibroblasts (Fitzgerald, 2001). In carcinoid heart disease, high serotonin levels were correlated with valve lesions (Robiolio, 1995). It was hypothesized that serotonin (5HT)2 released in excessive amounts stimulated 5-HT2B receptors on cardiac valves, exerting a trophic effect on myofibroblasts, which caused valvular fibrosis (Newman-Tancredi, 2002). Pergolide had been reported to have agonist properties at some 5HT receptors (Boess, 1994). Given this information, it was reasonable to discuss the report with patients as pergolide, an ergot derivative, could possibly have similar effects, although the medication had been approved for the treatment of PD in the United States for 14 years and no previous events had been reported.

The collaborating physician and I discussed the report findings and concluded that patients treated with pergolide needed (1) to be informed of review findings, (2) assessment of cardiac function, and (3) review of medication treatment history to determine all potential therapeutic options so individual treatment plans could be developed. The cases that follow discuss the care provided for a patient during a follow-up appointment and a patient presenting for initial consultation.

NARRATIVE FOR FIRST PATIENT

55-year-old, right-hand dominant, Dominican, Spanish-speaking woman diagnosed with PD 14 years ago; presenting symptoms bradykinesia, increased tone, and left-hand tremor, returns for follow-up of PD and review of medication regimen to evaluate the need for pergolide in treatment of PD. Patient is accompanied by her husband and home attendant. History provided by patient and husband.

Patient states she is doing well since her last appointment.

PD is a chronic, progressive neurodegenerative disease. Symptoms of PD usually begin between ages 40 and 70 years with peak age of onset during the sixth decade (Waters, 2002). The incidence of PD increases with age. A population-based investigation of PD conducted in Northern Manhattan (Mayeux, 1992) found the crude prevalence of idiopathic PD was 99.4/100,000 increasing from 2.3/100,000 for those under age 50 to 1145/100,000 for those over age 80. The prevalence ratios found in this study were comparable to the ratios of other population-based studies in the United States.

Symptoms of PD are caused by pathology within the extrapyramidal system. In Parkinson's disease there is destruction of the dopaminergic, pigmented neurons in the pars compacta of the substantia nigra. Degeneration of the nigrostriatal dopamine system leads to depletion of striatal dopamine. Lewy bodies — intracytoplasmic inclusions composed of protein aggregates — in the substantia nigra are the characteristic histological finding in PD (Forno, 1981).

Input from all areas of the cerebral cortex as well as dopaminergic pathways from the ventral midbrain and thalamus are received by the input zone of the basal ganglia which consists of the putamen, caudate nucleus, and ventral striatum (Fahn, Jancovic, Hallet, & Jenner, 2004). The output zone of the basal ganglia is comprised of the medial globus pallidus and the substantia nigra pars reticulata. The output zone projects to the thalamus and brainstem. Neurons in the thalamus project to premotor and prefrontal structures. There is also an intermediate zone, within the basal ganglia, consisting of the lateral globus pallidus and the subthalamic nucleus. Segregated circuits within the basal ganglia receive input from different areas of the cerebral cortex and send output to the final destination, the frontal lobe. These circuits may serve as the neural substrates for parallel processing of different functions. Dopamine abnormalities within these circuits cause the manifestations of PD.

Within the basal ganglia, connections are made by two balanced dopaminergic systems, the indirect and direct pathways. These pathways have opposite effects. The direct pathway facilitates cortically initiated movement. In this pathway input from the sensorimotor cortex, mediated by glutamate, or input from the substantia nigra pars compacta, mediated by dopamine, excite inhibitory pathways from the putamen to the medial globus pallidus and substantia nigra pars reticulata, resulting in disinhibition of thalamic targets that project excitatory input onto precentral motor fields. Dopamine activity in the direct pathway is mediated by the D1-like receptors, D1 and D5. In the indirect pathway, corticostriatal stimulation leads to increased inhibition of thalamic targets and reduced thalamo-cortical input onto precentral motor fields. In the nigrostriatal-pallidal system, dopamine inhibits the indirect pathway. Dopamine activity in the indirect pathway is mediated by the D2-like receptors, which include the D2 short, D2 long, D3, and D4 receptors.

Depletion of striatal dopamine upsets the balance between the indirect and direct systems. Dopamine activates excitatory D1-like receptors in the direct pathway and suppresses inhibitory D2-like receptors in the indirect pathway. Dopamine depletion results in decreased activity of the direct pathway and increased activity of the indirect pathway, resulting in inhibition of cortically initiated movement.

Symptom onset in idiopathic PD is gradual, occurring after 80% reduction in striatal dopamine (Waters, 2002). Initially, affected persons may not be aware of symptoms. Diagnosis may be made several years after symptom onset. Clinically, PD is characterized by variable combinations of resting tremor, rigidity, bradykinesia, and postural reflex impairment. The classic manifestation of PD is a resting tremor that begins unilaterally in an extremity before affecting the opposite side of the body. Rigidity, which is defined as an increase in resistance to passive movement, can cause pain in the affected extremity as well as stooped posture. Bradykinesia, which can progress to akinesia, is one of the most disabling symptoms. Manifestations of bradykinesia include decreased arm swing when walking, masked facies, drooling of saliva, hypokinetic dysarthria, and hypophonia. Freezing, the sudden, transient inability to move a body part for several seconds, is a manifestation of akinesia. Patients may also have impaired cognitive function that can progress to dementia (Delong, 2005).

HISTORY OF PRESENTING ILLNESS

At last appointment, two months previously, her symptoms included motor fluctuations, gait freezing, frequent falls, and mild hallucinations. Medications were not changed because she was comfortable with her ability to function. Physical therapy (PT) and consistent use of front-wheeled walker were recommended for impaired gait and postural instability.

As PD progresses, most patients should have a formal PT evaluation to assess needs and set specific goals. Prescribed exercises can improve gait and postural stability (de Goede, 2001).

Events since her last appointment: She did not keep her appointment for PT after the initial evaluation because appointments at a hospital-based center were only available in the afternoon when severe dyskinesias made ambulette travel too difficult.

Three weeks previously, she fell in the house and fractured two ribs. The fall occurred in the "off state." She was alone in the kitchen, bent forward to take a cup from a cabinet, lost her balance, and fell, striking the right side of her torso against the cabinet. She did not strike her head or lose consciousness. Her husband took her to the Emergency Room via 911 ambulance. She had X-rays and was discharged home with a prescription for Tylenol #2, which she did not purchase. Due to pain, she has been walking less at home and in the street. She denies fever, chills, chest pain, SOB, cough, nausea, or vomiting. Her husband has moved a set of dishes to the kitchen counter to prevent future falls.

Current symptoms: Motor fluctuation: Patient states motor symptoms have remained stable since the last appointment. She takes her first dose of medications before breakfast with ginger ale. The carbidopa/levodopa is chewed. She begins to feel the medication effect in ½ hour. She begins to feel slow and stiff 3½ hours after each carbidopa/levodopa dose, which she takes approximately every four hours during the day. When her medication "wears off," she moves slowly and requires assistance with cutting food but rates her activities of daily living (ADL), Schwab and England score 60%. In the "off" state she has gait freezing, which usually occurs in doorways or when she gets up from a seated position. She falls two to three times a day. According to her husband, her falls usually follow freezing episodes when she does not use her cane or walker. She states she does not use the cane or walker because it makes her feel like she is giving in to her illness. She is embarrassed being seen in public using a walker. For this reason, she recently stopped going to church. At night, she sleeps well in one position. Her husband states she appears confused and has difficulty concentrating in the "off" state.

In the "on" state, she is able to dress, bathe, cut food, and eat slowly without assistance; Schwab and England score 80%. Approximately 1½ hours after each carbidopa/levodopa dose she experiences peak dose dyskinesias for 20 minutes. The dyskinesias are not uncomfortable. She feels her mouth twist. Her dyskinesias do not affect eating, drinking, or speech.

She has bilateral arm and leg tremors that are not a source of disability. Her handwriting is micrographic and illegible.

An average of 4.1 years after starting levodopa therapy for Parkinsonian symptoms, 28 – 84% of patients develop motor response complications (Chase, 1993). Motor complications can occur as predictable "wearing off" fluctuations, unpredictable "on-off" fluctuations, and dyskinesias.

The "wearing off" phenomenon is the most common motor fluctuation. It is characterized by a progressive shortening of the benefit period following each dose of levodopa and progressive increase in "off" periods. Patients with "wearing off" demonstrate 2 – 4 hour benefit after each levodopa dose (Stern, 1993; Riley, 1993). "Wearing off" symptoms correlate with falling levodopa plasma levels (Fahn, 1982). Central factors including small dopamine storage capacity, dopamine receptor alteration, and peripheral pharmacokinetic factors have been studied as causes of the wearing off response (Mouradian, 1988; de la Fuente-Fernandez, 2001; Fahn, 2004).

Patients have reported that the "off" state with partial or full immobility is more troubling than the dyskinesias. During "off" periods, patients may experience sensory, psychiatric, and autonomic symptoms as well as motor "offs." Nonmotor "off" symptoms include paresthesias, pain, tachycardia, sweating, constipation, belching, and shortness of breath (Fahn, 1982).

Dyskinesias are related to severity of disease (Horstink, 1990; Luquin, 1992), duration of disease (Roos, 1990), and levodopa dosage (Poewe, 1986). Peak-dose dyskinesias represent an overdosed state with elevated plasma levodopa levels and excess striatal dopamine (Meunter, 1977). Ten percent of patients developed dyskinesias within the six months of initiating levodopa therapy. Thirty-six percent of patients developed dyskinesias within four to six years of initiating levodopa therapy. Eighty-eight percent of patients manifest dyskinesias after nine years of treatment with levodopa.

The Schwab and England Activities of Daily Living Scale is a quantitative, forced-choice rating scale routinely used in clinical practice to describe and monitor the patient's functional ability (Waters, 2002). The scale contains 10 descriptions of different levels of ability to complete self-care chores. The patient chooses the description that best matches his/her ability. A percentage (value) is assigned to each description. Clinically, the percentage is followed over time to assess changes in the patient's level of function. A score of 100% describes a person with no functional impairment. A score of 0 describes a person who is completely bedridden. A score of 80% "Completely independent in most chores. Takes twice as long. Conscious of difficulty and slowness." Score of 60%, "Some dependency. Can do most chores but exceedingly slowly and with much effort. Errors: some possible."

Hallucinations: She sees rats running around her bed every night. Sometimes she sees her grandchildren playing in the house. If she looks away from the hallucinations, they disappear. She also asks her husband, who tells her the hallucinations are not real, and they disappear. She does not find the hallucinations frightening.

> *PD medications that can cause hallucinations include levodopa, dopamine agonists (bromocriptine, pergolide, pramipexole, and ropinirole), selegiline, amantadine, apomorphine, and anticholinergic agents. Visual hallucinations are the most common feature of drug-induced psychoses and are found in 30% of levodopa treated patients. The hallucinations are usually nonthreatening and recurrent. In approximately 28% of patients, the hallucinations become threatening. Drug-induced psychoses are most likely caused by dysfunction of the central serotonergic pathways (Goetz, 1993).*

Depression: Treated with medication for two years, which she finds helpful. States she feels sad and angry intermittently during the day when she can't do things. The feelings are not persistent. Appetite is good. She is sleeping well. She does not feel hopeless or suicidal. She worries about being a burden to her husband. She does not want behavioral therapy. She finds comfort in prayer.

> *Forty percent of patients with PD suffer from depression, characterized by high levels of anxiety with milder self-punitive ideation (Cummings, 1992).*

CURRENT MEDICATIONS

Medication	Strength	8 AM	12 noon	4 PM	8 PM
Carbidopa/levodopa	25/100	2 tablets	2 tablets	2 tablets	1 tablet

> *Levodopa is the immediate metabolic precursor of dopamine. More than 95% of levodopa is rapidly decarboxylated in the periphery. Approximately 1% crosses the blood-brain barrier to permeate striatal tissue. Levodopa is administered with carbidopa, a peripheral inhibitor of dopadecarboxylase, which increases the amount of unmetabolized drug available to cross the blood brain barrier. Levodopa is the gold standard for treatment of PD. The most serious side effects of carbidopa/levodopa are dyskinesias, involuntary movements, paranoid ideation, psychotic episodes, nausea, cardiac irregularities, orthostatic hypotension, anorexia, vomiting, dizziness (Waters, 2002).*

> *This patient's pharmacological regimen is based on carbidopa/levodopa, the most effective medication currently available for the treatment of PD symptoms. Before levodopa became available, severe disability occurred in 16% of patients within five years of disease onset, in 37% of patients during the next five years, and in 42% of patients who survived 15 years (Fahn, 1995).*

Pergolide	1 mg tablet	½ tablet	½ tablet	½ tablet	XXXX

> *Pergolide is primarily a D2 receptor agonist with very weak D1 agonist effects and mild D3 agonist effects. Pergolide is one of the most frequently prescribed dopamine agonists worldwide (Kuniyoshi, 2005). Side effects are discussed on page 93 of this book.*

> *The long-term complications of levodopa therapy are discussed on page 96 of this book. Persons who develop symptoms of PD before age 40 are classified as having young onset PD (YOPD). Patients with YOPD are more likely to develop motor complications due to levodopa therapy. After five years of treatment with levodopa, 91% of YOPD patients*

developed motor fluctuations and dyskinesias. One hundred percent of patients were affected after 10 years of levodopa therapy (Schrag, 1998).

During the early stages of disease, when patients who are not elderly or extremely ill require pharmacological treatment, dopamine agonists are one of the classes of medication considered. The dopamine agonists directly stimulate receptors in the normal striatum and bypass the failing nigrostriatal pathway. They are the most effective class of PD medication for symptomatic treatment of PD after levodopa. There is a lower risk for the development of dyskinesias compared with levodopa. In the late stages of disease, the dopamine agonists can be used to supplement the effect of levodopa (Waters, 2002).

For this patient, pergolide is used to supplement carbidopa/levodopa in treatment of PD symptoms.

Medication	Strength	8 AM	12 noon	4 PM	8 PM
Amantadine	100 mg tablet	1 tablet	1 tablet	XXXX	XXXX

Amantadine is an antiviral agent (Shannon, 1987). While the mechanism of action is not known, it is reported to release dopamine from central neurons, delay neuronal dopamine uptake, and have anticholinergic effects. Adverse effects include confusion, hallucinations, and reversible lower-extremity edema (Waters 2002). Some studies have reported that amantadine decreases dyskinesias in advanced PD (Metaman Verhagen, 1998). Luginger (2000) found the antidyskinetic effect lasted less than eight months. Forty patients with advanced PD and levodopa-induced dyskinesias were treated with up to 300 mg of amantadine/day or placebo. Patients in the amantadine group demonstrated improvement in UPDRS IV questions 32 – 34, Dyskinesia Rating Scale, and Investigator Global Assessment scores at 15 and 30 days. Dyskinesia scores returned to baseline over the next seven months. Due to worsening dyskinesias, no patients in the amantadine group remained in treatment after eight months. No placebo group patients remained in treatment after three months. Systematic reviews (Thomas, 2004; Crosby, 2003) have reported that it was not possible to determine whether amantadine was a safe and effective treatment for patients with levodopa-induced dyskinesias due to a lack of evidence.

Amantadine is prescribed for this patient for two reasons: (1) to treat dyskinesias and (2) in advanced PD, when the effectiveness of levodopa is decreasing, an additive effect has been demonstrated between levodopa and amantadine. The addition of amantadine to levodopa can reduce symptoms (Waters, 2002).

Quetiapine	25 mg tablet	XXXX	XXXX	XXXX	3 tablets

Quetiapine is an atypical antipsychotic. The most common side effects include headache, agitation, dry mouth, constipation, vomiting, weight gain, and difficulty swallowing. Major potential risks and side effects of therapy include neuroleptic malignant syndrome, tardive dyskinesia, high blood sugar, low blood pressure, dizziness, increased heart rate, syncope, cataracts, seizures, hypothyroidism, elevated cholesterol or triglycerides, priaprism, and difficulty swallowing (U.S. Food and Drug Administration, 2004).

Torsade de pointe and sudden death due to arrhythmia have been reported with atypical antipsychotic medications (Haddad, 2002). Review of one-half million Tennessee Medicaid enrollees for an average of 2.5 years found 1,487 sudden unexpected cardiac deaths occurred. The risk of sudden death among adults treated with antipsychotic medication was 2.39 times that of nonusers (Ray, 2001). According to Glassman and Bigger (2001), although quetiapine binds to the IKr channel and can prolong the QTc interval, there is no evidence that it has caused torsade de pointe or ventricular fibrillation. In April 2005, the FDA issued a safety advisory that included quetiapine. Analyses of 17 placebo-controlled studies of atypical antipsychotic medications found the death rate for elderly persons with dementia was 1.6 – 1.7 that of placebo. Quetiapine is prescribed to treat this patient's hallucinations.

Venlafaxine	75 mg tablet	1 tablet	XXXX	XXXX	XXXX

Venlafaxine is a serotonin and norepinephrine reuptake inhibitor for treatment of depression. At doses up to 150 mg/day it functions like an SSRI. No controlled trials have been conducted with persons with PD. Adverse reactions include GI upset, dizziness, somnolence, insomnia, sexual dysfunction, sweating, dry mouth, nervousness, hypotension, abnormal dreams, yawn, paresthesia, agitation, anorexia, and weight change. It should be used with caution in patients with hepatic, renal, or cardiovascular disease (Karch, 2005). Venlafaxine is prescribed to treat this patient's depression.

Allergies: None known to medication, environment.

Social: She does not smoke, drink alcohol, or use recreational drugs. She lives with her husband in a first-floor handicapped-accessible apartment equipped with safety equipment. Her husband does not work and is her primary caregiver. She has a home attendant four hours Monday through Friday. Her children live in the Dominican Republic and visit twice a year. She uses ambulette services for transportation. She watches TV and reads for recreation. Neighbors in the building visit daily. Weather permitting, she and her home attendant sit in the park two blocks from her house several times a week.

PAST HISTORY

PMH: She denies history of cardiac disease, hypertension, diabetes, renal disease, or cancer.

PSH: Denies.

Psychological: See HPI.

FAMILY HISTORY

There is no family history of movement disorder or cardiac disease.

The cause of PD for the majority of patients is probably multifactorial, resulting from the interaction of a number of genetic and environmental risk factors. In a community-based study, researchers have shown that the lifetime risk of PD in a parent or sibling of an individual with PD is approximately 2%. This compares to a 1% lifetime risk of PD in an individual without a parent or sibling with PD (Marder, 1996).

REVIEW OF SYSTEMS

General: Denies fever, sweats, weight loss.

Skin: Denies history of skin disease, change in skin color, pruritus, rash, or melanoma.

Head: Occasional headache relieved with acetaminophen. Denies injury, dizziness, syncope, or vertigo.

Eyes: Denies blurred or double vision, transient vision loss, eye pain, discharge.

Ears: Denies hearing loss, tinnitus, and vertigo.

Nose: Denies nasal congestion, sinus pain.

Mouth: Denies difficulty swallowing, bleeding gums, or dental problems.

Neck: Denies pain, lumps, or swollen glands.

Respiratory: Denies wheezing, cough, hemoptysis, pneumonia, asthma, or SOB. PPD negative last year.

Cardiovascular: Denies chest pain, palpitations, SOB, orthopnea, edema, claudication angina, hypertension, heart murmur, MI, or CHF. Primary care provider did an EKG a few years ago that she was told was normal.

GI: Appetite good. Denies food intolerance, abdominal pain, nausea, vomiting. Bowel movement qd-qod without BRBPR or black stool. Uses rancho recipe to prevent constipation.

GU/GYN: Urinary urgency and occasional incontinence during the day due to difficulty ambulating to bathroom in "off" state. Wears liners during the day and adult diapers at night. Has a bedside commode that she does not use. During the day she empties bladder every two hours. No sexual dysfunction. Denies history of STIs or HIV risk. LMP eight years ago. Last gyn exam one year ago, no pathology reported.

Musculoskeletal: See HPI.

Neurological: Denies history of seizure disorder, fainting (see HPI).

Hematologic: Denies clots, anemia, transfusions, or excessive bruising.

Endocrine: Denies heat or cold intolerance, polydipsia, polyphagia, or polyuria.

Psychological: See HPI.

GENERAL EXAM

Blood pressure 130/80 regular size cuff, right arm sitting and standing. Pulse 80, Resp 12. Weight 150 pounds, height 62 inches.

Skin: Warm and dry with multiple ecchymotic areas on arms and legs in different stages of resolution. Patient and husband state these are due to falls.

Neck: Supple, thyroid without bruits or enlargement, no jugular venous distention.

Lungs: Vesicular breath sounds, without use of accessory muscles.

Cardiovascular: RR S$_1$, S$_2$, without murmurs, rubs, gallops, PMI 5th interspace left midclavicular line. The examination is limited by severe flexed neck and trunkal flexion.

Abdomen: Soft and nontender, without organomegaly. Bowel sounds present in all quadrants.

Musculoskeletal: Severe flexed neck and trunk flexion, unchanged since last exam.

Extremities: Radial, femoral, dorsalis pedis pulses 2+ and = bilaterally, without edema.

NEUROLOGICAL EXAM

Patient examined in the "on" state. A complete Unified Parkinson's Disease Rating Scale (UPDRS) performed. She has moderate dyskinesias of arms and legs.

> *The UPDRS consists of three separate sections (Fahn et al., 1987). The first section of the UPDRS can be completed by the patient and reviewed by the provider or completed by the patient and provider (Louis, Lynch, Marder, & Fahn, 1996). The section asks specific questions about symptoms and functional capacity. The section consists of 17 questions: four questions address mentation, behavior, and mood; 13 questions address activities of daily living. Each item has five forced-choice answers that are scored on a 0 to 4 scale. A score of zero represents the absence of symptomatology. A score of four represents severe symptomatology. The second section of the UPDRS consists of a 14-item motor examination that is performed by the clinician. For each item there are five forced-choice answers. A score of zero for an item represents the absence of abnormal motor findings. A score of four represents clinical findings of severe motor impairment for that item. The final section consists of 11 questions that address complications of therapy and clinical fluctuations in therapy. Four items have five forced-choice answers that are scored on a 0 to 4 scale. A score of zero represents the absence of symptomatology. A score of four represents severe symptomatology. Seven items require a yes or no answer regarding presence of specific complications. Validation of the UPDRS demonstrated high internal consistency (Cronbach's alpha = .96), satisfactory criterion-related and convergent validity, and satisfactory interrater reliability (Van Hilten, 1994; Richards, 1994; Martinez-Martin, 1994).*

Mental status: She is alert and cooperative. She cannot recall the date or address, cannot calculate change or perform serial subtraction. She names 3/5 presidents, recalls 2/3 objects, and draws a clock face with all numbers but is unable to set the time. Palmomental and glabellar reflexes present.

Cranial nerves: Pupils equal, round, reactive to light, without square wave jerks, without nystagmus. Extraocular movements intact. Facial sensation normal to light touch bilaterally. Facial movements are symmetric. She has a tendency to stare with a decreased blink rate. Her voice is hoarse and hypophonic. She has lower facial grimacing and purses her lips. Hearing grossly normal bilaterally to whisper. Her palate elevates symmetrically, tongue midline on protrusion, cough intact. Shoulder shrug asymmetric, left slower than right.

Sensory: Sensation was grossly intact to light touch and vibration in extremities.

Motor: Power 5/5 in all extremities. She has moderately increased tone in her upper extremities and neck. Left upper extremity tremor present at rest more than action. Finger tap, supination-pronation, hand grasps, and leg agility demonstrate moderate bradykinesia, left more severely affected than right. She has dyskinesias in all extremities that increase when she concentrates on performing tasks or becomes anxious. She arises from a chair briskly. Her posture is slightly stooped. Her gait is narrow based with good arm swing. She walks in a semi-circle to turn. She has retropulsion on pull testing, requiring assistance to recover.

CHART REVIEW:
PREVIOUS MEDICATION TREATMENT FOR PD

Year since Dx.	Intervention/Response
One	• Symptoms were mild and did not affect ADL. Symptoms were present for three years prior to diagnosis. • No medication required.
Two	• Selegiline 5 mg bid improved slowness and clumsiness with eating and preparing food. • Symptoms adequately relieved for five years. *Selegiline, an irreversible inhibitor of MAO-B, may have a neuro-protective effect (PSG, 1989), provide symptom benefit for patients with mild disease (Langston, 2000), and prolong the symptom benefit of levodopa in advanced disease (Waters, 2002). The medication should not be prescribed for patients over age 65 or persons with cognitive impairment as it can cause further decompensation and psychosis (PSG, 1989).*
Seven	• Gait increasingly narrow based with shuffling steps. • Pramipexole added. Pramipexole caused fatigue, sleepiness, and leg swelling. • Pramipexole was discontinued after six months. *Pramipexole is a nonergot dopamine benzothiazole agonist. Pramipexole binds to the D3 receptor subtype of the D2 receptor class (Mierau, 1995). In clinical trials of pramipexole, as monotherapy, patients receiving pramipexole demonstrated significant improvement in ability to perform activities of daily living and motor symptoms (Shannon, 1997; PSG, 1997). Pramipexole was compared to levodopa in a multicenter, randomized, parallel group double-blind study (PSG, 2000). At 23 months, the levodopa group demonstrated significant improvement in motor scores and ability to perform activities of daily living compared to the pramipexole group. The pramipexole-treated patients reported significantly less dyskinesias, motor fluctuation, and wearing-off symptoms compared with levodopa-treated patients. The most common side effects are nausea, dyskinesia, hallucination, confusion, and postural hypotension. A serious adverse effect of pramipexole is sleep attack. Seven patients have fallen asleep while driving, resulting in serious accidents. The sleep attacks occurred without warning (Frucht, 1999).*
Seven	• Ropinirole added to selegiline. • Ropinirole caused dizziness and somnolence. • Ropinirole discontinued after three months. *Ropinirole is a dopamine agonist with a nonergoline structure similar to dopamine (Tulloch, 1997). Ropinirole stimulates D2 and D3 receptors. Side effects of ropinirole include nausea, dizziness, postural hypotension, syncope, somnolence, confusion, and hallucinations.*
Eight	• Treatment with pergolide initiated. Gait improved with pergolide and no adverse effects were reported.

Eleven	• Gait freezing. Carbidopa/levodopa was added to selegiline and pergolide. Gait and bradykinesia responded.
Twelve	• Depressed about the impact of her disease on her life. • Treatment with venlafaxine, with improved mood. • Urinary urgency with incontinence. • Patient chose not to take medication.
Thirteen	• Painful peak dose dyskinesias. • Selegiline discontinued. • Pergolide dosage reduced with decrease in dyskinesias but increased bradykinesia.
Fourteen	• Amantadine added to treat dyskinesias with decrease in dyskinesias. • Patient subsequently developed hallucinations. No evidence of intercurrent illness; malignancy; stroke; electrolyte disturbance; renal, metabolic, or hepatic dysfunction; anemia; or infection. • Amantadine tapered with return of painful dyskinesias and no change in hallucinations. Amantadine benefit acknowledged. Amantadine increased to present dose with decrease in dyskinesias and no change in hallucinations. • Pergolide dosage reduced and quetiapine added with reduction in hallucinations. • Patient did not tolerate reduction in pergolide below present dosage (0.5 mg tid). She experienced deep "offs" with panic attacks in "off" state.

LABORATORY REVIEW

Mammogram without abnormal findings one year ago.
Bone density within normal limits five years ago.

IMPRESSION

55-year-old woman with PD, complicated by wearing off, dyskinesias, falls triggered by freezing episodes, medication-induced hallucinations, dementia, and depression treated with medication. The patient and husband feel quality of life is acceptable on the current medication regimen.

An article published in *Mayo Clinic Proceedings* has raised concerns about PAVHD. Discontinuing the pergolide, which augments carbidopa/levodopa, will result in more "off" time and further decrease her quality of life. Several months ago, pergolide dosage was reduced to eliminate hallucinations. This resulted in severe "off" freezing and precipitated panic episodes in the "off" state. She experienced side effects with two other dopamine agonists, so changing the agonist is not a therapeutic option. Other medications that improve motor function could cause cognitive impairment or increase dyskinesias, compromising her safety. Given her cognitive impairment, she is not a candidate for deep brain stimulation surgery.

PLAN

Pergolide and FVHD. The patient does not describe cardiac or respiratory symptoms. Murmur not appreciated on examination, however, examination is limited by dyskinesias and severe neck and trunkal flexion.

The Mayo Clinic case review was discussed with the patient and her husband who elected to continue treatment with pergolide based on symptom benefit. Echocardiogram ordered and pergolide continued, at current dosage, pending results.

Diagnostic	• Baseline echocardiogram/EKG
	  ▪ If echocardiogram is without pathology, will continue present dose and monitor cardiac status according to center-specific guidelines.
	  ▪ If pathology demonstrated, taper & d/c pergolide with referral to cardiology.

Education & Counseling	• Cardiac symptoms
	  ▪ Possible association of pergolide and FVHD.
	  ▪ If symptoms experienced, contact PCP and this office.
	  ▪ Continued use of pergolide and cardiac monitoring plan will be revised as data become available.

Medications	• Continue pergolide as prescribed.
Referral	• Letter to PCP regarding treatment plan and rationale.

Hallucinations without change since last appointment. Patient and husband are comfortable with mild hallucinations.

Thirty percent of PD patients treated with medication experience visual hallucinations (Waters, 2002; Naimark, 1996), which appear as animals or familiar people (Inzelberg, 1998). Patients with mild hallucinations have insight and know they are false. These hallucinations can progress and the person becomes confused and paranoid. Atypical antipsychotic drugs do not aggravate parkinsonism while treating the psychoses. Treatment is usually initiated with quetiapine.

Education & Counseling	• If change in hallucinations, contact this office.
Medications	• Continue as prescribed.

Hallucinations and dyskinesias: While patient is comfortable with current treatment for her hallucinations, clozapine could treat hallucinations and dyskinesias. She will consider changing to clozapine after decision is made regarding pergolide.

Clozapine can suppress dyskinesias while increasing "on" time (Bennet, 1993, 1994; Pierelli, 1998). Clozapine is a tricyclic dibenzodiazepine with minimal central dopaminergic antagonism. Clozapine demonstrates D4 receptor antagonism, serotonin receptor antagonism, alpha 2 receptor blockade, and partial M1 cholinergic agonist activity. Clozapine does not cause parkinsonism.

Diagnostic	• Baseline CBC prior to initiation of treatment.
	Regular monitoring of CBC is required as there is a 1 – 2% risk of severe idiosyncratic agranulocytosis (Friedman, 1999). Before intensive monitoring was instituted, 75 deaths in the United States were related to this adverse medication effect.
Education & Counseling	• Clozapine: side effects including sedation, sialorrhea, and orthostatic hypotension, and need for CBC monitoring given risk of agranulocytosis, development of diabetes mellitus, lipid abnormalities, question of sudden death due to cardiac effects.
	Adverse cardiac effects of clozapine have been discussed in the literature. Merril (2005) reviewed articles published from 1970 – 2004 and concluded that clozapine is associated with a low risk of fatal myocarditis or cardiomyopathy (0.015% to 0.188%). Clozapine did not independently prolong QTc interval.
Medications	• No change at present.
Referral	• Weekly CBC monitoring if clozapine initiated, at lab near patient's house.

Neck and trunkal flexion, gait impairment, and postural instability: assistive devices and PT to maintain independence and maximize safety.

Education & Counseling	• Benefit of assistive devices and physical therapy in maintaining independence and maximizing safety.
Referral	• I called PT center near patient's house. Motor fluctuations discussed and a.m. appointments scheduled.

Depression: While patient reports symptoms are controlled with medication and friends visit her at home, she recently stopped going to church because she does not want to be seen with walker. Mood requires monitoring.

Education & Counseling	• Depression and PD, medication benefit, effect of mood on current ADL decisions.
Referral	• Declines behavioral therapy.
Medication	• Declines increase in venlafaxine.

Cognitive dysfunction: No change in examination. Monitor symptoms at each appointment.

The DSM-IV defines dementia as development of multiple cognitive deficits that affect memory and result in aphasia, apraxia, or executive dysfunction impairing functional status and social function (APA, 1994).

Dementia is a symptom of an underlying disorder. Dementia is characterized by an alteration in mental capacity. Dementia may affect memory, language, cognition, spatial orientation, or personality. Usually several of these functions are impaired.

> *Causes of dementia include tumor, subdural hematoma, cerebral contusion, lacunar stroke, multiple sclerosis, Huntington's disease, Pick's disease, normal pressure hydrocephalus, multi-infarct dementia, Parkinson's disease, progressive supranuclear palsy, olivopontocerebellar degeneration, pernicious anemia, syphilis, uremia, hypo/hyperkalemia, hypo/hypermagnesemia, hypo/hyperthyroidism, hepatic encephalopathy, alcoholism, Cushing's disease, Addison's disease, AIDS encephalopathy, heavy metal intoxication, lupus cerebritis, brain abscess, chronic meningitis, Creutzfeldt-Jacob disease, post-concussive syndrome, Alzheimer's disease, depression, senile dementia, Wernicke encephalopathy, and medications (Aminoff, 2001).*
>
> *A prospective community-based population study examined prevalence of dementia in PD patients over eight years. Patients were examined at baseline, four, and eight years later. The mean duration of disease at baseline was nine years. Dementia was found in 26% of patients at baseline examination, in 52% of patients in study year four, and in 78% at study year eight. The mean duration of disease was 14 years at the time patients developed dementia (Aarsland, 2003).*
>
> *Only one randomized clinical trial has been conducted in PD patients with dementia. Fourteen patients were treated with donepezil for 20 weeks. Mini-mental state score in the experimental group subjects improved 2.1 points versus 0.3 points for controls. PD motor symptoms were not affected (Aarsland, 2002).*

Urinary incontinence: No change in symptoms, adequately treated nonpharmacologically.	
Education & Counseling	• Regular voiding during day. • Medications if requested.

Follow-up appointment scheduled in two months.

ADDENDUM

The patient had a normal echocardiogram. She continued the pergolide, and cardiac function was monitored according to center-specific guidelines.

Following normal echocardiogram report and decision to continue pergolide, quetiapine was slowly tapered and discontinued as clozapine was substituted. This resulted in decrease in dyskinesias and resolution of hallucinations.

NARRATIVE FOR SECOND PATIENT

57-year-old, right-hand dominant, Puerto Rican, Spanish-speaking woman referred for evaluation of PD by community neurologist. Referral note provides the following information: PD x 10 years. Medications: carbidopa/levodopa, pergolide, gabapentin, amantadine, quetiapine, entacapone. Patient is accompanied by her husband. History provided by husband, who appears to be a reliable historian. The patient's speech is soft and difficult to understand. She has dyskinesias and needs to concentrate to speak more than a few sentences.

She would like to know if there are other medications to treat her PD. Her biggest problems are painful dyskinesias and frightening hallucinations.

HISTORY OF PRESENT ILLNESS

PD diagnosed 10 years ago. Initial symptoms were right arm tremor, stiffness, slow movement, and fatigue. She was referred to a neurologist, who diagnosed PD and began treatment with carbidopa/levodopa 10/100 tid. She felt less stiff and slow with the medication. About one year later, she developed tremor and stiffness in her right leg that impaired her gait. Carbidopa/levodopa CR was added and her gait improved, but she was unable to continue working in the local grocery store due to fatigue and tremor. Over the next few years she developed left upper and lower extremity tremor. Her symptoms were treated with selegiline, carbidopa/levodopa 25/100, and bromocriptine. She does not recall her response to the medications or reasons for dose changes. Three years ago, she developed peak dose dyskinesias. She was taking two kinds of carbidopa/levodopa, pergolide, and several other medications, names not recalled. Multiple medication changes were made to decrease the dyskinesias that resulted in increased "off" time while peak dose dyskinesias persisted. For the past two years she has delayed time to "on," wearing off after two hours, and unexpected dose failures that make it necessary for her to use a wheelchair outside the house. Six months ago she began having hallucinations. She sees strangers in the closet. The hallucinations usually occur in the evening. When she is in bed at night, the furniture changes shape and she sees frightening animals. Her neurologist did "a lot of blood tests and an MRI" and began treatment with quetiapine. The hallucinations have persisted despite increase in quetiapine dosage. Last week she became so frightened she called the police.

> Carbidopa/levodopa ER is a continuous-release preparation of carbidopa/levodopa. It has 70% of the bioavailability of standard carbidopa/levodopa preparation (Stern, 1993). The mechanism that causes motor fluctuation in response to levodopa therapy has not been determined. In animal models, continuous administration of levodopa results in fewer receptor alterations and behavioral changes, providing a rationale for the use of the extended-release levodopa preparation (Koller, 1994). Carbidopa/levodopa CR has no peak effect and is used to decrease symptoms that could awaken the person from sleep.

> Bromocriptine is an ergot alkaloid D2 agonist. Side effects include nausea, dyskinesia, hallucinations, confusion, and postural hypotension (Waters, 2002).

She currently awakens at 6 a.m. Her husband helps her dress. She takes her medications before breakfast at 7 a.m. She feels sleepy after she takes the medicine and goes to bed until 8 a.m. She has dyskinesias from 8 a.m. – 9 a.m. She feels restless with the dyskinesias, as if she has to move. The medication wears off before 9:30 a.m. The same pattern occurs with the 10 a.m. medication dose. When she takes the 1 p.m. dose, she develops dyskinesias at 2 p.m., which lasts until 6 p.m. She is exhausted and goes to bed at 7 p.m. The 7 p.m. medication may not have any effect. During this period she has vivid hallucinations. She stays in her bedroom, dozes intermittently, and falls asleep by 11 p.m. She awakens at 1 a.m., and then sleeps for one- or two-hour intervals until 6 a.m. She does not know why she awakens during the night. She wears adult diapers at night. She does not have pain, feel stiff or cold, or experience symptoms consistent with restless legs or periodic movements. She sleeps in a separate bed in the same room as her husband. She is not awakened by environmental stimuli. When she awakens during the night, she sees people and the furniture become animals. She awakens her husband, who reassures her, and the visions disappear. She does not feel refreshed when awakening in the morning. She naps intermittently during the day. Her husband states she does not snore, vocalize, or have episodes of apnea at night.

She spends most of the day sitting in the house watching TV, listening to the radio, or spending time with friends who visit. She lives in a third-floor apartment in a non-elevator building. She has a bedside commode, wheelchair, and front-wheeled walker. She does not have shower bars or chair. Her husband assists her with bathing, dressing, and cutting food. She prefers to hold his arms for walking in the house rather than use the walker. She uses the wheelchair when they go grocery shopping. She has not fallen in the past year because she does not walk when her husband is not present to assist. She reports Schwab and England score 20%. "Nothing alone. *Can be a slight help with some chores. Severe invalid" (Waters, 2002)*. Her sister-in-law comes once a week to help with housekeeping. Her two children live in Puerto Rico and visit occasionally.

Medications: Taken as prescribed.

Medication	Dose	7 AM	10 AM	1 PM	4 PM	7 PM	10 PM
Gabapentin	100 mg	1 tablet	XXXX	1 tablet	XXXX	XXXX	1 tablet
Gabapentin is used to treat neuropathic pain. Adverse effects include dizziness, somnolence, peripheral edema, GI upset, ataxia, visual disturbance, thought disorder, and incoordination (Karch, 2005).							
Nortriptyline	50 mg	XXXX	XXXX	XXXX	XXXX	XXXX	1 tablet
Tricyclic antidepressants are the first choice to improve depression in patients with difficulty initiating sleep, maintaining sleep, and early awakening (Poewe, 1986). Adverse reactions include anticholinergic effects, arrhythmias, extrapyramidal symptoms, alteration in blood pressure, nausea, fatigue, rash, increased perspiration, headache, changes in blood sugar, photosensitivity, jaundice, and blood dyscrasias (Karch, 2005).							
Amantadine	100 mg	1 tablet	XXXX	1 tablet	XXX	XXXX	XXXX
Entacapone	200 mg	1 tablet	1 tablet	1 tablet	1 tablet	1 tablet	XXXX
Entacapone is a peripherally acting COMT inhibitor. In patients with levodopa-related fluctuations, entacapone increases the elimination half-life of levodopa, increasing "on" time without increasing the magnitude of response to levodopa (PSG, 1997). The North American PD Study found that entacapone-treated patients increased the percent "on" time by five percentage points compared with placebo at weeks 1, 8, 16, and 24. The effect of entacapone was more prominent in patients with smaller baseline "on" time. At week 24, mean UPDRS scores improved by approximately 10% among entacapone-treated patients versus placebo. Symptom benefit was lost with withdrawal of the study drug. *Entacapone is usually given with every dose of levodopa. Each tablet is 200 mg. The total dose/day should not exceed 1600 mg. It is eliminated in two hours. Adverse effects include nausea, vomiting, dyskinesias, hypotension, sedation, headache, constipation, and diarrhea (Karch, 2005).* *Entacapone is prescribed for this patient to supplement levodopa and extend "on" time. The addition of entacapone to levodopa increases "on" time for approximately one hour/day.*							

Medication	Dose	7 AM	10 AM	1 PM	4 PM	7 PM	10 PM
Carbidopa/ levodopa	25/100	1 tablet	1 tablet	1 tablet	1 tablet	1 tablet	XXXX
Pergolide	1 mg	1 tablet	XXXX	1 tablet	1 tablet	1 tablet	XXXX
Quetiapine	100 mg	XXXX	XXXX	XXXX	XXXX	XXXX	3 tablets

Patient explanation for reason medications are prescribed and assessment of effectiveness:

Medication	Reason for taking medication	Assessment of effectiveness
Gabapentin prescribed	Leg pain with dyskinesias	No change since medication
Nortriptyline	Sleep	Doesn't help sleep
Amantadine	PD	Not sure
Entacapone	PD	Not sure
Carbidopa/levodopa	PD	Varies
Pergolide	PD	Not sure
Quetiapine	Hallucinations	Not helping

Allergies: None to food, environment, or medication.

ADULT ILLNESSES

Denies HTN, CHF, CAD, diabetes, hypertension, liver disease, pulmonary disease, renal disease, or cancer.

PSH: Tonsillectomy as child.

Psychiatric: Denies history of depression. Hallucinations for six months (See HPI).

FAMILY HISTORY

Affected family members developed PD after age 40. She does not recall her parents' ages when they died. Patient has never spoken with a clinical geneticist.

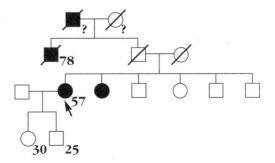

SOCIAL

Completed seventh-grade education in Puerto Rico. Came to this state at age 17 and was employed in grocery store and child care. No known exposure to environmental toxins.

Denies cigarettes, alcohol, and recreational drug use. Husband is her primary caregiver. He is not employed. He assists patient with all ADL, cooks, does laundry, pays bills, and cleans the house. Patient does not recall having referral for home attendant services. Assistance would be appreciated. She has never completed an advance directive. Husband would be health-care proxy.

REVIEW OF SYSTEMS

General: Experiences drenching sweats when "off" and needs to change clothes, denies fever. During the past year she has lost 10 pounds without change in food intake or increased activity. She doesn't understand why this happened.

Skin: Denies history of skin disease, rash, pruritus, or melanoma.

Eyes: Wears glasses. Denies blurred vision, diplopia, transient vision loss, or pain.

Ears: Denies hearing loss, discharge, tinnitus, or vertigo.

Nose: Denies nasal congestion or epistaxis.

Mouth: Denies difficulty swallowing, dental problems. Voice is soft and she has difficulty being understood on telephone.

Neck: Denies pain, lumps, or swollen glands.

Breast: Denies pain, lumps, and nipple discharge. Does not perform breast self-examination. Last mammogram three years ago.

Respiratory: Denies asthma, pneumonia, lung disease, wheezing, cough, hemoptysis, or SOB. Last PPD negative (year not recalled).

Cardiovascular: She feels dizzy when getting out of bed in the morning and sits at the side of the bed for a few minutes before getting up. She denies chest pain, palpitations, SOB, orthopnea, edema, claudication, angina, hypertension, MI, CHF, murmers, or EKG abnormalities. Has never had an echocardiogram.

GI: Appetite good. Denies food intolerance, change in eating habits, abdominal pain, nausea, vomiting. Bowel movement every three to five days without BRBPR or black stool. Constipation is longstanding. Uses natural tea for bowel movement. Has not had colonoscopy.

GU/GYN: Has urinary incontinence when she is "off" because she cannot ambulate to bathroom quickly enough; wears liners during the day and diapers at night. Occasionally loses some urine when coughs. Denies dysuria, hesitancy, or straining. No sexual dysfunction. No history of STIs. Denies vaginal pruritus, discharge, sores, or lesions. LMP 10 years ago. Last gynecological exam and mammogram five years ago, told everything was fine.

Musculoskeletal: See HPI. Doesn't recall bone density screening.

Neurological: Denies history of seizure disorder, syncope, stroke, headache (see HPI).

Hematologic: Denies excessive bruising, anemia, transfusions.

Endocrine: Denies heat or cold intolerance, polydipsia, polyphagia, or polyuria.

Psychiatric: See HPI. Denies depression. Does not feel hopeless. Sometimes feels a little sad.

Does not have regular care with primary provider, doesn't recall last comprehensive examination or provider's name, "his office closed."

Physical exam

General: Patient in no acute distress; examined in the "on" state with marked dyskinesias, right greater than left. BP 100/60 P76, right (sitting) 100/60 P78, right (standing), Resp. 14, Wt. 124 pounds, Ht. 63 inches.

Skin: Warm and dry, without lesions or bruises.

HEENT: Normocephalic, oropharynx with moist mucosal membranes, sclera anicteric.

Neck: Supple without carotid bruits or jugular venous distention.

Thyroid: Not palpable, without nodules or bruits.

Lungs: Vesicular breath sounds, without use of accessory muscles.

Heart: RR S_1, S_2, without murmurs, gallops, rubs. PMI 5th interspace at left midclavicular line. Examination limited by dyskinesias.

Abdomen: BS normoactive; abdomen soft, nondistended, nontender, without masses or organomegaly.

Extremities: Radial, femoral, dorsalis pedis pulses 2+ and = bilaterally, without cyanosis or edema.

Neurological exam

Mental status: Alert and oriented to person, place, and time.

Mini-mental state exam score is 40/57. Patient's dyskinesias and hypophonic, tachyphemic speech affect her ability to follow directions and influenced the scope of the examination.

Mood: Appropriate to situation. Thought is coherent. Denies delusions, illusions, hallucinations, ideas of reference, suicidal ideation.

Cranial nerves: Discs yellow with sharp borders; without arteriolar narrowing, AV nicking, hemorrhages, or exudates. Pupils equal, round, reactive to light. No visual field cuts, EOMs full, without nystagmus, square wave jerks, blepharospasm, or apraxia of eyelid opening. Facial sensation intact to light touch bilaterally. Strong mastication muscles. She has facial masking and asymmetric smile, right lower than left. Hearing is grossly normal bilaterally to whisper. Palate elevates bilaterally; voice is hypophonic, tachyphemic, and dysarthric. She has pooled secretions and cough is feeble. Shoulder shrug slower on right than left. Tongue protrusion midline, without tremor.

Motor: Normal muscle bulk, dyskinesias in all extremities and dystonia right foot. Tone increased with moderate rigidity, right greater than left. Power 4/5 throughout, without pronator drift. Rapid alternating movements are incomplete, right is affected more than left. Generalized dyskinesias prevent full examination. No apraxia.

Reflexes: Biceps, triceps, brachioradialis, patellar, ankle are 2+ and symmetric, downgoing toes, nonextinguishing glabellar.

Sensory: Sensation grossly normal to pinprick, light touch, and vibration in all extremities. Recognizes keys by manipulation. Romberg negative.

Coordination: FNF intact.

Gait: Unable to stand without assistance. Walks five feet assisted by husband and examiner. Narrow-based, shuffling, unsteady gait, cadence irregular, slower on right. Dyskinesias and right foot dystonia further impair gait. Unable to tandem. Pull test is positive, she would spontaneously fall if not assisted by examiner.

LABORATORY REVIEW

Community neurologist contacted by telephone with patient's consent. Chem 7, LFTs, CBC, TSH, B12, RPR, and U/A were within normal limits. MRI was unremarkable.

> *Patients with PD do not demonstrate abnormalities on MRI (Waters, 2002).*

IMPRESSION

57-year-old right-hand dominant woman with family history of PD, residing in walk-up apartment building, wheelchair bound due to advanced PD, dependent on husband for all care, presents in deconditioned state with motor fluctuations, questionable cognitive impairment, hallucinations, sleep disorder, constipation, and unexplained 10-pound weight loss this year.

Dyskinesias and hallucinations, which are upsetting to the patient, are most likely related to over-medication with antiparkinson agents. Diffuse Lewy Body Disease could be considered as persons with longstanding PD can present with cognitive impairment, visual hallucinations, fluctuating awareness, and falls. The mental state examination was limited today. She has postural instability and would fall if not continuously assisted by her husband.

As the patient is essentially wheelchair bound, reduction in medication should not further compromise her ADL or place her at increased risk for falls, whereas psychosis presents significant risk for skilled nursing facility placement and morbidity. Medication reduction should begin with pergolide which can cause hallucinations, somnolence, insomnia, and dyskinesias. There may also be an association between pergolide and valvular heart disease that requires evaluation.

Sleep fragmentation is most likely related to nocturnal hallucinations secondary to antiparkinson medications. Tricyclic antidepressant can also cause nocturnal delirium, and the patient cannot recall when she started taking nortriptyline in relation to sleep disorder. It is unclear if tremor, akinesia, or dyskinesias are related to frequent awakening. The description of her sleep pattern is not consistent with REM behavior disorder, periodic limb movements, restless legs, or nocturnal respiratory disorder. Sleep environment appears satisfactory. Will monitor sleep disorder as antiparkinson and antipsychotic medication are adjusted.

> *One of the earliest, most common sleep disorders found in PD patients is sleep fragmentation. Compared with healthy elderly, PD patients have greater difficulty with sleep maintenance (Nausieda & Leo, 1994).*

Constipation is most likely related to advanced disease and medications, as delayed colonic transit time is common in persons with PD. Malignancy must be excluded, especially with recent weight loss.

> *Constipation is reported in 20 – 29% of PD patients (Edwards, 1991; Siddiqui, 2002). Jost (1991) reported abnormally prolonged colonic transit time in 80% of patients studied. Life-threatening complications of constipation in PD patients include megacolon, intestinal pseudo obstruction, and bowel perforation (Rosenthal, 1987).*

Weight loss: While progressive weight loss has been described in PD, evaluation is required to exclude other etiologies. Patient has not received age-appropriate health screening and regular primary care.

> *Weight loss has been reported in PD patients. Chen (2003) reported an average weight loss of 5.2 pounds in the 10 years prior to diagnosis and 7.7 pounds in the eight years following diagnosis. According to Abott (1992), 52% of patients demonstrated weight loss; 22% lost more than 28 pounds. The reason for weight loss in PD is not known. Weight loss has been correlated with disease progression (Beyer, 1995).*

Family history of PD, age of onset after 40 years, to be discussed with genetic counselor.

INITIAL INTERVENTION

Hallucinations and dyskinesias related to advanced disease and overmedication:	
Medication	• Taper schedule for pergolide provided. • After assessing symptoms with pergolide taper and d/c will consider taper to d/c of entacapone. • As hallucinations have not resolved with quetiapine, will initiate treatment with clozapine and taper quetiapine.
Diagnostic	• Baseline CBC today before initiation of clozapine.
Referrals	• Skilled nursing home care for (1) medication evaluation (2) supervision of weekly in-home of CBC monitoring.

Pergolide and FHVD. Pergolide taken for three years. The patient did not describe cardiac or respiratory symptoms. Cardiac examination was limited by dyskinesias.

Diagnostic	• Baseline echocardiogram ▪ If pathology demonstrated, referral to cardiology.
Education & Counseling	• The Mayo Clinic case review discussed. • Rationale for echocardiogram provided.
Medications	• Taper and d/c pergolide.

Constipation	
Education & Counseling	• Therapeutic plan • Potential complications of constipation in PD
Medication	• Stool softener • Fiber supplementation
Referral	• Gastroenterology for colonoscopy

General health, safety, and environment	
Referrals	• Primary care provider (1) Health screening (2) 10-pound weight loss in one year
	• Home skilled nursing (1) Home safety evaluation (2) Assess need and supervision of home attendant (3) Coordination of home PT
Forms completed	• Durable medical equipment (bathchair with transfer bar) • M11Q for home attendant services • Medical necessity for Section 8 housing *Section 8 housing refers to public housing. This program is administered by the New York City Housing Authority. To be considered for public housing, an application is completed. Applicants select first and second borough choices and provide information about total household income, family composition, and current living situation (New York City Housing Authority, 2004).*

FOLLOW-UP

Weekly telephone follow-up.

Return in two weeks.

ADDENDUM

Pergolide and FHVD: Echocardiogram without pathology.

Hallucinations: Resolved with clozapine 50 mg q hs. Quetiapine was then tapered and discontinued.

Sleep fragmentation: Sleep improved with resolution of hallucinations. Nortriptyline was subsequently discontinued without symptoms of depression.

Motor fluctuation and functional status: Pergolide was discontinued without further decline in motor function. Discontinuation of entacapone increased "off time" but did not affect patient or husband's perception of quality of life. Dyskinesias became less painful after pergolide and entacapone were discontinued. Power improved 5/5 with home PT and patient was able to ambulate 20 feet with assistance of husband at an appointment six months after initial evaluation.

Gabapentin was discontinued as it was not indicated for the symptoms.

Health care proxy was completed at a subsequent appointment.

Clinical geneticist met with patient and husband at a subsequent appointment. Information about PD and participation in research were discussed.

DISCUSSION

THERAPEUTIC INTERVENTIONS

This case study examines the care provided for two patients with advanced PD, treated with pergolide, after a case report described FVHD in three PD patients treated with pergolide. The case report was discussed with both patients, cardiac function was assessed, medication history was reviewed, and care plans developed. The patients' medication regimens were not changed based on the preliminary report of PAVHD. Therapeutic interventions focused on improving patients' health-related quality of life. The decision to continue pergolide for one patient and discontinue pergolide for the other patient can be examined using a health-related quality of life outcome model.

Health-related quality of life examines an individual's sense of well-being, purpose in life, autonomy, ability to maintain a meaningful role, and ability to participate in meaningful relationships (Spilker, 1996). Outcome models examine patients' health-related quality of life and include epidemiological data, continuum of disease state, and patient self-report of functional status (Hobart, 1999).

A conceptual model for quality of life in PD has been proposed (Welsh, 2005). The approach to patient care described in these two narratives can be examined using the Parkinson's Disease Health Related Quality of Life model (PDHRQOL).

According to the PDHRQOL, the quality of life in PD is determined by five domains: (1) the individual's general health, (2) personality and psychological state, (3) social and environmental conditions, (4) economic and spiritual factors, and (5) stage of PD and therapy for PD. Sources within the individual and outside the individual influence the quality of life within the five domains. Table One discusses these factors in relation to the assessment for the two patients.

Table One: Application of PDHRQOL concepts in this case study

Concept	Definition	Case One	Case Two
General health	Comorbid conditions that add stress; can increase PD symptoms and interfere with efficacy of treatment	Urinary incontinence Constipation	Weight loss No preventive care Sleep disorder Urinary incontinence
Personality	Personality characteristics influence adaptation to disease. Individual characteristics such as mastery, health beliefs, values, and health perceptions contribute to HRQOL	Religious beliefs Need for functional independence	Adaptation to wheelchair-bound status
Psychological influence	Cognitive impairment, depression, hallucinations	Hallucinations Cognitive impairment Depression	Hallucinations Cognitive impairment

Concept	Definition	Case One	Case Two
Disease stage & therapy	Stage of disease Therapeutic interventions	*Stage 4 Hoehn & Yahr Multiple medications **Pergolide and risk of FVHD**	*Stage 5 Hoehn & Yahr Multiple medications **Pergolide and risk of FVHD**

*The Hoehn and Yahr Rating Scale is used to describe the extent of clinical disability exhibited by an individual with PD based on motor examination findings. This scale divides the severity of disease into five stages. The scale begins with stage 0, no signs of disease, and progresses to stage 5, describing an individual who is wheelchair-bound or bedridden unless aided. This scale was developed based on clinical observation of 856 PD patients followed at Columbia Presbyterian Medical Center from 1949 to 1964 (Hoehn & Yahr, 1967).

Concept	Definition	Case One	Case Two
Social Environmental	Assessment of social engagement and environmental contacts that can affect health outcomes	Formal and informal caregiver support	Informal caregiver support No formal caregiver support Inadequate housing
Economic	Assessment of financial burden	Medicaid	Medicaid
Spiritual	The values that guide and influence all social behavior. Discussion of spiritual preferences, beliefs, and practices	Faith provides comfort	Not assessed at initial encounter
Intra-individual sources	Individual resources within the patient	Able to state symptoms that have negative effect on QOL and participate in care	Able to state symptoms that have negative effect on QOL and participate in care
Extra-individual sources	Sources outside of the individual	Family, friends, and home attendant	Husband and sister-in-law

Both patients required interventions to address psychological influences, disease state, and medication therapy. The second patient required interventions to modify comorbid conditions, social and environmental factors, and extra-individual sources of care.

The first patient determined that pergolide improved motor function and fostered independent physical activity, which contributed to her quality of life. For this patient, the plan of care related to pergolide focused on continuing the medication and monitoring patient for symptoms and signs of VHD. The second patient's quality of life was negatively affected by severe dyskinesias and hallucinations. It was hypothesized that discontinuing pergolide would decrease these symptoms and improve quality of life. Cardiac function was assessed as part of the plan of care, as the patient had been exposed to pergolide for three years.

Pergolide: a selection of subsequent reports and opinions

At the conclusion of the initial case report of PAVHD, Pritchett and colleagues (2002) discussed the need to determine the incidence of disease and the spectrum of abnormalities. They recommended that patients treated with pergolide have a cardiovascular examination, echocardiography when a new murmur was identified or a stable murmur worsened, and pergolide be discontinued for patients with VHD and no other identified etiology.

In the editorial that accompanied Dr. Pritchett's report, cardiologist S. Rahimtoola (2002) discussed the need to determine the incidence of PAVHD, severity of disease, relationship of pergolide dosage and duration to disease, effect of discontinuing the drug on valve disease, and the progression of disease if pergolide was continued. He recommended that prospective studies be conducted at centers where adequate numbers of pergolide-treated PD patients could be evaluated by clinical cardiologists experienced in VHD.

In 2003, a letter from Eli Lilly and Company posted on the FDA Medwatch Website stated that 500,000 people had been treated with pergolide since 1989 and valvulopathy had been reported in less than 0.005%. This indicated that up to 25 persons could have been registered with the FDA (Lanier, 2003). Collaboration between multiple sources determined that in addition to the three cases described by Pritchett and colleagues (2002), 12 cases of PAVHD had been reported to the FDA (Flowers, 2003). Limited information about the 12 cases was summarized in a brief communication. Patients ranged in age from 49 to 77 years and had been treated with pergolide from nine months to four years. Two patients had been treated with other ergot dopamine agonists. Presenting symptoms were described in seven patients. Cough and SOB were the most common presenting symptoms. Three of these patients had alveolitis, exudative pleuritis, or pneumonitis. Abnormalities were found in single and multiple valves. The mitral, tricuspid, and aortic valves were affected. Pergolide was discontinued for 10 patients. Five patients reported symptomatic improvement. Data regarding the five other patients was not available. The authors noted that pergolide already had a warning for pleural and retroperitoneal fibrosis which was being updated. In the accompanying editorial, Dr. Lanier, Editor-in-Chief of Mayo Clinic Proceedings (2003), discussed the need for data collection. Formal prospective study was required to determine incidence, typical presentation, dose and duration effect, and reversibility with discontinuation. Longitudinal study of individual patients should examine evolution of valvulopathy.

To clarify frequency, severity, dose relationship, and reversibility of PAVHD, 78 persons treated with pergolide and 18 control subjects were evaluated by echocardiography using a valvular scoring system ranging from one (proven ergot-like restrictive valve disease) to four (no disease) (Van Camp, 2004). Tenting areas and distances were measured for the mitral valve and systolic pulmonary artery pressure. Subjects were recruited from the ambulatory neurology departments of four hospitals. Persons were excluded if they had a history of coronary heart disease, valvular disease, use of anorectic medications, ergot-derived drugs, or Chinese herbs. Restrictive valvular disease of any type was present in 33% of pergolide-treated patients and no controls. Important restrictive disease was found in 19% of pergolide-treated patients. Significant correlation was found between cumulative doses of pergolide and tenting areas of the mitral valves. Pergolide was discontinued in six patients because restrictive valvular disease was demonstrated. Two of these patients demonstrated regression of disease. The authors concluded that restrictive valvular heart disease was not a rare finding. Patients needed to be informed of the risk. Close clinical and echocardiographic follow-up was mandatory. They recommended that clinicians consider changing to a non-ergot drug if restrictive disease was diagnosed. When a new murmur appeared and was confirmed with echocardiography, endocarditis prophylaxis *was indicated. The validity of the scoring system used in this study and the clinical implication of tenting distances were subsequently questioned in a letter to the editor of* Movement Disorders *(Chaudhuri, 2003).*

To determine prevalence of valvular disease, Baseman (2004) used a historical case design comparing echocardiograms scored for valvular regurgitation in PD patients treated with pergolide and age-matched controls from the Framingham study database. The valve regurgitation score was modeled as a linear function of total mg lifetime use of pergolide, controlling for age. Eighty-nine percent of the 46 pergolide-treated patients had some degree of valvular insufficiency. There was a 14-fold increased risk of tricuspid regurgitation (OR = 18.4) in patients treated with pergolide.

Horvath et al. (2004) reported on four cases of FHVD in PD patients treated with pergolide and cabergoline and proposed that asymptomatic patients have clinical cardiac assessment at three- to six-month intervals. They recommended that echo-cardiography be performed if a new murmur was detected.

Agarwal and Frucht (2004) presented two patients treated at Columbia University Medical Center and reviewed 12 studies that described 24 pergolide-treated patients who developed symptomatic fibrosis. The most common presenting symptom was dyspnea. Other symptoms included edema in one or both legs, cough, and chest pain. Most patients gained weight, although three patients lost weight. Time from first symptom to diagnosis ranged from one to 36 months. The total daily dosage of pergolide in published cases ranged from 1 mg/day to 8 mg/day. The duration of exposure ranged from 11 months to eight years. In six patients, the ESR was elevated, ranging from 40 to 127 mm. Anemia was reported in four patients. In all cases, pergolide was discontinued upon diagnosis. The authors recommended all patients be counseled about the rare possibility of fibrosis before starting pergolide, all patients already taking the drug be informed of the possibility of this adverse event, and pergolide be avoided in patients with a known elevated ESR, abnormal renal function, congestive heart failure, or valvular heart disease. They recommended non-ergot dopamine agonists for initial first-line therapy.

In a letter to the editor, pulmonary specialists from the University of Western Ontario commented on Dr. Agarwal and Frucht's article and discussed their experience with pergolide-induced pleural disease in a patient with low-level asbestos exposure who developed mesothelioma (Hirani, 2005). Their literature review suggested a synergistic relationship between pergolide and asbestos exposure with pleural disease. They recommended that before initiating treatment with pergolide, all patients be asked about asbestos exposure and have baseline CXR and PFTs. Dr. Frucht responded to Dr. Hirani's comments (2005), stating he supported careful monitoring with imaging of the chest and abdomen and serial echocardiograms for patients who required treatment with pergolide.

In 2005, a case review described two patients with organ changes associated with pergolide therapy (Roth, 2005). One year after initiation of treatment with pergolide, a 56-year-old woman with PD developed lower extremity edema. Echocardiography demonstrated minor mitral regurgitation. Six months later the patient developed left-sided heart failure with multivalvular insufficiency and severe mitral regurgitation. The second patient, a 66-year-old man treated with pergolide for five years, developed edema, bilateral hydronephrosis with ureteric strictures, and renal insufficiency. The authors reviewed the literature and suggested four guidelines.

1. Ergot dopamine agonists should not be first-line therapy.

2. Persons treated with ergot dopamine agonists should be monitored for dyspnea, cough, SOB, chest pain, and heart murmur. Elevated C-reactive protein and anemia support a diagnosis.

3. Symptomatic patients should be evaluated for serosal fibrosis.

4. Prior to initiating treatment with an ergot dopamine agonist, renal function, CXR, and echocardiography should be examined. Screening echocardiography should be performed in three to six months and subsequently every six to 12 months.

An editorial in Movement Disorders *discussed pharmacovigilance — the study of the undesirable effects of drugs on a long-term basis (Rascol, 2004) — and the need to assess safety, the true benefit/risk ratio of treatment, the importance of clinician-based observations, and international cooperation to improve underreporting. In the author's opinion, data on pergolide was too limited for definitive answers. Incidence and prevalence were not known, risk factors had not been identified, the mechanisms causing fibrosis were not completely understood, it was not known if patients had undetected valvulopathies prior to treatment, and the role of dose, duration of exposure, and reversibility after drug withdrawal was not known. Most important, Dr. Rascol discussed the need for neutral data collection and large prescription databases to address pharmacoepidemiological questions.*

The journal articles reviewed for this case study consisted of small studies that examined valvular function in pergolide-treated patients and controls, case reports of PAVHD, and case reports of pergolide-associated fibrosis affecting different organ systems. Some authors recommend serial echocardiography to monitor for VHD in these patients, while other authors recommend echocardiography as indicated by history and clinical examination.

The articles reviewed did not reference studies of medications thought to cause FVHD through similar mechanisms. This literature deserves attention. For patients exposed to dexfenfluramine, cardiac auscultation has been found to be the screening method of choice to detect valvular regurgitation (Roldan, 2000). Two hundred and twenty-three patients receiving dexfenfluramine for 6.9 months and 189 matched controls had history and physical examination performed by noncardiologists. Color Doppler echocardiograms were interpreted by cardiologists blinded to patient treatment information. Grade I-II/VI systolic heart murmurs were heard in 14% of dexfenfluramine-treated patients and 11% of controls. Among patients treated with dexfenfluramine, heart murmurs were associated with mild or abnormal regurgitation. When cardiac auscultation did not identify murmurs, most valves had normal morphology and mild regurgitation. Among patients treated with dexfenfluramine, the absence of heart murmur was predictive of the absence of mild, worse, or abnormal regurgitation of any heart valves.

In 2003, the American College of Cardiology (ACC), the American Heart Association (AHA), and the American Society of Echocardiography (ASE) task force recommended that echocardiography be used to assess valve morphology and regurgitation in patients with history of anoretic drug use or use of any drug associated with VHD who have symptoms, technically inadequate auscultatory examination, or murmurs. Routine screening of patients exposed to anoretic medications was not recommended. This was a class one recommendation.

I would welcome expert discussion of the dexfenfluramine/fenfluramine literature and the ACC/AHA/ASE (2003) recommendations relevant to cardiac monitoring of patients requiring treatment with pergolide.

References

Aarsland, D., Anderson, K., Larsen, J.P., Lolk, A., Nielson, H., Ragh-Sorensen, P. (2001). *Risk of dementia in Parkinson's disease — a community based prospective study.* Neurology, 56, 730 – 736.

Aarsland, D., Laske, K., Larsen, J.P., Janvin, C. (2002). *Donezepril for cognitive impairment in Parkinson's disease: a randomized controlled study.* Journal of Neurology, Neurosurgery, and Psychiatry, 72, 708 – 712.

Aarsland, D., Anderson, K., Larsen, J.P., Lolk, A., Kragh-Sorensen, P. (2003). *Prevalence and characteristics of dementia in Parkinson's disease: an 8 year prospective study.* Archives of Neurology, 60, 387 – 392.

Abott, R.A. (1992). *Diet, body size, and micronutrient status in Parkinson's disease.* European Journal of Clinical Nutrition, 46, 879.

Agarwal, P., Fahn, S., Frucht, S.J. (2004). *The diagnosis and management of pergolide induced fibrosis.* Movement Disorders, 19, 699 – 704.

ACC/AHA/ASE (2003). *Guideline update for the clinical application of echocardiography: summary article.* Journal of American Society of Echocardiography, 16, 1091 – 1110.

American Psychiatric Association. *Diagnostic and Statistical Manual of Mental Disorders* (4th ed.), 1994. Washington D.C.: American Psychiatric Association.

Aminoff, M.J. (2001). *Neurology and General Medicine* (3rd edition). New York: Churchill Livingstone.

Bana, D.S., MacNeal, P.S., LeCompte, P.M., Shah, Y., Graham, J.R. (1974). *Cardiac murmurs and endocardial fibrosis associated with methysergide therapy.* American Hospital Journal, 88, 640 – 655.

Baseman, D.G., O'Suillebain, P.E., Reimhold, S.C., Laskar, S.R., Baseman, J.G., Dewey, R.B. (2004). *Pergolide use in Parkinson's disease is associated with cardiac valve regurgitation.* Neurology, 63, 301 – 304.

Bennett, J.P., Landrow, E.R., Schuh, L.A., (1993). *Suppression of dyskinesias in advanced Parkinson's disease. II. Increasing daily clozapine doses suppress dyskinesias and improve parkinsonism symptoms.* Neurology, 43 (8): 1551 – 1555.

Bennett, J.P., Landrow, E.R., Dietrich, S., Schuh, L.A. (1994). *Suppression of dyskinesias in advanced Parkinson's disease: moderate daily clozapine doses provide long-term dyskinesia reduction.* Movement Disorders, 9, 409 – 414.

Beyer, P.L. (1995). *Weight change and body composition in patients with Parkinson's disease.* Journal of the American Dietetic Association, 95, 979.

Boess, F.G., Martin, I.L. (1994). *Molecular biology of 5-HT receptors.* Neuropharmacology, 33, 275 – 317.

Chase, T.N., Mouradian, M.M., Engber, T.M. (1993). *Motor response complications and the function of striatal efferent systems.* Neurology, 43.6, S23 – 26.

Chaudhuri, K.R., Dhawan, V., Basu, S., Jackson, G., Odin, P. (2003). *Valvular heart disease and fibrotic reactions may be related to ergot dopamine agonists, but non-ergot agonists may also not be spared.* Movement Disorders, 19 (12): 1522 – 1523.

Chen, H. (2003). *Weight loss in Parkinson's disease.* Annals of Neurology, 53, 676.

Connolly, H.M., Crary, J.L., McGoon, M.D. (1997). *Valvular heart disease associated with ergot alkaloid use: echocardiographic and pathologic correlations.* Annals of Internal Medicine, 337, 581 – 589.

Crosby, N.J., Deane, K.H., Clarke, C.E. (2003). *Amantadine for dyskinesia in Parkinson's disease.* Cochrane Database System Revision, 2, CD003467.

Cummings, J. (1992). *Depression and Parkinson's disease: a review.* American Journal of Psychiatry, 149 (4): 443 – 454.

de Goede, C., Keus, S., Kwakkel, G., Wagenaar, R. (2001). *The effects of physical therapy on Parkinson's disease: a research synthesis.* Archives of Physical Medical Rehabilitation, 82.

de la Fuente-Fernandez, R., Lu, J.Q., Sossi, V., Jivan, S., Schulzer, M., Holden, J.E., Lee, C.S., Ruth, T.J., Clame, D.B., Stoessl, A.J. (2001). *Biochemical variations in the synaptic level of dopamine precede motor fluctuations in Parkinson's disease: PET evidence of increased dopamine turnover.* Annals of Neurology, 49, 298 – 303.

Delong, M.R., Juncos, J.L. (2005). *Parkinson's disease and other movement disorders*. In: D. Kasper, A.E. Fauci, D. Longo, E. Braunwald, S. Hauser, & J.L. Jameson (Eds.), Harrison's Principles of Internal Medicine, 2406 – 2415. New York: McGraw-Hill.

Edwards, L.L. (1991). *Gastrointestinal symptoms in Parkinson's disease*. Movement Disorders, 6, 151.

Fahn, S. (1982). *Fluctuations of disability in Parkinson's disease: pathophysiological aspects*. In: C.D. Marsden, & S. Fahn (Eds.), Movement Disorders, 123 – 145. London: Butterworth Scientific.

Fahn, S., Elton, W., et al. (1987). *Unified Parkinson's disease rating scale*. In S. Fahn, C.D. Marsden, D.B. Calne, & M. Goldstein (Eds.), Recent Developments in Parkinson's Disease, Vol. 2, 153 – 164. Florham Park, N.J.: Macmillian Health Care Information.

Fahn, S. (1995). *Parkinsonism*. In L.P. Roland (Ed.), Merrit's Textbook of Neurology, 9th ed., 713 – 730. Baltimore, MD: Lea and Febiger.

Fahn, S. (2004). *Medical treatment of Parkinson's disease*. In: S. Fahn, J. Jancovic, M. Hallet, & P. Jenner, In 14th Annual Course: A Comprehensive Review of Movement Disorders for the Clinical Practitioner, 439 – 536. New York: Columbia University.

Fernandez, H.H., Friedman, J.H., Jacques, C., Rosenfeld, M. (1999). *Quetiapine for the treatment of drug-induced psychosis in Parkinson's disease*. Movement Disorders, 14, 484 – 487.

Fitzgerald, L.W., Burn, R.C., Brown, B.S. (2001). *Possible role of valvular serotonin 5-HT (2B) receptors in the cardiopathy associated with fenfluramine*. Molecular Pharmacology, 57, 75 – 81.

Flowers, C.M., Rascoosin, J.A., Lu, S.L., Beitz, J.G. (2003). *The U.S. Food and Drug Administration's registry of patients with pergolide associated valvular heart disease*. Mayo Clinic Procedures, 78, 730 – 731.

Forno, S. (1981). *Pathology of Parkinson's disease*. In C.D. Marsden & S. Fahn (Eds.), Movement Disorders, Neurology 2, 21 – 40. Cornwall: Butterworth Scientific.

Friedman, J., Lannon, M., Cornella, C. (1999). *Low dose clozapine for the treatment of drug-induced psychosis in Parkinson's disease*. New England Journal of Medicine, 340, 757 – 763.

Frucht, S., Rogers, J.D., Greene, P., Fahn, S. (1999). *Falling asleep at the wheel: motor vehicle mishaps in people taking pramipexole and ropinirole*. Neurology, 52, 1908 – 1910.

Frucht, S., Agarwal, P., Fahn, S. (2005). *Reply: diagnosis and management of pergolide-induced fibrosis*. Movement Disorders, 20 (4): 513.

Glassman, A.H., Bigger, J.T. (2001). *Antipsychotic drugs: prolonged QTc interval, torsade de pointes and sudden death*. American Journal of Psychiatry, 158, 1774 – 1782.

Goetz, C.G., Stebbins, G.T. (1993). *Risk factors for nursing home placement in advanced Parkinson's disease*. Neurology, 43, 2227 – 2229.

Goetz, C.G., Koller, W.C., Poewe, W., Rascol, O., Sampaio, C. (2002). *Amantadine and other antiglutamate agents*. Movement Disorders, 17, S13 – 22.

Haddad, P.M., Anderson, I.M. (2002). *Antipsychotic related QTc prolongation, torsade de pointe and sudden death*. Drugs, 62 (11): 1649 – 1671.

Hauck, A.J., Freeman, D.P., Ackerman, D.M., Danielson, G.K., Edwards, W.D. (1988). *Surgical pathology of the tricuspid valve: a study of 363 cases spanning 25 years*. Mayo Clinic Procedures, 63, 851 – 863.

Hauck, A.J., Edwards, W.D., Danielson, G.K., Mullany, C.J., Bresnahan, D.R. (1990). *Mitral and aortic valve disease associated with ergotamine therapy for migraine: report of two cases and review of literature*. Archives of Pathology Laboratory Medicine, 114, 62 – 64.

Hirani, N., Bayliff, C.C., McCormack, D.G. (2005). *Diagnosis and management of pergolide-induced fibrosis*. Movement Disorders, 20 (4): 512 – 513.

Hobart, J.C., Lamping, D.L., Thompson, A.J. (1999). *Evaluating neurological outcome measures: the bare essentials*. Journal of Neurology, Neurosurgery, and Psychiatry, 127.

Hoehn, M.M., Yahr, M.D. (1967). *Parkinsonism: onset, progression, and mortality*. Neurology, 17, 427 – 442.

Horvath, J., Fross, R.D., Kleiner-Fisman, G., Lerch, R., Stalder, H., Liaudat, S., Raskoff, W.J., Flachsbart, K.D., Rakowski, H., Pache, J.C., Burkhard, P.R., Lang, A.E. (2004). *Severe multivalvular heart disease: a new complication of the ergot dopamine agonists.* Movement Disorders, 19, 611 – 613.

Horstink, M.W., et al. (1990). *Severity of Parkinson's disease is a risk factor for peak dose dyskinesia.* Journal of Neurology, Neurosurgery, and Psychiatry, 53, 224.

Inzelberg, R., Kipervasser, S., Korczyn, A.D. (1998). *Auditory hallucinations in Parkinson's disease.* Journal of Neurology, Neurosurgery, and Psychiatry, 64, 533 – 535.

Jimenez-Jimenez, F.J., Lopez-Alvarez, J., Sanchez-Chapado, M. (1995). *Retroperitoneal fibrosis in a patient with Parkinson's disease treated with pergolide.* Clinical Neuropharmacy, 18, 277 – 279.

Jost, W.H., Schrimrigk, K. (1991). *Constipation in Parkinson's disease.* Klin Wochenschr, 69, 906.

Karch, A. (2005). *Lippincott's Nursing Drug Guide.* Philadelphia: Lippincott Williams & Wilkins.

Koller, W.C., Pahwa, R. (1994). *Treating motor fluctuations with controlled release levodopa preparations.* Neurology, 44 (6): S323 – 328.

Kuniyoshi, S., Jancovic, J. (2005). *Dopamine agonists in Parkinson's disease.* In: Ebadi and Pfeiffer, Parkinson's Disease, 729 – 744. Florida: CRC Press.

Lanier, W. (2003). *Additional insights into pergolide associated valvular heart disease.* Mayo Clinic Proceedings, 78 (6): 684 – 686.

Langston, J.W., Tanner, C.M. (2000). *Selegiline and Parkinson's disease: it's deja vu again.* Neurology, 55, 1770 – 1771.

Ling, L.H., Ahlskog, J.E., Munger, T.M., Limper, A.H., Oh, J.K. (2004). *Constrictive pericarditis and pleuropulmonary disease linked to ergot dopamine agonist therapy for Parkinson's disease.* Mayo Clinic Proceedings, 74, 371 – 375.

Louis, E.D., Lynch, T., Marder, K., Fahn, S. (1996). *Reliability of patient completion of the historical section of the unified Parkinson's disease rating scale.* Movement Disorders, 11 (2): 185 – 192.

Luginger, E., Weaning, G.K., Bosch, S., Poewe, W. (2000). *Beneficial effects of amantadine on L-Dopa-induced dyskinesias in Parkinson's disease.* Movement Disorders, 15, 873 – 878.

Luquin, M.R., Scipioni, O., Vaamonde, J., Gershanik, O., Obeso, J.A. (1992). *Levodopa induced dyskinesias in Parkinson's disease: clinical and pharmacological classification.* Movement Disorders, 7, 117 – 124.

Marder, K., Tang, M.X., Mejia, H., Alfaro, B., Cote, L., Louis, E., Groves, J., Mayeux, R. (1996). *Risk of Parkinson's disease among first degree relatives: a community based study.* Neurology, 47, 155 – 160.

Martinez-Martin, P., Gil-Nagel, A., Garcia, L.M., et al. (1994). *Unified Parkinson's disease rating scale characteristics and structure.* Movement Disorders, 9, 76 – 83.

Mayeux, R., Denaro, J., Hemenegildo, N., Marder, K., Tang, M.X., Cote, L., Stern, Y. (1992). *A population based investigation of Parkinson's disease with and without dementia: relationship to age and gender.* Archives of Neurology, 49, 492 – 497.

Metman Verhagen, L., Del Dotto, P., Van den Munckhopf, P., Fang, J., Mouradian, M.M., Case, T.N. (1998). *Amantadine as treatment for dyskinesias and motor fluctuations in Parkinson's disease.* Neurology, 50, 1323 – 1326.

Merril, D.B., Dee, G.W., Geoff, D.C. (2005). *Adverse cardiac effects associated with clozapine.* Journal of Clinical Psychopharmacy, 25, 32 – 41.

Mierau, J., Schneider, F.J., Ensinger, H.A., Chio, C.L., Lajiness, M.E., Huff, R.M. (1995). *Pramipexole binding and activation of cloned and expressed dopamine D2, D3, and D4 receptors.* European Journal of Pharmocology, 290, 29 – 36.

Mizuno, Y., Kondo, T., Narabyashi, H. (1995). *Pergolide in the treatment of Parkinson's disease.* Neurology, 45 (supp 3): S13 – 21.

Mondal, B.K., Suri, S. (2000). *Pergolide induced retroperitoneal fibrosis.* International Journal of Clinical Practice, 54, 403.

Mouradian, M.M., Juncos, J.L., Fabbrini, G., Schlegel, J., Bartko, J.J., Chase, T.N. (1988). *Motor fluctuations in Parkinson's disease: central pathophysiological mechanisms.* Part II. Annals of Neurology, 24, 372 – 278.

Muenter, M.D., Sharpless, N.S., Tyce, G.M., Darley, F.L. (1997). *Patterns of dystonia ("I-D-I" and "D-I-D") in response to L-dopa therapy of Parkinson's disease.* Mayo Clinic Proceedings, 52, 163 – 174.

Naimark, D., Jackson, E., Rockwell, E., Jeste, D.V. (1996). *Psychotic symptoms in Parkinson's disease patients with dementia.* Journal of the American Geriatric Society, 44, 296 – 299.

Nausieda, P.A., Leo, G.J., Chesney, D. (1994). *Comparison of regular sinemet and sinemet CR on the sleep of Parkinsonian patients.* Neurology, 44, 219.

Newman-Tancredi, A., Cussac, D., Quentric, Y. (2002). *Differential actions of anti-Parkinsonian agents at multiple classes of monoaminergic receptor. Agonist and antagonist properties at serotonin 5-HT1 and 5 HT2 receptor subtypes.* Journal of Pharmacology Experimental Therapy, 303, 815 – 822.

New York City Housing Authority (2004). *Section 8 housing.* Retrieved Feb. 2005 from http://www.nyc.gov/html/nycha/html/section8pro.html.

Oertel, W.H. (2001). *Pergolide vs. levodopa (PELMOPET).* Movement Disorders, 15 (suppl 3): 5.

Parkinson's disease study group. (1989). *Effect of deprenyl on the progression of disability in early Parkinson's disease.* New England Journal of Medicine, 321, 1364 – 1371.

Parkinson Study Group (1997). *The COMT inhibitor entacapone improves motor fluctuations in patients with levodopa-treated Parkinson's disease.* Annals of Neurology, 42, 747 – 755.

Parkinson Study Group (1997). *Safety and efficacy of pramipexole in early Parkinson's disease: a randomized dose ranging study.* Journal of the American Medical Association, 278, 125 – 130.

Parkinson Study Group (2000). *Pramipexole vs. levodopa as initial treatment for Parkinson's disease: a randomized controlled trial.* Journal of the American Medical Association, 284, 1931 – 1938.

Pfitzenmeyer, P., Foucher, P., Dennewald, G., Chevalon, B., Debieuvre, D., Bensa, P., Piard, F., Camus, P. (1996). *Pleuropulmonary changes induced by ergoline drugs.* European Respiratory Journal, 9, 1013 – 1019.

Pierelli, F., Adipietro, A., Soldati, G., Fattapposta, F., Pozzessere, G., Scoppetta, C. (1998). *Low dosage clozapine effects on L-dopa induced dyskinesias in Parkinsonian patients.* Acta Neurology of Scandinavia, 97, 295 – 299.

Poewe, W., Lees, A.J., Stern, G.M. (1986). *Low dose L-dopa therapy in Parkinson's disease: a six year follow-up study.* Neurology, 36, 1528 – 1530.

Pritchett, A.M., Morrison, J.F., Edwards, W.D., Schaff, H.V., Connolly, H.M., Espinosa, R.E. (2002). *Valvular heart disease in patients taking pergolide.* Mayo Clinic Proceedings, 77, 1280 – 1286.

Rahimtoola, S.H. (2002). *Drug related valvular heart disease: here we go again: will we do better this time?* Mayo Clinic Proceedings, 77 (12): 1275 – 1277.

Rascol, O., Pathak, A., Bagheri, H., Montastruc, J.L. (2004). *New concerns about old drugs: valvular heart disease on ergot derivative dopamine agonists as an exemplary situation of pharmacovigilance.* Movement Disorders, 12, 1524 – 1525.

Ray, W.A., Meredith, S., Thapa, P.B., Meador, K.G., Hall, K., Murray, K.T. (2001). *Antipsychotics and the risk of sudden death.* Archives of General Psychology, 58 (12): 1161 – 1167.

Redfield, M.M., Nicholson, W.J., Edwards, W.D., Tajik, A.J. (1992). *Valve disease associated with ergot alkaloid use: echocardiographic and pathologic correlations.* Annals of Internal Medicine, 117, 50 – 52.

Richards, M., Marder, K., Cote, L., et al. (1994). *Interrater reliability of the unified Parkinson's disease rating scale motor examination.* Movement Disorders, 9, 89 – 91.

Riley, D.E., Lang, A.E. (1993). *The spectrum of levodopa-related fluctuations in Parkinson's disease.* Neurology, 43, 1459 – 64.

Robiolio, P.A., Rigolin, V.H., Wilson, J.S., et al. (1995). *Carcinoid heart disease. Correlation of high serotonin levels with valvular abnormalities detected by cardiac catheterization and echocardiography.* Circulation, 92 (4): 790 – 795.

Roldan, C.A., Gill, E.A., Shively, B.K. (2000). *Prevalence and diagnostic value of precordial murmurs for valvular regurgitation in obese patients treated with dexfenfluramine.* American Journal of Cardiology, 86 (5): 535 – 539.

Roos, R.A.C., Vredevoogd, C.B., Vandervelde, E.A. (1990). *Response fluctuations in Parkinson's disease.* Neurology, 40, 1344 – 1346.

Rosenthal, M.J., Marshall, C.E. (1987). *Sigmoid volvulus in association with parkinsonism: report of four cases.* Journal of the American Geriatric Society, 35, 683.

Roth, J., Ulmanova, O., Ruzzicka, E. (2005). *Organ changes induced by ergot derivative dopamine agonist drugs: time to change treatment guidelines in Parkinson's disease?* Cas Lek Cesk, 144 (2): 123 – 126.

Shannon, K.M., Bennet, J.P., Friedman, J.H. (1997). *Efficacy of pramipexole, a novel dopamine agonist, as monotherapy in mild to moderate Parkinson's disease.* The Pramipexole Study Group. Neurology, 49, 724 – 728.

Shannon, K.M., Goetz, C.G., Carroll, V.S., Tanner, C.M., Klawans, H.L. (1987). *Amantadine and motor fluctuations in chronic Parkinson's disease.* Clinical Neuropharmacology, 10, 522 – 526.

Shaunak, S., Wilkins, A., Piling, J.B., Dick, D.J. (1999). *Pericardial, retroperitoneal, and pleural fibrosis induced by pergolide.* Journal of Neurology, Neurosurgery, and Psychiatry, 66, 79 – 81.

Schrag, A., Ben-Schlomo, Y., Brown, R., Marsden, C.D., Quinn, N. (1998). *Young onset Parkinson's disease revisited — clinical features, natural history, and mortality.* Movement Disorders, 13, 885 – 894.

Siddiqui, M. (2002). *Autonomic dysfunction in Parkinson's disease: a comprehensive survey.* Parkinsonism Related Disorders, 8, 277.

Simula, D.V., Edwards, W.D., Tazelaar, H.D., Connolly, H.M., Schaff, H.V. (2002). *Surgical pathology of carcinoid heart disease: a study of 139 valves from 75 patients spanning 20 years.* Mayo Clinic Proceedings, 77, 139 – 147.

Spilker, B. (1996). *Quality of Life Studies: Definitions and Conceptual Issues.* Philadelphia: H. Schipper, Lipincott-Raven.

Stern, M.B. (1993). *Sinemet CR: rational and clinical experience.* Neurology, 43 (Suppl. I): S34 – 35.

Thanvi, B.R., Munshi, S.K., Vijamkumar, N., Lo, T.C. (2003). *Neuropsychiatric non-motor aspects of Parkinson's disease.* Postgraduate Medicine Journal, 79, 561 – 565.

Thomas, A., Iacono, D., Luciano, A.L., Armellino, K., Di Iorio, A., Onofri, M. (2004). *Duration of amantadine benefit on dyskinesia of severe Parkinson's disease.* Journal of Neurology, Neurosurgery, and Psychiatry, 75, 141 – 143.

Tulloch, I.F. (1997). *Pharmacologic profile of ropinirole: a nonergoline dopamine agonist.* Neurology, 49, S58 – 62.

U.S. Food and Drug Administration (2004). *Quetiapine FDA patient information sheet.* Retrieved Feb. 2005 from http://www.fda.gov/cder/drug/InfoSheets/patient/quetiapinePIS.htm.

U.S. Food and Drug Administration (2005). *Health advisory for antipsychotic drugs used for treatment of behavioral disorders in elderly patients.* http://www.fda.gov/cder/drug/advisory/antipsychotics.htm.

Van Camp, G., Flamez, A., Cosyns, B., Weytjens, C., et al. (2004). *Treatment of Parkinson's disease with pergolide and relation to restrictive valvular heart disease.* The Lancet, 363 (9416): 1179 – 1183.

Van Hilten, J.J., Van der Zwan, A.D., Zwinderman, A.H. (1994). *Rating impairment and disability in Parkinson's disease: evaluation of the unified Parkinson's disease rating scale.* Movement Disorders, 9, 84 – 88.

Waters, C. (2002). *Diagnosis and Management in Parkinson's Disease.* New York: Professional Communications, Inc.

Weissman, N.J., Tighe Jr., J.F., Gottdiener, J.S., Gwynne, J.T. (1998). *An assessment of heart-valve abnormalities in obese patients taking dexfenfluramine, sustained release dexfenfluramine or placebo.* New England Journal of Medicine, 339, 725 – 732.

Welsh, M. (2005). *Quality of life in Parkinson's disease: a conceptual model.* In: M. Pfeiffer and M. Ebadi (Eds.), Parkinson's Disease, 1009 – 1014. Boca Raton, FL: CRC Press.

A 34-year-old woman with bipolar I depression requiring hospitalization

Bipolar depression is frequently unrecognized, misdiagnosed, and treated as unipolar depression (APA, 2004; Hirschfeld, 2004; Ghaemi et al., 2000). The case presents an individual suffering from bipolar depression who demonstrates the complexities found in treating individuals with this disorder. All diagnoses are based on *Diagnostic and Statistical Manual of Mental Disorders*, 4th Edition, Revised (DSM-IV-TR) (APA, 2000).

INTRODUCTION

Jennifer was involuntarily admitted to a psychiatric hospital for further treatment and stabilization of an acute psychotic disorder. The patient's initial diagnosis was major depression, recurrent, severe, with psychotic symptoms.

> *The first step in effective treatment is an accurate diagnosis. A patient presenting with a prior diagnosis of major depression, recurrent requires consideration of a differential diagnosis of bipolar depression. A diagnosis of bipolar disorder is often missed in individuals who report depressive rather than manic symptoms (Ghaemi et al., 1999). Bipolar mania is well-recognized by practitioners in all practice settings, but bipolar depression is often misdiagnosed and mistreated as unipolar depression. (Kupfer, 2004; Bowden, 2001a; Ghaemi et al., 2000).*

DEMOGRAPHIC DATA

The patient is a 34-year-old woman who resides with her son and daughter, ages 8 and 6, who are both in grammar school. The patient is a high-school graduate. She attended college but left school just before completing her associate's degree. The patient has been employed as an office manager for the last five years. The patient's estranged husband left the family shortly after gaining citizenship in the United States when the children were preschoolers. His whereabouts are unknown. Jennifer had been living with her boyfriend, Brian, age 45, for the past three years. They terminated their relationship one month prior to this admission.

> *Bipolar I disorder affects approximately 0.8% of the adult population, with estimates from community samples ranging between 0.4% and 1.6% (APA, 2004). These rates are consistent across diverse cultures and ethnic groups. Bipolar I disorder affects men and women equally (Weisman et al., 1996). Bipolar I disorder is generally an episodic, lifelong illness with a variable course. The first episode of bipolar disorder can be mania, hypomania, and/or depression. Men are more likely than women to be initially manic, but both are more likely to have a first episode of depression (APA, 2004). Bipolar I disorder causes substantial psychosocial morbidity, frequently affecting the patients' relationships with spouses or partners, children, and other family members as well as their occupation and other aspects of their lives (Kessing et al., 2004).*

Chief complaint: "They tell me I had a nervous breakdown, but I think I'm depressed."

> *Current evidence suggests that many patients with bipolar depression are misdiagnosed, primarily because their bipolar disorder is not recognized. The literature is rich with*

studies that describe the epidemiology of the disorder and the misdiagnosis of bipolar I depression. In one study, 69% of bipolar patients had been misdiagnosed (Hirschfield et al., 2003). In another study, the most common misdiagnosis of bipolar I depression was unipolar depression (Angst, 1998; Angst et al., 2005). In this case, looking at only the chief complaint can lead to grave errors in managing this patient's illness. The treatment of choice in major depressive disorders is antidepressants. The treatment of bipolar disorder with antidepressants alone often has adverse consequences that complicate the patient's treatment outcome (Ghaemi et al., 2004; Bowden, 2001a; Bowden, 2001b; Kahn et al., 2000).

History of present illness

Jennifer, a 34-year-old female, was brought to a community hospital emergency room (ER) because of escalating psychotic behavior. Her admission to the ER was precipitated by her neighbors calling the local police because she was making odd noises and bizarre gestures. The neighbors expressed concern for Jennifer's two children, whom they had not seen for two days. When the police arrived at Jennifer's residence, she would not allow them to enter her apartment. She expressed paranoid ideation to the responding police officers, reporting she knew they were at her residence to kidnap her children. She eventually allowed the police to enter her apartment, having been coaxed into doing so by a neighbor.

The police brought Jennifer and her two children to the local community hospital ER. Jennifer's medical examination was unremarkable. All laboratory tests were within normal. The drug screen profile was negative. Jennifer's presenting diagnosis was acute psychotic state. She presented with paranoid delusions, auditory hallucinations, and labile mood state. She was easily agitated by the ER staff and required lorazepam 2 mg IM to prevent her from acting on her threats to the staff.

Upon arrival at the ER, Jennifer's children were placed with State Child Protective Services for assessment and placement. When the State Child Protective Services case manager questioned Jennifer about appropriate placement with relatives for the children, she responded that she would rather "kill" her children than have family members take custody of her children. Jennifer refused to permit the treatment staff to have any contact with relatives and refused to give the names of family members who could care for the children while she was hospitalized. The children were placed in protective custody with foster families until Jennifer's mental status improved.

On the psychiatric unit, she was medicated with Zoloft, Zyprexa, and Klonopin. Her overt psychotic symptoms continued despite compliance with the prescribed medications. After a 10-day stay on the community psychiatric inpatient unit, Jennifer was transferred to our psychiatric setting, where I admitted her for further stabilization and treatment. Her admitting diagnosis was major depression with psychotic features.

Upon transfer to my service, Jennifer described the symptoms she had been experiencing over the last three months, which were indicative of a major depressive disorder. Jennifer reported she has been having difficulty falling asleep, early morning awakening, inability to concentrate, inability to attend, and psychomotor retardation. Her predominant symptom was one of a sad mood state. She described feeling like she could not live another day. She lost 20 pounds in eight weeks. She denied suicidal ideation, plans, and/or attempts. She denied homicidal ideation, plans, and/or attempts.

Bipolar depressive symptoms are beginning to surface in the literature as being more common than manic symptoms and causing greater disruption of occupational, family, and social functioning (Calabrese et al., 2004). Jennifer was initially diagnosed by the transferring hospital because they had limited information regarding past psychiatric history. Whereas antidepressants are the treatment of choice for major depression, current guidelines recommend that antidepressants not be used in the absence of mood stabilizers in patients with bipolar disorder (APA, 2004; Sachs et al., 2000).

Medications upon admission: I admitted Jennifer to our psychiatric unit and initially continued the medications ordered at the community hospital. These medications were: Zoloft 75 mg, bid; Zyprexa 10 mg, PO q am; and Klonapin 0.5 mg, PO bid. She had been on the above medications for approximately 10 days with no considerable decrease in her psychosis.

Allergies: Patient reported being allergic to penicillin. Patient denied any other known drug allergies.

Emergency room visits: Two emergency room visits resulting in two psychiatric hospitalizations, including the current hospitalization.

Medical hospitalizations: Denied.

ADULT HEALTH

The medical history and physical examination are performed by the hospitalist. I review and cosign the findings and provide follow-up.

Review of systems/medical history: The review of systems was unremarkable for skin, eyes, respiratory, cardiac, GI, GU, GYN, endocrine, and neurological symptoms. She described a 20-pound weight loss during the past eight weeks. She reported normal menses. Her last Pap smear was six months ago and reported normal. She denied pregnancy, and pregnancy test done at time of ER admission was negative. Reports use of birth control via three-month injection. Gravida 2, Para 2. Denies hepatitis A, B, or C. Denies HIV/AIDS. Denies sexually transmitted diseases. Tuberculosis screening at community hospital was negative (RPR was nonreactive). Chest X-Ray was negative.

Habits: Patient denied a history of drug and alcohol abuse/use. Patient denied history of cigarette smoking. She also denied use of illicit drugs. Urine screen in emergency room was negative.

PHYSICAL EXAM

Vital signs: RR 16, P 76, T 98 degrees F, BP 120/80.

HEENT: Normocephalic, pupils equal and reactive to light. No sinus tenderness. Throat was not congested. Thyroid not enlarged.

Back: No scoliosis noted.

Lungs: Clear to auscultation. No rales. No wheezing noted.

Cardiovascular: S_1, S_2, regular rate and rhythm. No murmur appreciated. PMI 4th intercostal space at left midclavicular line.

Abdomen: Soft, nontender. Bowel sounds are normoactive. No organomegaly noted. Negative for costovertebral angle tenderness.

Rectal: Refused examination.

Extremities: No edema. No cyanosis noted. Pedal pulses equally bilaterally.

Skin: Warm and dry. No rash noted.

Neurological: Cranial Nerves II – XII intact. Power 5/5 in all extremities. Sensation intact to sharp, dull, and vibration. Motor: finger taps, supination, pronation without decrement. Gait regular without abnormality. Coordination intact. DTRs 2+ equal bilaterally, toes downgoing.

Laboratory data from community hospital reviewed: Thyroid function test, SMA-7, U/A, CBC, were within normal limits. Urine toxicology screen and serum pregnancy test were negative. RPR was nonreactive.

> *Psychiatric prescribers must be sensitive to the possibility of comorbid medical illness in their patients (Sadock & Sadock, 2003). Medical workup is an expected part of the psychiatric evaluation to determine contributing factors that impact on the patient's care and treatment. Although no laboratory test can establish or rule out a diagnosis of bipolar depression, it is an integral part of treatment to evaluate the patient's hematologic status on a regular basis (APA, 2002a).*

Mental status examination: I completed the psychiatric assessment following the hospitalist's physical examination.

Jennifer presented as a disheveled women appearing her stated age of 34. Her dress was age appropriate. Her posture was rigid and tense. She had intermittent eye contact with the interviewer. Her facial expressions were constricted. Affect was blunted. Her affect was appropriate to her thought content. Motor activity was underactive, but at times she paced and was restless.

Jennifer became easily agitated when participating in the clinical interview. Both the clinical interview and the mental status examination had to be done in short time intervals as Jennifer could not tolerate more than 10 minutes of contact. Her mood was irritable, anxious, and dysphoric. Her predominant symptom was her dysphoric mood. Speech was low, initially monosyllabic, and guarded. Her thinking was illogical. She had delusional thoughts of a paranoid nature. "Why are they putting medicine in my food?" She was overly suspicious of others. She admitted to experiencing Schneiderian First Rank Symptoms of thought control, thought withdrawal, and thought insertion. She reported the television was removing her thoughts. Although she currently denied auditory hallucinations, she experienced "God talking to me" at the time of admission to the ER. She denied suicidal ideation, plans, and/or attempts. She did report a suicide attempt at the age of 13 as being the last time she had "thought about it." She denied homicidal ideation, plans, and/or attempts. Her concentration and attention were problematic. She frequently stopped mid-sentence to remark about her distrust of the hospital. She displayed unpredictable behaviors by quickly becoming agitated and yelling at staff and/or other patients. She denied episodes of derealization, depersonalization, and deja vu experiences.

Formal cognitive mental status examination found she was oriented times three. Her ability to concentrate and attend was impaired relative to her paranoid thought process. Her memory was intact. She was able to perform digital spans forward and backward. Serial sevens were not calculated related to her mood irritability. Later she was able to complete serial three calculations. She was able to do similarities and proverbs, displaying an ability to perform abstract thinking. Her judgment and lack of insight into her illness was grossly impaired. She continued to state, "They just tried to hurt my kids." In response to three wishes, Jennifer replied, "Go back to work, have my kids with me, and be out of the hospital."

> *Successful evaluation and treatment of psychopathologic symptoms, cognitive impairment, and emotional distress can be based only on thorough and objective assessment of the patient, utilizing the Mental Status Examination (MSE) (Trzepacz & Baker, 1993). The mental status examination is the part of the clinical assessment that describes the sum total of the examiner's observations and impressions of the psychiatric patient at the time of the interview. The patient's history remains stable, but mental status can fluctuate sometimes*

from hour to hour (Sadock & Sadock, 2003). Jennifer's mental status examination clearly describes an individual who is suffering from depression. This is just one piece of the data. Most frequently the mental status examination displays the patient's presenting problem and does not reflect the critical historic data needed to determine an accurate diagnosis, thus accurate treatment. In Jennifer's situation, her psychopharmacological treatment addressed only the presenting problem of depression. Jennifer refused involvement of family and refused to consent to the prior hospitalization records. This prevented important and critical data from entering into the clinical diagnosis.

The psychiatric treatment of major depressive disorder is distinctly different than the treatment of bipolar depression (Goldberg, 2003; Compton & Nemeroff, 2000; Thase & Sachs, 2000). The treatment of choice for a major depression is the initiation of antidepressants; however, in bipolar depression the guidelines recommend that antidepressants not be used in the absence of mood stabilizers in patients with bipolar depression (APA, 2004). The outcomes of not addressing the history of an earlier bipolar disorder could have devastating results for Jennifer.

HOSPITAL COURSE

As Jennifer's psychotic symptoms abated, she became more cooperative and was able to account a history of episodes where she experienced bursts of energy, decreased sleep, increased mood lability, increased energy, spending sprees, and expanded moods.

As she improved, she agreed that the treatment team could contact family members, allowing the opportunity to evaluate all elements of her case.

PAST PSYCHIATRIC HISTORY

Hospitalization as an adolescent: Patient was hospitalized at age 13 for treatment of "depression." Patient reported she overdosed on asthma pills. She was treated at the pediatric unit and sent home with aftercare arrangements for psychotherapy. Patient participated in psychotherapy for about one year. She denied other suicidal ideation, plans, and/or attempts.

Twenty to 40% of adolescents with major depression develop bipolar disorder within five years after depression onset (NIMH, 2000). All patients with a history of adolescent depression are at higher risk to experience bipolar episodes later in life (Birmaher et al., 1998; Sadock & Sadock, 2003). The early history of this patient indicates that she is at higher risk for developing bipolar disorder later in life. With a suicide attempt at age 13, the advanced practice nurse must seek information that either confirms or denies that this patient could have experienced an earlier bipolar manic episode.

First hospitalization as an adult: Both the patient and the family accounted that the patient presented quite differently five months ago. At that time the patient was described as having too much energy, experiencing mood swings, and just not being herself. The patient was taking on extra projects and spending more money than she had done in the past. She was brought to a community hospital in the area of her employment because she began to yell at all of her co-workers that she was having a "breakdown." Upon discharge, both the patient and the family were told that Jennifer was experiencing a bipolar episode, manic.

During that hospitalization, Jennifer was placed on Zyprexa, Depakote, and a low dose of Zoloft. The final diagnosis was bipolar disorder, single manic episode. Aftercare and discharge plans included referral to the Community Mental Health Center for continued medication management.

Psychosocial stressors: Jennifer and her family accounted the death of their oldest sister as a significant event that contributed to the patient's current difficulties. Patient accounts she had recently lost her sister who died of "colon cancer." Jennifer was raised by this oldest sister, reporting that this sister had been "a mother to me." Although Jennifer was aware of her sister's chemotherapy treatments, her sister's death came as a shock to Jennifer. The family recounted that when Jennifer was told of her sister's colon tumor, Jennifer became increasingly agitated and irritable. Jennifer's first hospitalization occurred three months after her sister was diagnosed with colon cancer. Initially Jennifer's sister responded well to surgery and chemotherapy. Several months later when Jennifer's sister had a reoccurrence, Jennifer's family were fearful that Jennifer would have another serious episode if she learned of her sister's prognosis. In an effort to protect Jennifer, the family did not let Jennifer know about the reoccurrence. During chemotherapy, Jennifer's sister became gravely ill with a complication and died within a week. The family did not tell Jennifer of her death until two days later.

Jennifer became increasingly depressed after her sister's death. The week prior to this admission, Jennifer reported that she was fearful that someone was "putting something like poison" in her food. She described auditory hallucinations. "They were telling me to protect my children... I thought it was God talking to me." In addition, Jennifer reported she experienced diurnal variations of feeling worse in the morning and better in the afternoon. Eventually, she "felt numb, helplessness, and hopelessness." She described not being able to concentrate or attend during this time. She had also lost interest in pleasurable activities. Although she denied suicidal ideation, she did feel like she did not want to live any longer. She began experiencing psychotic symptoms that someone would take her children. She reported that she believed her bizarre gestures were protective towards her children.

> *Psychosocial stress and loss of social support appear to play a role in bipolar episodes and may be particularly relevant to precipitating depressive episodes (Miklowitz, 2004). The Jorvi Bipolar Study (JoBS) findings reported that women who suffer from a psychosocial loss are more likely to present with bipolar depression than men (Mantere et al., 2004).*

FAMILY MEDICAL AND PSYCHIATRIC HISTORY

Patient's biological parents divorced when the patient was two years of age. Father died from prostate cancer. Mother, who suffered from hypertension, died of a CVA one year ago. Patient's stepfather died of lung cancer two years ago. Patient's sister, who raised her, died of colon cancer four months ago. There is no family history of diabetes, heart disease, alcoholism, and/or drug abuse. Patient and her sister report a family history of psychiatric illness. Jennifer's maternal grandmother suffered from depression. A maternal aunt had been hospitalized for several months for postpartum depressions after the birth of each of her children.

> *Evidence suggests that bipolar disorder is an inheritable illness. First-degree relatives of persons with bipolar disorder experience higher rates of major depressive disorder and bipolar disorder than first-degree relatives of persons without bipolar disorder (APA, 2004b; Kupfer, 2004; Chaudron & Pies, 2003; Sadock & Sadock, 2003). The issue that complicates the family studies is the wide variety of symptoms that frequently fluctuate over time with all mood disorders of which bipolar depression is a subset (Kupfer, 2004). Studies are being conducted to determine if the psychiatric disorders should be classified by psychotic disorders and nonpsychotic disorders.*

PSYCHOSOCIAL HISTORY

Jennifer reports she was the fifth and youngest child born of her parents' marriage. Jennifer grew up in a large extended family of older half-siblings both on her maternal and paternal side of the family. Jennifer was raised by her oldest half-sister whom she considered her mother. Jennifer had no academic difficulties in school. She has numerous peer relationships which she has maintained since grammar school. Jennifer reported dating her husband for approximately two years before the couple married.

Despite the patient not knowing the whereabouts of her husband, Jennifer has never filed for divorce. Family reports the patient's children are doing well in school. Presently Jennifer's family and friends are very distressed over the patient placing the children in foster care instead of with one of her many siblings. The patient now reports she was just "too paranoid" to do anything else. The patient had been with her estranged boyfriend until one month ago. The family was not supportive of this relationship, reporting the patient was verbally abused by the boyfriend. The patient has no history of legal difficulties. Jennifer considers herself to be religious and participates actively in the Baptist church in her town. She has had an excellent work history with few interruptions until this past year.

Jennifer has experienced two significant losses over this last year. She considers the death of her mother and then her sister to be the precipitants to her psychiatric hospitalizations. Her siblings have remorse and regret about not telling Jennifer when the oldest sibling was hospitalized with extensive metastasis. According to the siblings, this oldest sister was extremely protective of Jennifer and did not want Jennifer to know of her continued struggle. The family felt unprepared when this sister died. Jennifer was not told of sister's death until two days later, as her siblings felt she was too fragile to manage the loss. In retrospect, Jennifer's siblings recognize that excluding Jennifer from the bereavement process may have contributed to Jennifer's current difficulties.

There is an increasing focus on the impact of psychosocial factors and life stressors on the course of bipolar disorders. The life event research has rendered multiple research biases with conflicting study results. In a prospective study, Christensen et al. (2003) examined the relationship between life events and affective phases in a group of bipolar patients. This study's results supported earlier studies by Leibenluft (1996) and Perugio et al. (1990) reporting gender differences in an individual's course of bipolar disorders and life events. Somatic health problems and conflicts in the family were significant factors preceding new depressive phases in women. Christensen et al. (2003) found that in bipolar patients with long duration of disease, a significant number of depressive episodes in women were preceded by negative life events. In men, there was a higher frequency of manic episodes following a life stressor.

The loss of her sister to colon cancer was a devastating loss. The family dynamic of attempting to protect the patient in fact only contributed more to the patient's paranoia toward her family and contributed to the placement of her children in a foster home during her hospitalization. By the time of Jennifer's admission, her psychosis was acute and her inability to trust the family in providing for her children was predictable, given the family dynamics of an inability for "truth telling" in all situations. The addition of psychosocial treatments for Jennifer and her family of origin may further improve patient outcomes (Jindal et al., 2003).

Diagnosis

Axis I: Bipolar I, Most Recent Episode Depressed

Axis II: Deferred

Axis III: Medically Stable

Axis IV: Chronic Illness

Axis V: Current GAF: 20; Highest GAF: 80

Case formulation

Jennifer presented with symptoms that were indicative of a bipolar I depression. Over the last two months she had experienced escalating difficulties with mood modulation. Her predominant symptoms of dysphoria and depression were severe. In addition, she exhibited sleep disturbances, with difficulty falling asleep and early morning awakening, chronic feelings of fatigue, decreased concentration and attention, lack of interest in pleasurable activities, as well as feelings of helplessness and hopelessness. Although she denied suicidal ideation, plans, and/or attempts, she acknowledged she was "better off dead." With the addition of psychosis, Jennifer entered into a high-risk category for both a slow resolution of symptoms and danger of suicidal attempts. Impacting on the medication management of Jennifer is the history of a past manic episode that led to her prior psychiatric hospitalization earlier this year. At that time she cycled into a depressive phase. She was treated with Zyprexa, Depakote, and Zoloft successfully.

> *Although pharmacotherapy is the mainstay of a comprehensive plan of care for the management of a patient with bipolar depression, the additional benefits of psychosocial interventions for the patient, family, and caregivers is increasingly supported by recent clinical evidence (Vieta, 2005).*

> *Distinguishing between major depressive (unipolar) disorder and bipolar depressive disorders is extremely critical to providing the best possible outcomes in treatment planning. "Unipolar" depression is characterized by a single mood pole, that of major depression, and fulfills specific defined criteria (APA, 2000a). Bipolar episodes can be seen as having three distinct phases: the depressed phase, which mimics the clinical picture of major depression; the manic or hypomanic phase (upper pole); and euthymia, or the asymptomatic phase. Bipolar episode subsets exist with the diagnosis of bipolar I disorder, requiring only one lifetime manic or mixed episode. For a diagnosis of bipolar II disorder, the DSM-IV-TR specified that at least one hypomania and one depressive episode occur in the absence of manic or mixed episodes (APA, 2004b). Distinguishing between unipolar and bipolar depression is a priority in cases that present with similar history.*

Initial plan

Week 1:   • Increase Zyprexa to alleviate psychotic symptoms.

   • Add lamotrigine (Lamictal) at 25 mg/od for bipolar depressive symptoms and as mood stabilizer. Monitor for adverse effects of medications, especially rash development with lamotrigine (Lamictal).

   • Continue Zoloft at lower dose of 25 mg/bid for depressive symptoms.

- Maintain patient on 15-minute checks for protection of self and others.

Week 2:
- Continue lamotrigine 25 mg/od as a mood stabilizer; continue Zyprexa and Zoloft at current dose. Improvement in mood state and reality with discontinuation of 15-minute checks for protection of self and others.

Week 3:
- Titrate lamotrigine 25 mg/bid as a mood stabilizer. Monitor for adverse reaction to lamotrigine, especially development of rash.

- Voluntary status: Discontinue involuntary commitment.

Week 4:
- Titrate lamotrigine 50 mg/bid. Monitor for adverse reaction to medications, especially rash development with lamotrigine (Lamictal).

- Discharge meds: Zoloft 25 mg/bid; Zyprexa 30 mg/hs; lamotrigine (Lamictal) 50 mg/bid.

CASE CONCLUSIONS

Jennifer has a positive response to the lamotrigine. Her depressive symptoms abated by the second week of hospitalization. Concurrently her psychotic symptoms responded to treatment with increased Zyprexa. She was able to leave the hospital with mood stability. Jennifer verbalized a commitment to remaining on these medications as she was experiencing no side effects to this medication regime.

Continuity of care: Aftercare arrangements were completed by the second week of Jennifer's hospitalization. Jennifer became an active participant in this process as a partner in the health-care plan. On third week of hospitalization, she was sent to one visit with her community prescriber so that the medications would be continued and adjusted as Jennifer returned to work.

Employee assistance program was a vital link in Jennifer's aftercare plan. Assessment of her ability to complete her job responsibilities was discussed, and a realistic plan was developed for her return to work. In addition to pharmacotherapy, Jennifer participated in adjunctive psychosocial interventions, including psychoeducational programs and cognitive-behavioral therapy (CBT). *The adjunctive psychosocial interventions were phase-specific, with the goal of helping Jennifer move toward a more comprehensive functional recovery (Zarestsky, 2003).* The continuations of Jennifer's psychosocial treatments were followed through with the aftercare and discharge plans. Psychoeducational programs included medication education, reproductive education, and relapse prevention. The psychoeducational programs would continue on an outpatient basis with Jennifer attending the Community Mental Health Service and the Visiting Nurse Services Relapse Prevention Program.

CLINICAL CONCLUSIONS

The World Health Organization identified bipolar disorder as the sixth leading cause of disability-adjusted life years in the world among people ages 15 to 44 years. Bipolar I mania/depression is often not recognized as an illness, and people may suffer for years before it is properly diagnosed and treated. Like diabetes or heart disease, bipolar disorder is a long-term illness that must be carefully managed throughout a person's life (NIMH, 2004).

Pharmacotherapy is the mainstay of the comprehensive program of care for the management of patients with bipolar disorder. However, several facets of bipolar depression can be addressed more effectively by instituting adjunctive psychosocial interventions. The adjunctive psychosocial interventions were phase-specific and provided in direct linkage to Jennifer's fluctuating mood state (Swartz & Frank, 2001). Evidence suggests that combining pharmacotherapy with psychosocial interventions which are tailored to the patient's individual needs may decrease the risk of relapse, improve patient adherence, and decrease the number and length of hospitalizations (Vieta, 2005; Colom & Vieta, 2004; Zarestsky, 2003).

CASE DISCUSSION

The following issues are raised in this case study:

1. The patient's right to truth came in direct conflict with the dying sibling's right to autonomy.

Patients' end-of-life decisions challenge nurses to improve palliative care, symptom management, patient advocacy, and to examine ethical issues. When a terminally ill patient takes charge of the last stages of life, they may challenge nurses to re-examine attitudes about lifesaving technology as well as autonomy and values about preserving life. Family members can become benevolent and believe that they know what is best despite the patient's independent decisions (Valente, 2004). In this instance, the family and dying sibling practiced benevolence with Jennifer. Jennifer's dying sibling and family made a conscious decision to exclude Jennifer from the process of end-of-life care. Several studies have highlighted the patient-family and practitioner relationship in decision-making and autonomy (Arnold & Egan, 2004; Valente, 2004; Tulsky et al., 1998; Bradley et al., 1998). However, despite the literature, families often report that they remained dissatisfied with such communications. Although patients, family members, and providers consider the conversation about end-of-life decisions, the conversations continue to happen too infrequently (Valente, 2004; Hanson et al., 1997). In this instance, the family reported that they were all essentially "frozen" by the imminent death of this sibling. The family also reported that they were not aware of how imminent the death was for this sibling. In an attempt to protect (benevolence) Jennifer, they essentially created an irreversible event. These issues will need further treatment on an outpatient basis once Jennifer's mood is stabilized.

2. Complications of treating a patient with bipolar I depression with an antidepressant.

The goal of treatment of bipolar I depression is remission of the symptoms of major depression and a return to normal levels of psychosocial functioning. There are concerns about precipitation of a manic or hypomanic episode in the treatment of bipolar depression that do not exist for major depression. Upon admission, Jennifer was being treated with an antidepressant. This practice would have eventually precipitated the patient into a bipolar I manic episode. Therefore the continuation of this antidepressant without a mood stabilizer was not a consideration.

There are significant negative risks associated with treating an individual with bipolar I depression with antidepressants (Sadock & Sadock, 2003). The anti-depressant treatment can "switch" this individual into a manic, hypomanic, and/or rapid cycling episode literally overnight. In one study, more than 50% of patients with bipolar depression did not respond to antidepressant therapy (Ghaemi et al., 2004). In a separate study, 55% of patients with bipolar depression who received anti-depressants monotherapy developed hypomania or mania, and 23% experienced illness destabilization, including new or worsening rapid cycling (Ghaemi et al., 2000). With this population the use of mood stabilizers is less effective in treating a depressive episode (Sadock & Sadock, 2003).

3. A complication of untreated bipolar I depression is suicide.

Jennifer was being treated for a major depressive episode. She was being inadequately medicated since she had not been placed on a mood stabilizer. The complication of suicide was and still remains a clear risk.

> *Completed suicide occurs in an estimated 10 – 15% of individuals with bipolar I disorder (Suppes et al., 2005; APA, 2004a; APA, 2004b; Kupfer et al., 2002; Watson & Young, 2001). Suicide is more likely to occur during a depressive episode (Burgess et al., 2004). Suicide rates average 0.4% per year in men and women diagnosed with bipolar disorder; however in patients experiencing bipolar I depression, the suicide rates are >20-fold higher than in the bipolar population (Tondo et al., 2001; Tondo & Baldessarini, 2000).*

4. Choice of mood stabilizers.

The goal of the treatment is to reduce depressive symptoms and suicidal thoughts, restore function, prevent mood switching and cycling, and build a therapeutic alliance.

Jennifer clearly met the criteria for bipolar I depression. Of the mood stabilizers (lithium, Lamictal, Depakote, Tegretol, etc.), which choice would be based on the best clinical evidence, also taking into account that Jennifer is of child-bearing age?

> *The treatment of bipolar I depression is challenging to all clinicians. There are several treatment guidelines based on expert consensus (APA, 2004a; Kahn et al., 2000; Sachs et al., 2000; Frances et al., 1998). There are three RCT on the treatment of bipolar I depression that are considered the "gold standard" for medication management (Kupfer, 2004). These three studies demonstrate that lamotrigine has significant antidepressant efficacy in bipolar I depression and that clinical improvement becomes evident as early as the third week of treatment (Bowden, 2001a; Calabrese et al., 1999a; Calabrese et al., 1999b; Frye et al., 2000). These studies resulted in the revision of the APA guidelines for treatment of bipolar disorder in 2004. These studies improved the outcome for numerous patients suffering from this disorder. With the high suicide rate of individuals who experience bipolar I depression coming to the forefront of the psychiatric literature, these three studies have become "gold standard" for evidence-based practice. It has been assimilated into the American Psychiatric Association Guidelines revisions of treatment of bipolar disorders in 2004. The cited literature describes the scope and depth of the problem of treating this population.*

Question: Why not prescribe lithium for treatment of bipolar I depression?

Lithium selection for Jennifer was also considered as a first-line mood stabilizer. If lamotrigine failed to alleviate her depressive symptoms, then lithium would have been an excellent choice. However, lithium is fraught with monitoring guidelines which often are difficult for working individuals to maintain. The side effects of lithium can adversely affect patient adherence. *This is of particular importance since a sudden withdrawal of lithium can increase the likelihood of relapse and the risk of suicide (Baldessarini et al., 1999).* Jennifer as a child-bearing age female presents with additional challenges when profiling the comparison between lithium and lamotrigine. Although there are many considerations in comparing side effect profiles, teratogenicity must be considered in medication selections for all women of child-bearing age. Lamotrigine is the first-line choice when comparing the drug profiles of these two mood stabilizers in the treatment of bipolar I depression.

> *The somatic treatments that have been studied in bipolar I depression include lithium, anticonvulsants, antidepressants, and electroconvulsive therapy (ECT). The literature on the use of lithium as a mood stabilizer in bipolar disorder is compelling for bipolar I*

mania. Although lithium has shown superior efficacy in the treatment of bipolar I manic episodes, it has not demonstrated comparable efficacy in the treatment of bipolar I depression. Lamotrigine, compared to lithium, has shown to be more effective for bipolar I depression (Goldsmith et al., 2003; Sacks et al., 2000). However, it is important to note that lamotrigine has not demonstrated efficacy in treating bipolar I manic episodes (Keck, 2005).

When treating female patients with bipolar disorder, the provider must consider the patient's child-bearing plans, sexual side effects, and fetal teratogenicity along with other side effect profile issues such as the development of hypothyroidism with lithium. Many women with bipolar disorder who are contemplating pregnancy will not be dissuaded by the information regarding risk either to themselves or to their fetus. This is illustrated in a study by Viguera et al., in 2002. Most Expert Consensus Guidelines report variability with females' responses, concerns with reproductive health issues, and urge the need for further study in this area to assist in the delivery of appropriate care to women with bipolar disorder (Freeman & Gelenberg, 2005). The standard of practice currently is to educate every woman of reproductive age. The patient education includes (besides the known risks and benefits of her pharmacologic treatment options) what we know about risks in pregnancy, as well as the risks of untreated mood disorder in pregnancy and postpartum. Further study is critical in these areas to determine an evidenced-based standard of care that is appropriate to women with bipolar disorder (Freeman & Gelenberg, 2005).

5. Review the DSM-IV-TR criteria after information gathering and reviewing of pertinent records from transferring hospital.

Jennifer was experiencing a mood disorder. There are four main syndromes that are considered when assessing and evaluating an individual who is experiencing a mood disorder. Of all the disorders, the diagnosis of bipolar I depression presents the most challenges, as a provider must purposefully review the symptoms and course of this illness with the patient and their family (Sachs, 2003; Fauman, 2001).

The most important diagnostic decision in the mood disorders groups is usually the determination of whether the patient fulfills the criteria for one or more of the four main syndromes: major depressive episode, manic episode, hypomania episode, or mixed episode. Once this diagnostic question is answered, the range of possible diagnoses is considerably narrowed (First et al., 2002; Fauman, 2001).

6. Knowledge of the evidence-based practice literature is critical in the practice of psychiatric assessment and evaluation.

Upon completion of Jennifer's assessment and evaluation, the clinical treatment was changed to reflect evidence-based practices. If Jennifer had been maintained on Zoloft, Zyprexa, and Klonapin, eventually Jennifer may well have experienced dramatic complications that could be life-threatening. If an accurate diagnosis could have been made with the records from the first adult hospitalization, the additional costs to Jennifer for the longer-term hospitalization would not have financially cost her and the State. She also was dealing with the social loss of her siblings and the occupational losses. Clinicians should keep in mind that guidelines provide direction for addressing common clinical dilemmas that arise in the pharmacologic treatment of psychiatric disorders. The guidelines are used to inform clinicians and educate patients and families regarding the relative merits of a variety of interventions.

The psychiatric literature documents the pitfalls of diagnosis in depression. Numerous peer-reviewed articles describe beneficial outcomes when utilizing best-practice guidelines in clinical practice, yet there remains a discord in health care in general, and in behavioral health care specifically, between research and clinical practice. Multiple factors are proposed as causing the continuation of this discord, yet there exists a basic lack of research in addressing the factors that continue this discord (Haynes, 2005). In 1999 the American Psychiatric Association Practice Research Network Study of Psychiatric Patients and Treatment reported the best-practice guidelines were not being followed when studying outcomes of practice. They reported 20% of the bipolar population did not receive treatment with a mood stabilizer and 40% did not receive any type of psychotherapy, both of which are recommended in the APA's best-practice guidelines (APA, 2004a; APA, 2002b). Soon after, "Mental Health: Report of the Surgeon General" emulated these findings (USDHHS, 1999). This extensive report emphasized that these state-of-the-art treatments refined through years of research were not being transferred into actual practice in community settings (Hayes, 2005).

In response to the Surgeon General's Report, the National Institute of Mental Health put forth an initiative in seeking a public health intervention model that could generate externally valid answers to the continued treatment effectiveness questions related to bipolar disorder (Sachs et al., 2003). The complexity of the condition, lack of a common intervention model, and the need for a large sample present daunting obstacles to the researchers and provide compelling rationale for NIMH sponsorship of multi-site collaborative research. The Systematic Treatment Enhancement Program for Bipolar Disorder (STEP-BD), a large national multi-site study, is one of the several large initiative studies with funding provided by NIMH. STEP-BD disease-management model is a national multi-site study built on evidence-based practices and collaborative care approaches designed to maximize specific and nonspecific treatment interventions (Morris, 2005). The data from the STEP-BD prospective studies will greatly improve quantity and quality of data available to guide clinicians and policy makers as they attempt to meet the needs of a population with severe mental illness (Sachs et al., 2003).

References

Angst, J. (1998). *The emerging epidemiology of hypomania and bipolar II disorder.* Journal of Affective Disorders, 50, 143 – 151.

Angst, J., Sellaro, R., Stassen, H.H., Gamma, A. (2005). *Diagnostic conversion from depression to bipolar disorders: results of a long-term prospective study of hospital admissions.* Journal of Affective Disorders, 84 (2 – 3): 149 – 157.

American Psychiatric Association (2000). *Diagnostic Statistical Manual of Mental Disorders,* Fourth ed., text revised (DSM-IV-TR). Washington, D.C.: American Psychiatric Publishing, Inc.

American Psychiatric Association (2002a). *Practice guidelines for the treatment of patients with bipolar disorder (revision).* American Journal of Psychiatry, 159 (supplement 4): 1 – 50.

American Psychiatric Association (2002b). *Guidelines for Practice.* Washington, D.C.: American Psychiatric Association Publishing, Inc.

American Psychiatric Association (2004a). *Practice guidelines for the treatment of patients with major depressive disorder (2nd ed.); Practice guidelines for the treatment of patients with bipolar disorder (2nd ed.).* Found in Practice Guidelines for the Treatment of Psychiatric Disorders: Compendium 2004. Washington, D.C.: American Psychiatric Association, 441 – 612.

American Psychiatric Association (2004b). *APA Guidelines for Bipolar Disorder, revised.*

American Psychiatric Association (2004). *Practice Guidelines.* Abstract retrieved Nov. 19, 2004, from http://www.psych.org/ psych pract/treatg/pg/bipolar revisebook index.cfm.

Arnold, R.L., Egan, K. *Breaking the "bad" news to patients and families: preparing to have the conversation about end-of-life and hospice care* (2004). American Journal of Geriatric Cardiology, 13 (6): 307 – 312.

Baldessarini, R.J., Tondo, L., Hennen, J. (1999). *Effects of lithium treatment and its discontinuation on suicidal behavior in bipolar manic-depressive disorders.* Journal of Clinical Psychiatry, 60 (supplement 2): 77 – 84.

Birmaher, B., Brent, D.A., Benson, R.S. (1998). *Summary of the practice parameters for the assessment and treatment of children and adolescents with depressive disorders.* Journal of the American Academy of Child and Adolescent Psychiatry, 37 (11): 1234 – 1238.

Bowden, C.L. (2001a). *Novel treatment for bipolar disorder.* Expert Opinion on Investigative Drugs, 10 (4): 661 – 671.

Bowden, C.L. (2001b). *Strategies to reduce misdiagnosis of bipolar depression.* Psychiatric Services, 52 (1): 51 – 77.

Bradley, E.H., Peiris, V., Wetle, T. (1998). *Discussions about end-of-life care in nursing homes.* Journal of the American Geriatric Society, 46 (10): 1235 – 1241.

Burgess, S., Geddes, J., Hawton, K., Townsend, E., Jamison, K., Goodwin, G. (2004) (Version 5-25-04). *EBM Reviews: Cochrane Depression, Anxiety and Neurosis Group [Data file].* Cochrane Database of Systematic Reviews. Available from http://http:gateway.ut. ovie.com/gwl/ovidweb.cg.

Calabrese, J.R., Bowden, C.L., McElroy, S.L. (1999a). *Spectrum of activity of lamotrigine in treatment-refractory bipolar disorder.* American Journal of Psychiatry, 156, 1019 – 1023.

Calabrese, J.R., Bowden, C.L., Sachs, C.L., Ascher, J.A., Monaghan, E., Rudd, G.D. (1999b). *A double-blind placebo-controlled study of lamotrigine monotherapy in outpatients with bipolar I depression.* Journal of Clinical Psychiatry, 60 (2): 79 – 88.

Calabrese, J.R., Hirschfeld, R., Frye, M.A., Reed, M.L. (2003). *Impact of depressive symptoms compared with manic symptoms in bipolar disorder: results of a U.S. community-based sample.* Journal of Clinical Psychiatry, 65 (11): 499 – 504.

Calabrese, J.R., Hirschfeld, R.M., Frye, M.A., Reed, M.L. (2004). *Journal of Clinical Psychiatry,* 65 (11): 1499 – 1504.

Chaudron, L.H., Pies, R.W. (2003). *The relationship between postpartum psychosis and bipolar disorder: a review.* Journal of Clinical Psychiatry, 64 (11): 1284 – 1292.

Christensen, E.M., Gjerris, A., Larsen, J.K., Bendtsen, B.B., Larsen, B.H., Rolff, H., et al. (2003). *Life events and onset of a new phase in bipolar affective disorder.* Bipolar Disorders, 5, 356 – 351.

Colom, F., Vieta, E. (2004). *A perspective on the use of psychoeducation cognitive-behavioral therapy and interpersonal therapy for bipolar patients.* Bipolar Disorders, 6, 480 – 486.

Compton, M.T., Nemeroff, C.B. (2000). *The treatment of bipolar depression.* Journal of Clinical Psychiatry, 61 (Supplement 9): 57 – 67.

Fauman, M. (2001). *Study Guide to DSM-IV-TR.* Washington, D.C.: American Psychiatric Association Publishing, Inc.

First, M.B., Frances, A., Pincus, H.A. (2002). *Handbook of Differential Diagnosis.* Washington, D.C.: American Psychiatric Publishing Company (Original work published 1956).

Frances, A.J., Kahn, D.A., Carpenter, D., Docherty, J.P., Donovan, S.L. (1998). *The expert consensus guidelines for treating depression in bipolar disorder.* Journal of Clinical Psychiatry, 59 (Supplement 4): 73 – 79.

Freeman, M.P., Gelenberg, A.J. (2005). *Bipolar disorder in women: reproductive events and treatment considerations.* Acta Psychiatrica Scandinavica, 112 (2): 88 – 96.

Frye, M.A., Ketter, T.A., Kimbrell, T.A., Dunn, R.T., Speer, A.M., Osuch, E.A., Luckenbaugh, D.A., Cora-Ocatelli, G., Leverich, G.S., Post, R.M. (2000). *A placebo-controlled study of lamotrigine and gabapentin monotherapy in refractory mood disorders.* Journal of Clinical Psychopharmacology, 20 (6): 607 – 614.

Ghaemi, S.N., Rosenquist, K., Ko, J.Y., Baldassano, C.F., Kontos, N.J., Baldessarini, R.J. (2004). *Antidepressant treatment in bipolar versus unipolar depression.* American Journal of Psychiatry, 161 (1): 163 – 165.

Ghaemi, S.N., Boisman, E.E., Goodwin, F.K. (2000). *Diagnosing bipolar disorder and the effect of antidepressants: a naturalistic study.* Journal of Clinical Psychiatry, 61 (10): 804 – 808.

Ghaemi, S.N., Sachs, G.S., Chiou, A.M., Pandurangi, A.K., Goodwin, K. (1999). *Is bipolar disorder still underdiagnosed? Are antidepressants overutilized?* Journal of Affective Disorders, 52 (1 – 3): 135 – 144.

Goldberg, J. F. (2003). *When do antidepressants worsen the course of bipolar disorder?* Journal of Psychiatric Practice, 9 (3): 181 – 194.

Greenhalgh, T., Donald, A. (2000). *Evidence Based Health Care Workbook.* London: BMJ Publishing Group.

Hanson, L.C., Danis, M., Garrett, J. (1997). *What is wrong with end-of-life care? The opinions of bereaved family members.* Journal of the American Geriatric Society, 45, 1339 – 1344.

Hayes, R.A. (2005). *Introduction to evidence-based practices.* In: C.E. Stout & R.A. Hayes, (Eds.), Evidence-Based Practice: Methods, Models, and Tools for Mental Health Professionals (pp. 1 – 9). Hoboken, NJ: John Wiley & Sons.

Hirschfeld, R.M. (2004). *Diagnosis of bipolar disorder.* In D.J. Kupfer (Ed.), Bipolar Depression: The Clinician's Reference Guide (pp. 15 – 25). Montvale, NJ: Current Psychiatry.

Hirschfeld, R.M., Calabrese, J.R., Weissman, M., Reed, M., Davies, M.A., Fry, M.A., Keck, P.E., Lewis, L., McElroy, S.L., McNulty, J.P., Wagner, K.D. (2003). *Screening for bipolar disorder in the community.* Journal of Clinical Psychiatry, 64 (1): 53 – 59.

Jenicek, M. (2001). *Clinical Case Reporting in Evidence-Based Medicine* (2nd ed.). New York, NY: Oxford University Press, Inc. (Original work published 1999).

Jindal, R.D., Thase, M.E. (2003). *Integrating psychotherapy and pharmacotherapy to improve outcomes among patients with mood disorders.* Psychiatric Services, 54 (11): 1484 – 1490.

Kahn, D.A., Sachs, G.S., Printz, D.J., Carpenter, D., Docherty, J.P., Ross, R. (2000). *Medication treatment of bipolar disorder 2000: a summary of the expert consensus guidelines.* Journal of Psychiatric Practice, 6 (4): 197 – 211.

Kaye, N.S. (2005). *Is your depressed patient bipolar?* Journal of the American Board of Family Practice, 18 (4): 271 – 281.

Keck Jr., P.E., (2005). *Bipolar depression: a new role for atypical antipsychotics.* Bipolar Disorders, 7 (supplement 4): 34 – 40.

Keck Jr., P.E., Perlis, R.H., Otto, M.W., Carpenter, D., Ross, R., Docherty, J.P. (2004). *Expert consensus guideline series: treatment of bipolar disorder 2004 [A special report].* Postgraduate Medicine — A Special Report, Dec. 2004, 1 – 116.

Kessing, L.V., Hansen, M.G., Andersen, P.K. (2004). *Course of illness in depressive and bipolar disorders: naturalistic study, 1994 – 1999.* British Journal of Psychiatry, 185, 372 – 377.

Kupfer, D.J., Frank, E., Grochocinski, V.J., Cluss, P.A., Houch, P.R., Stapf, D.A. (2002). *Demographic and clinical characteristics of individuals in a bipolar disorder case registry.* Journal of Clinical Psychiatry, 63 (11): 120 – 125.

Kupfer, D.J. (2004). *Epidemiology and clinical course of bipolar disorder.* In D.J. Kupfer (Ed.), Bipolar Depression: The Clinician's Reference Guide (BD-CRG) (pp. 1 – 13). Montvale, NJ: Current Psychiatry.

Leibenluft, E. (1996). *Women with bipolar illness: clinical and research issues.* American Journal of Psychiatry, 153, 163 – 173.

Mantere, O., Suominen, K., Leppamaki, S., Valtonen, H., Arvilommi, P., Isometsa, E. (2004). *The clinical characteristics of DSM-IV bipolar I and II disorders: baseline findings from the Jorvi Bipolar Study (JoBS).* Bipolar Disorders, 6, 395 – 405.

March, J.S., Silva, S.G., Compton, S., Shapiro, M., Califf, R., Krishnan, R. (2005). *The case for practice clinical trials in psychiatry.* American Journal of Psychiatry, 162 (5): 836 – 846.

Miklowitz, D.J. (2004). *Psychosocial issues in bipolar depression.* Bipolar Depression: The Clinician's Reference Guide (pp. 61 – 78). Montvale, NJ: Current Psychiatry.

Morris, C.D., Miklowitz, D.J., Wisniewski, S.R., Giese, A.A., Thomas, M.R., Allen, M.H. (2005). *Care satisfaction, hope, and life functioning among adults with bipolar disorder: data from the first 1000 participants in the Systematic Treatment Enhancement Program.* Comprehensive Psychiatry, 46, 98 – 104.

National Institute of Mental Health (2000, September). *Depression in Children and Adolescents.* In A Fact Sheet for Physicians (chapter) retrieved Dec. 1, 2004, from Department of Health and Human Services; Public Health Services; and National Institutes of Health: http://www.nimh.nih.gov/publicat/NIMHdepchildresfact.pdf.

National Institute of Mental Health (2004). *Introduction: Bipolar Disorder.* Abstract retrieved Dec. 4, 2004, from National Institutes of Health: http://www.nimh.nih.gov/publicat/bipolar.cfm#readNow.

Norquist, G.S., Magruder, K.M. (1998). *Views from funding agencies: National Institute of Mental Health.* Medical Care, 36 (9): 1306 – 1308.

Perugio, G., Musetti, L., Simonini, E., Piagentini, F., Cassano, G.B., Akiskal, H.S. (1990). *Gender-mediated clinical features of depressive illness: the importance of temperamental differences.* British Journal of Psychiatry, 157, 835 – 841.

Sachs, G.S., Thase, M.E., Otto, M.W., Bauer, M., Miklowitz, D., Wisniewski, S.T., Lavori, P., Lebowitz, B., Rudorfer, M., Frank, E., Nierenberg, A.A., Fava, M., Dowden, C., Ketter, T., Marangell, L., Calabrese, J., Kupfer, D., Rosenbaum, J.F. (2003). *Rationale, design, and methods of the systematic treatment enhancement program for bipolar disorder (STEP-BD).* Biological Psychiatry, 53, 1028 – 1042.

Sachs, G.S. (2003). *Decision tree for the treatment of bipolar disorder.* Journal of Clinical Psychiatry, 64 (supplement 8): 35 – 40.

Sachs, G.S., Printz, D.J., Kahn, D.A., Carpenter, D., Docherty, J.P., Donovan, S.L. (2000). *The expert consensus guideline series: medication treatment of bipolar disorder 2000.* Postgraduate Medicine 2000, No. 1, 1 – 104.

Sadock, J.B., Sadock, V.A. (2003). *Kaplan and Sadock's Synopsis of Psychiatry.* New York: Lippincott Williams & Wilkins.

Schatzberg, A.F., Cole, J.O., DeBattista, C. (2003). *Manual of Clinical Psychopharmacology* (4th ed.). Washington, DC: American Psychiatric Publishing, Inc.

Suppes, T., Kelly, D.I., Perla, J.M. (2005). *Challenges in the management of bipolar depression.* Journal of Clinical Psychiatry, 66 (Supplement 5): 11 – 6.

Swartz, H.A., Frank, E. (2001). *Psychotherapy for bipolar depression: a phase-specific treatment strategy?* Bipolar Disorders, 3 (1): 11 – 22.

Thase, M., Sachs, G. (2000). *Bipolar depression: pharmacotherapy and related therapeutic strategy?* Biological Psychiatry, 48 (6): 558 – 572.

Tondo, L., Ghiani, C., Albert, M. (2001). *Pharmacologic interventions in suicide prevention.* Journal of Clinical Psychiatry, 61 (Supplement 25): 51 – 55.

Tondo, L., Baldessarini, R.J. (2000). *Reduced suicide risk during lithium maintenance treatment.* Journal of Clinical Psychiatry, 61 (supplement 9): 97 – 104.

Trzepacz, P.T., Baker, R.W. (1993). *The Psychiatric Mental Status Examination.* New York: Oxford University Press.

Tulsky, J.A., Fisher, G.S., Rose, M.R., Arnold, R.M. (1998). *Opening the black box: how do physicians communicate about advance directives?* Annual of Internal Medicine, 129 (8): 441 – 449.

United States Department of Health and Human Services (1999). *Mental Health: A Report of the Surgeon General.* Rockville, MD. Retrieved on Jan. 5, 2004 from http://www.surgeongeneral.gov/library/mentalhealth/home.html.

Valente, S.M. (2004). *End-of-life challenges: honoring autonomy.* Cancer Nursing, 27 (4): 314 – 319.

Vieta, E. (2005). *The package of care for patients with bipolar depression.* Journal of Clinical Psychiatry, 66 (Supplement 5): 34 – 39.

Viguera, A.C., Cohen, L.S., Bouffard, S., Whitfield, T.H., Baldessarini, R.J. (2002). *Reproductive decisions by women with bipolar disorder after prepregnancy psychiatric consultation.* American Journal of Psychiatry, 159, 2102 – 2104.

Watson, S., Young, A.H. (2001). *Bipolar disorders: new approaches to therapy.* Expert Opinion Pharmacotherapy, 2 (4): 601 – 612.

Weisman, M.M., Bland, R.C., Canino, G.J., Faravelli, C., Greenwald, S., Hwu, H.G., Joyce, P.R., Karam, E.G., Lee, C.K., Lellouch, J., Lepine, J.P., Newman, S.C., Rubino-Stipec, M., Wells, J.E., Wickramaratne, P.J., Wittchen, H., Yeh, E.K. (1996). *Cross-national epidemiology of major depression and bipolar disorder.* Journal of the American Medical Association (JAMA), 276 (4): 293 – 299.

Woods, S.W. (2000). *The economic burden of bipolar disease.* Journal of Clinical Psychiatry, 61 (Supplement 13): 38 – 41.

Yonkers, K.A., Wisner, K.L., Stowe, Z., Leibenluft, E., Cohen, L., Miller, L., et al. (2004). *Management of bipolar disorder during pregnancy and the postpartum period.* American Journal of Psychiatry, 161 (4): 608 – 620.

Zarestsky, A. (2003). *Targeted psychosocial interventions for bipolar disorder.* Bipolar Disorders, 5 (Supplement 2): 80 – 87.

Zerhouni, E. (2003). *Medicine: the NIH roadmap.* Science, 302, 63 – 72.

CASE EIGHT:
A 57-year-old woman with back pain treated with traditional Chinese medicine

This case study summarizes the care provided by an APN acupuncturist for a woman with back pain.

TRADITIONAL CHINESE MEDICINE PRIMER (TCM)

The concepts and philosophy of TCM may seem peculiar to the outside observer because the terminology and explanations of the theory are not always congruent with those of Western ideology. A brief discussion of the history and philosophy of TCM is included to provide reviewers with a basis for understanding the TCM protocol prescribed for this patient.

Traditional Chinese acupuncture has a history of approximately 3,000 years (Riddle, 1974). It is based upon the concept that health is determined by a balanced flow of qi (also referred to as chi), a vital life energy that runs through energy pathways called "meridians" (Ulett, Han, & Han, 1998). Qi is believed to exist in all living things, thus, the essence of qi can be taken into the body by consuming plant and animal food sources. In addition to qi, blood and fluids are the other major components of TCM (Beijing College of Traditional Chinese Medicine, 1987).

Clinical approach to TCM

In TCM, the cause of illness is determined by the TCM practitioner's assessment of the patient by using the "8 principles of TCM." They are hot/cold, excess/deficiency, interior/ exterior, and yin/yang. The practitioner is looking for imbalances in the patient by applying those principles. In addition, there are three major components which include qi, blood, and fluids. The diagnosis is based on five organ networks: the lungs/colon, spleen/ stomach, heart/small intestine, kidneys/ bladder, and liver/gallbladder. Each network correlates to one of five elements (metal, earth, fire, water, and wood); cycles of development; seasons (fall, late summer, summer, winter, and spring); climates; and personality types. Each organ network is capable of creating TCM pathogenic factors. They are: wind, heat, dampness, phlegm, dryness, and cold. Therefore, when organ networks are in a state of imbalance or when there is an excess or deficiency in qi, blood, or fluids, then symptoms, disease, injury, or stress may ensue. A typical TCM evaluation consists of: the interview, assessment, TCM diagnosis, and treatment plan.

FIRST ENCOUNTER

Chief complaint

57-year-old Caucasian female presents for initial acupuncture treatment. "My family doctor referred me to you because I have back pain. I over-did it with shoveling the snow."

Present illness

The low back pain started approximately two months ago when she was shoveling snow. According to the patient, she "over-did" shoveling her sidewalks and driveway. She initially experienced left

145

leg pain that started from the buttocks and traveled to the back of her left thigh. She felt extreme pain at that time, rated as a 10 from a scale of 1 to 10; 10 being the worst pain. She recalled taking ibuprofen 400 mg every four to six hours for pain management that reduced the pain to approximately 9. She described the pain as sharp and shooting, which was exacerbated by walking and sitting for extended periods of time, and relieved by lying down. She had not experienced any back pain prior to this incident, but reported that she has gained an additional eight pounds since the holidays and felt that the extra weight could be contributing to her discomfort. She did not experience urine retention/incontinence, bowel changes, numbness in the perineal area, or numbness/weakness in extremities.

After two days of over-the-counter ibuprofen therapy, the patient saw her primary care physician (PCP) for an examination. The PCP prescribed Naprosyn 500 mg bid prn for pain management. After one week of Naprosyn, the back pain continued with little relief from the medication, the PCP was contacted, and he added tramadol 50 mg tid for pain relief. The patient could not tolerate tramadol, she felt nauseous and lethargic. She contacted her PCP again and he ordered an MRI and CBC, discontinued tramadol, and added acetaminophen with codeine. The patient did not tolerate the acetaminophen with codeine due to the lethargy it caused and requested an alternative therapy for pain management.

The patient reports a normal MRI and CBC. The PCP referred her to a physiatrist for pain management, who subsequently sent her to physical therapy. After four weeks and eight sessions of physical therapy, the patient did not feel her condition improved. The patient was unhappy that she could not walk or sit for extended periods of time despite two months of various treatments. She contacted her PCP for additional assistance, and the PCP referred her for acupuncture for pain management.

Past history

Childhood illnesses
Chicken pox age 6, measles age 8.

Adult illnesses
Hypertension for 10 years.
Hypercholesterolemia for eight years.
Denies history of diabetes, CAD, cancer, liver disease, or renal disease.

Psychiatric illness
Although she denied a history of depression or suicidal ideation, she is worried that she will not be able to regain her full range of mobility. At present, she feels hopeful about the acupuncture treatments since the treatments did not involve taking medications, potentially limiting her ability to tolerate the treatments.

Accidents and injuries
Denies previous accidents or injuries.

Operations/hospitalizations
Denies.

Current health status

Allergies
No known allergies or reactions to food, drugs, or environment.

Immunizations
Influenza vaccine four months ago.
Hepatitis B, completed the series three years ago.

Screening tests
Eye exam one year ago.
Colonoscopy seven months ago, negative.
Mammogram six months ago, negative.

Environmental hazards/use of safety measures
Employed as an elementary school teacher. Uses an ergonomic chair and wrist rest when using the computer. Always uses a seat belt when in the car. Smoke and carbon monoxide detector in the house and batteries checked every three months.

Diet and exercise
Prior to low back pain, enjoyed gardening in her yard. No regular physical activity.

> Average daily intake:
> Breakfast: coffee with skim milk, Special K cereal — two bowls with skim milk
> Lunch: tuna fish on wheat bread, French fries or chips, and diet soda
> Dinner: baked chicken without skin, salad, and water
> Snacks: two peanut butter cups or one Milky Way bar

Risk factors contributing to weight status include her food selection and choices. She reported that while she knows which foods are healthy and which ones are not, she indulges in many foods that have contributed to her weight gain. When she has "energy lows" in the afternoon, would go to the vending machine for a snack on a daily basis (Monday – Friday). Her favorite snacks and selection are peanut butter cups and Milky Way bars. Both of these snacks contain a significant amount of fat, carbohydrates, and calories. Over the course of the year, this is a significant number of calories that translate to weight gain. She also mentioned that she either has potato chips or French fries along with her meal (meal is generally healthy in terms of fat and calorie intake). Some of her poor food choices are due to her cravings for sweet and salt, but another component to her selection has to do with the constant temptation of fast food on and near the school grounds. (See addendum on food label contents of snacks eaten.)

> *According to Jonas (2004), some of the risk factors that contribute to obesity are:*
> *1. High-calorie overweight: adult onset overeating/under-exercising.*
> *2. Family-induced overweight: commences in childhood through eating/exercise patterns established in the family.*
> *3. Genetically predisposed overweight: a genetic anomaly leads to a metabolic imbalance.*
> *4. Diet-induced low-calorie overweight: the result of the negative impact on resting metabolic rate of the sudden-calorie-restriction "weight-loss" diets that are so popular in this culture.*

Current medications
Lipitor 10 mg daily.

> *Lipitor (atorvastatin calcium) inhibits HMG CoA, the enzyme that catalyzes the first step in the cholesterol synthesis pathway, resulting in a decrease in serum cholesterol, serum LDLs (associated with increased risk of CAD), and increases serum HDLs (associated with decreased risk of CAD); increases hepatic LDL recapture sites, enhances reuptake and catabolism of LDL; lowers triglyceride levels (Lacey, 2004).*

Lisinopril 10 mg daily.

ACE inhibitor prescribed to treat hypertension alone or in conjunction with other anti-hypertensive agents (Lacey, 2004).

Aspirin 81 mg daily.

Aspirin-inhibition of platelet aggregation is attributable to the inhibition of platelet synthesis of thromboxane A2, a potent vasoconstrictor and inducer of platelet aggregation. This effect occurs at low doses and lasts for the life of the platelet (eight days). Higher doses inhibit the synthesis of prostacyclin, a potent vasodilator and inhibitor of platelet aggregation (Lacey, 2004). When used for secondary prevention of CHD, an overview of randomized trials from the Antiplatelet Trialists' Collaboration found that aspirin was beneficial in women. Although not as well-studied for primary prevention as in men, aspirin may provide the same benefit in women with at least one risk factor (Lacey, 2004).

Naprosyn 500 mg prn od-bid for pain.

Naprosyn is a nonsteroidal anti-inflammatory with analgesic and antipyretic properties (Lacey, 2004).

Social/habits
She was born and raised in New York State. She majored in education in college and currently works at a local public elementary school. She has been married for 25 years to her high school sweetheart. They have two daughters, ages 21 and 25. The youngest daughter is an undergraduate student and lives on campus at a Northeastern university. The oldest daughter is attending graduate school in California. She reports being very close to her children. She speaks to them on a weekly basis.

She denies using tobacco or illicit drugs. She reports drinking white or red wine during the holidays and special occasions. She drinks one cup of coffee or tea and one can of diet soda on a daily basis. She usually sleeps five to six hours per night and does not use any sleep aids.

Family history
Mother — 77: Alive and well. History of HTN, hypercholesterolemia.
Father — 82: Alive and well. History of asthma, HTN.
Brother — 50: Alive and well. History of HTN, hypercholesterolemia.
Brother — 54: Alive and well. History of HTN, hypercholesterolemia.

REVIEW OF SYSTEMS

General health
Reports general health as "good." Has gained approximately 40 pounds in the past 20 years with recent gain of eight pounds. Her goal is to lose 20 pounds. Denies fatigue, weakness, fever, chills, or sweats. Her energy level is adequate for work and home responsibilities.

Skin
No changes in skin color. Denies pruritus, rashes, or lesions. No hair loss.

Head
Denies headache or head injury.

Eyes

Has worn contact lenses since the age of 16 and has been wearing reading glasses since the age of 40. Denies double vision, loss of vision, inflammation, or eye pain.

Ears, nose, throat

No history of hearing loss, vertigo, tinnitus, sinus pain, obstruction, or epistaxis. Has had a history of gingivitis, sees dentist one to two times a year. Currently, denies bleeding of the gums. Brushes teeth after each meal, uses a dental rinse nightly, and flosses daily.

Neck

No history of thyroid disease, swollen glands, or limitation of movement.

Breast

Denies breast pain, lumps, or nipple discharge. No history of breast augmentation or reduction. Performs monthly breast self-examination. Last mammogram six months ago, negative.

Respiratory

Denies wheezing and shortness of breath. No history of asthma, lung disease, or pneumonia. PPD negative one year ago.

Cardiac

Denies chest pain, SOB, PND, palpitations. Sleeps with one pillow, nocturia x 1 without peripheral edema. No history of myocardial infarction, angina. Last EKG two years ago — within normal.

Gastrointestinal

Good appetite; no nausea, vomiting, indigestion. Denies food intolerances or allergies. Daily bowel movement, soft, formed, and brown. Denies blood in stool.

Urinary

No history of renal disease, stone, or urinary tract infections. Denies dysuria, frequency, urgency, hesitancy, or straining.

Genitalia

Gravida 2, Para 2. Menarche age 13. Used oral contraceptive for approximately 15 years, stopped 10 years ago. Last menstrual period seven years ago. Last Pap smear two years ago with negative findings. Denies discharge, bleeding, or post-coital pain.

Musculoskeletal

See history of present illness.

Peripheral vascular

Positive for varicose veins in both legs post-initial pregnancy. No history of leg pain or phlebitis prior to current presenting complaint.

Neurologic

Denies history of syncope, seizures, motor or sensory loss.

Hematologic

No history of coagulopathies or anemia.

Endocrine

No history of nervousness, tremors, appetite changes, or unintended weight loss. Denies problems with hot or cold environments.

Psychiatric

See past medical history.

> *TCM interview. The interview is based on the "10 questions," which involves asking and evaluating the patient's sleep, thirst, urinary output, bowel movements, appetite, digestion, energy level, sweating patterns, menses, and emotions. These aspects are evaluated as they relate to the patient's main complaint. In addition, questions on the onset of the condition, treatments used, what makes it (the condition) better or worse are also discussed in the interview (Beijing College of Traditional Chinese Medicine, 1987).*

PHYSICAL EXAM

General survey

Well-dressed Caucasian female who responds appropriately and quickly to all questions.

Height (without shoes) 5' 2"   Weight (undressed) 160 pounds   BMI: 29.3

Blood pressure: 119/78 right arm, sitting, pulse 82
                120/80, right arm, standing, pulse 86

Skin

Warm and dry, no lesions noted.

Head

Hair texture medium. Scalp without lesions.

Eyes, ears, nose

Conjunctiva pink and sclera anicteric. Good acuity to whispered voice. Nares patent bilaterally. Septum midline. No sinus tenderness.

Mouth

Teeth in good repair. Tongue midline. Tonsils without exudate.

Neck

Supple, FROM. Trachea midline. Thyroid nonpalpable.

Lymph nodes

No axillary or epitrochlear or inguinal lymphadenopathy.

Thorax and lungs

Symmetrical expansion. Bilateral breath sounds without adventitious sounds.

Cardiac

S_1, S_2, no murmurs, rubs, gallops.

Abdomen

Nondistended, soft, bowel sounds present. No vascular bruits. No hepatomegaly or splenomegaly. No CVA tenderness.

Genital/rectal

Refused.

Peripheral vascular

Peripheral pulses 2+ equal bilateral. No edema. + superficial varicosities, - Homan's.

Neuro/musculoskeletal

+ tenderness to palpation over lumbar spine L>R. SLR negative. DTRs 2+ throughout, downgoing toes. No diminished ankle jerks. Motor: muscle bulk without atrophy, normal tone. Power 5/5. Sensory: pain and soft touch grossly intact. Position sense intact. Gait: antalgic. Spinal ROM limited related to pain.

TRADITIONAL CHINESE MEDICINE EXAM

TCM tongue assessment
- **Color:** red tip, prickles, slight darkish, blue/purplish (*blood stagnation*)
- **Coat:** thin white coating
- **Shape:** normal
- **Moisture:** moist (*kidney yang deficiency*)
- **Other:** prickles on tip (*prickles usually indicate blood stagnation*), blue/purplish (*stagnation, pain*)

Pulse diagnosis:
Left hand rear position corresponds to *Kidney Yin*
Left hand middle position corresponds to *Liver*
Left hand front position corresponds to *Heart*
Right hand rear position corresponds to *Kidney Yang*
Right hand middle position corresponds to *Spleen*
Right hand front position corresponds to *Lungs*

Left hand:
1st position: wiry
2nd position: wiry
3rd position: weak, deep

Right hand:
1st position: superficial
2nd position: soggy
3rd position: deep

> *The pulse and tongue assessment are cardinal to TCM. The pulse evaluation is comprised of palpating for three separate pulses and three separate levels on each wrist corresponding to the organ networks, based on the pulse location. The pulse indicates the basic condition of the patient according to the eight-principle theory of yin and yang; excess and deficiency; heat and cold; and interior and exterior. The tongue evaluation consists of assessing color, texture, shape, and coating. The tongue has a geographic mapping of the organ system (Kirschbaum, 2000). The assessment also includes an evaluation of the patient's entire demeanor, from the brightness of the eyes to the color of the nail beds. Analysis indicates the involvement of a particular organ(s) as well as the specific substance (qi, blood, fluid) excess or deficiency.*

IMPRESSION

57-year-old overweight female referred by PCP for acupuncture treatment for two-month history of back pain related to snow shoveling. Patient with history of personal and family history of HTN and hypercholesterolemia.

TCM DIFFERENTIAL DIAGNOSIS/ PATTERN DIFFERENTIATION

1. Qi and blood stagnation: Pain along bladder channel, tender to touch, does not respond to changes in the weather, and is much worse after sitting for prolonged periods of time (20 – 30 minutes).

Treatment principle: Move qi and blood, relieve pain, focus on bladder meridian.
Points: LV-3, LI-4, Ah Shi (tender) points along the bladder channel, L-posterior leg: BL-25, BL-26, BL-54, BL-36, BL-37.

2. Kidney deficiency: Weakness in the lumbar area, fatigue symptoms, symptoms aggravated by exertion and alleviated by rest.
Treatment principle: Tonify kidney energy, strengthen kidney.
Points: Ki-3, BL-23, BL-40, BL-59, BL-62, DU-4.

The interview information, pulse, and tongue diagnoses are recorded by the acupuncturist. The TCM diagnosis is established, the treatment method is determined, and the treatment plan follows. Accurate TCM diagnosis based on the assessment of symptoms and differentiation of syndromes will indicate the appropriate point selection and methods to be administered. In Chinese medicine the treatment plan can include acupuncture, herbs, and massage. The plan for this patient has been limited to acupuncture, massage, and dietary counseling (Beijing College of Traditional Chinese Medicine, 1987).

TRADITIONAL CHINESE MEDICINE PERSPECTIVE OF THE PATHOGENESIS OF LOWER BACK PAIN

The pathogenesis of back pain in TCM is explained through pattern differentiation (also called syndrome analysis) and related symptoms. This process is similar to making a differential diagnosis in Western medicine.

The organ systems largely associated with this condition are the kidney and liver (Lyttleton, 2004). Prior to discussing the TCM diagnoses, it is important to have an understanding of TCM organ function as it relates to the low back pain.

In TCM, the lower back is most closely related to the health of the kidney system and is often referred to as the "palace of the kidney." The kidneys have a powerful influence over the tissues of the lower back, therefore if the kidney qi, yin/yang are weak, then the lower back is likely to be affected. Kidney deficiency will give rise to a chronic lower backache or low back pain with soreness and weakness, which is improved by applied pressure (massage) and general rest. Lower back pain is often recurring and is aggravated after exertion, prolonged standing, or sexual activity. The treatment principle is to "tonify kidney (qi, yin, or yang)," thereby strengthening the lower back (Lyttleton, 2004).

The function of the liver (in TCM) is to maintain the free flow of qi and blood in the body. When the liver fails to maintain a free flow of qi, blood, or fluids, there will be symptoms of stagnation, which can result in pain. The pain may have a distending quality that may move from place to place, or may remain in a fixed area and worsen with applied pressure. Lower back pain tends to be aggravated by stress and emotional upset and often radiates from the lower back to the lower abdomen or hypochondriac region. The treatment principle is to "invigorate, move qi and blood," thereby moving the stagnation and relieving pain (Beijing College of Traditional Chinese Medicine, 1987).

Common TCM diagnoses/pattern differentiation for low back pain
- *Liver qi and blood stagnation*
- *Kidney deficiency (qi, yin, yang types)*
- *External invasions (wind, damp, cold)*

TREATMENT PLAN

Encounter 1: Evaluation and treatment.
Focus of encounter: Move qi and blood stagnation, promote relaxation, reduce pain. Tonify and strengthen qi (energy). After needling, moxa and massage to bladder meridian, and provided patient with instructions on how to locate acupressure points (via diagram). In addition, patient was instructed to have her husband massage the bladder meridian every day. Instructed not to massage or put pressure on the spine, only massage lateral to the spine.
Patient teaching: Lifestyle — encouraged adequate rest and massage of specific points.

Encounter 2: Treatment.
Focus of encounter: Continue to move qi and blood (the source of pain), tonify, and reinforce kidney energy. Patient reported that she felt improved. On a 1 – 10 scale she rated her pain to be at 4. She reported that the pain was still present but she could tolerate it now.

Encounter 3: Treatment.
Focus of encounter: Continue to move qi and blood (the source of pain), tonify, and reinforce kidney energy. Patient reported that her pain was improving more, now at 3.

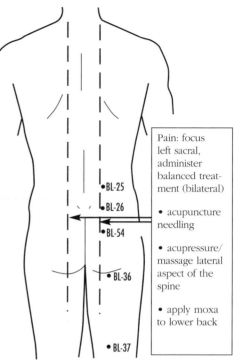

Pain: focus left sacral, administer balanced treatment (bilateral)

- acupuncture needling

- acupressure/massage lateral aspect of the spine

- apply moxa to lower back

Course of acupuncture treatment: The patient started to feel better after the first treatment. She was given instruction on an acupressure massage technique that could be administered by her husband on a nightly basis to maintain pain relief. The massage focused on the lateral aspects of the spine. She experienced sustained pain relief with this technique.

Most Western practitioners are knowledgeable about acupuncture, as acupuncture is a technique where very thin solid needles are inserted in specific locations on the body called acupuncture points. The points correspond to the 14 meridians/channels. According to TCM theory, these points carry qi. The needles are inserted in order to access and stimulate qi. The aim of acupuncture is to restore qi when the body is deficient, reduce when the body has excess, move qi when there is a stagnation, and to redirect qi to ultimately create balance. When qi is stimulated, it also benefits circulation of blood and fluids.

The main needle techniques are reinforcing/tonification and reducing/sedation.

- *Reinforcing/tonification: needle insertion(s) using manual tonification method. The purpose of this technique is to reinforce, strengthen, and move qi and blood.*

- *Reducing: needle insertion(s) using manual reducing, also called sedating or dispersing techniques. The purpose is to eliminate pathogenic factors and to harmonize hyperactive physiological functions (Beijing College of Traditional Chinese Medicine, 1987).*

Although the mechanism of these effects still requires further investigation, many investigators have proposed that needling may exert these effects through the neuroendocrine, immunological, specific channel, or traditional qi systems (Hammerschlag, 1997).

PATIENT EDUCATION

Low back pain management: Continue acupressure massage on a nightly basis for one month and evaluate the need based on symptoms. Apply gentle heat over the area for 10 – 15 minutes. Never sleep with a heating pad. She was also instructed on appropriate body mechanics for lifting, desk work, and sitting. She was instructed to stretch from her desk every 20 minutes to prevent muscle stiffness. She was also instructed to notify me or PCP if she experienced numbness, weakness, or bladder/bowel changes. Weekly acupuncture treatments for at least three sessions.

Cardiovascular risk:
Aspirin: Emphasized the importance of taking her baby aspirin on a daily basis to reduce likelihood of cardiovascular events.
Nutrition: I advised her to consult with PCP about recent cholesterol laboratory results. I discussed the National Cholesterol Education Therapeutic Lifestyle Changes Program. I encouraged her to prepare healthy snacks for work and provided nutritional facts on her current snacks (candy, fries, chips) (NHLBI, 2002). (See sample of nutrition facts on snacks attached.)
Exercise: She was instructed to see her primary care provider prior to initiating exercise.

> *Due to age and cardiovascular risks (weight, HTN, & cholesterol level), a stress test may be appropriate prior to undertaking exercise (Task force, 1997).*

Weight: She was informed that, due to her height and weight, her body mass index is considered overweight — borderline obesity. BMI = 29.3 (www.nhlbisupport.com/bmi/bmicalc.htm)

REFERRALS

1. Follow-up with primary care provider for health-care maintenance and discussion of individualized cardiovascular risk assessment.
2. Follow-up with nutritionist (Henkin, 2000).

FOLLOW-UP

1. Continue back exercises and increase physical activity as tolerated.
2. Continue acupressure massage every night for one month.
3. Resume weekly acupuncture treatments.

CASE SUMMARY

This case study summarizes the care provided by an APN acupuncturist for a 57-year-old female with low back pain induced by strenuous physical activity. Acupuncture, in combination with Western medical diagnostics and therapeutics, can reduce the pain and disability associated with low back pain. The incorporation of Western diagnostics is important to ensure that "red flags" for back pain are not missed. The acupuncture treatment plan utilized for this case study involved weekly acupuncture treatments for three weeks and nightly acupressure massage delivered by the patient's spouse for four weeks. Reduction of back pain was reported by the patient after the first acupuncture treatment, from a pain level of 9 to a pain level of 4 on a scale of 1 to 10. The acupuncture treatments also involved patient education on appropriate body mechanics, exercise, and stretching. The prognosis for this patient to resume her usual daily physical activities are excellent, assuming that she follows proper body mechanics, exercise, and stretching.

ADDENDUM

Current snacks:

Reese's Peanut Butter Cup

Serving Size   1 package (42 g)

Total Calories 230
   Calories from Fat 120

Amount per Serving . . . . . . **%DV***

Total Fat 13 g 20%
   Saturated Fat 4.5 g 23%
   Trans Fat 0 g

Cholesterol less than 5 mg. . 1%

Sodium 130 mg 5%

Total Carbohydrate 23 g . . . 8%
   Dietary Fiber 1 g 4%
   Sugars 20 g

Protein 4 g

</TD
   Vitamin A 0%
   Vitamin C 0%
   Calcium 2%
   Iron 2%

*Percent Daily Values are based on a 2,000 calorie diet.
Your daily values may be higher or lower depending on
your calorie needs:

	Calories:	2,000	2,500
Total Fat	Less than	. . . 65 g	. . . . . 80 g
Sat Fat	Less than	. . . 20 g	. . . . . 25 g
Cholesterol	Less than	. . . 300 mg	. . . 300 mg
Sodium	Less than	. . . 2,400 mg	. . 2,400 mg
Total Carbohydrate		. . . . 300 g	. . . . . 375 g
Dietary Fiber		. . . . 25 g	. . . . . . 30 g

Milky Way bar
Nutrition Facts

Calories	423.00
Protein (g)	4.50
Fat Total (g)	16.10
Carbohydrate (g)	71.70
Fiber — Total (g)	1.70
Sugar — Total (g)	60.66
Calcium (mg)	130.00
Iron (mg)	0.76
Magnesium (mg)	34.00
Phosphorus (mg)	144.00
Potassium (mg)	241.00
Sodium (mg)	240.00
Zinc (mg)	0.71
Copper (mg)	0.15
Manganese (mg)	0.23
Selenium (mg)	5.60
Vitamin C (mg)	1.00
Thiamin (mg)	0.04
Riboflavin (mg)	0.22
Niacin (mg)	0.35
Vitamin B6 (mg)	0.05
Folate — Total (mcg)	6.00
Food — Folate (mcg)	6.00
Folate — DFE (mcg_DEF) . .	6.00
Vitamin B12 (mcg)	0.32
Vitamin A (IU)	64.00
Retinol (mcg)	18.00
Vitamin E (mg)	1.25
Vitamin K (mcg)	3.80
Fat — Saturated (g)	7.79
Fat — Monosaturated (g) . . .	6.02
Fat — Polysaturated (g)	0.60
Cholesterol (mg)	14.00

Potato Chips 1.5 oz
Nutrition Facts

Calories	237.29
Protein (g)	2.51
Fat Total (g)	6.33
Carbohydrate (g)	21.69
Fiber — Total (g)	1.53
Sugar — Total (g)	2.13
Calcium (mg)	10.21
Iron (mg)	0.64
Magnesium (mg)	24.66
Phosphorus (mg)	66.76
Potassium (mg)	428.65
Sodium (mg)	278.96
Zinc (mg)	0.25
Copper (mg)	0.07
Manganese (mg)	0.15
Selenium (mg)	3.44
Vitamin C (mg)	3.49
Thiamin (mg)	0.09
Riboflavin (mg)	0.05
Niacin (mg)	1.34
Vitamin B6 (mg)	0.06
Folate — Total (mcg)	2.98
Food — Folate (mcg)	2.98
Folate — DFE (mcg_DEF)	2.98
Vitamin B12 (mcg)	0.00
Vitamin A (IU)	0.00
Retinol (mcg)	0.00
Vitamin E (mg)	0.93
Vitamin K (mcg)	3.06
Fat — Saturated (g)	4.02
Fat — Monosaturated (g)	3.09
Fat — Polysaturated (g)	8.50
Cholesterol (mg)	0.00

McDonald's French Fries
Medium size

Nutrition Facts

Calories	411.54
Protein (g)	4.45
Fat Total (g)	21.97
Carbohydrate (g)	48.86
Fiber — Total (g)	4.33
Sugar — Total (g)	—
Calcium (mg)	19.38
Iron (mg)	1.00
Magnesium (mg)	42.18
Phosphorus (mg)	151.62
Potassium (mg)	687.42
Sodium (mg)	194.94
Zinc (mg)	0.63
Copper (mg)	0.16
Manganese (mg)	0.25
Selenium (mg)	0.46
Vitamin C (mg)	2.39
Thiamin (mg)	0.20
Riboflavin (mg)	0.12
Niacin (mg)	3.04
Vitamin B6 (mg)	0.65
Folate — Total (mcg)	9.12
Food — Folate (mcg)	9.12
Folate — DFE (mcg_DEF)	—
Vitamin B12 (mcg)	—
Vitamin A (IU)	0.00
Retinol (mcg)	—
Vitamin E (mg)	0.89
Vitamin K (mcg)	18.24
Fat — Saturated (g)	4.93
Fat — Monosaturated (g)	11.56
Fat — Polysaturated (g)	4.43
Cholesterol (mg)	0.00

Healthy alternatives: snacks

Almonds (15)

Nutrition Facts

Calories	81.93
Protein (g)	3.01
Fat Total (g)	7.18
Carbohydrate (g)	2.80
Fiber — Total (g)	1.67
Sugar — Total (g)	0.68
Calcium (mg)	35.15
Iron (mg)	0.61
Magnesium (mg)	38.98
Phosphorus (mg)	67.19
Potassium (mg)	103.19
Sodium (mg)	0.14
Zinc (mg)	0.48
Copper (mg)	0.16
Manganese (mg)	0.36
Selenium (mg)	0.40
Vitamin C (mg)	0.00
Thiamin (mg)	0.03
Riboflavin (mg)	0.11
Niacin (mg)	0.56
Vitamin B6 (mg)	0.02
Folate — Total (mcg)	4.11
Food — Folate (mcg)	4.11
Folate — DFE (mcg_DEF)	4.11
Vitamin B12 (mcg)	0.00
Vitamin A (IU)	0.71
Retinol (mcg)	0.00
Vitamin E (mg)	3.67
Vitamin K (mcg)	0.00
Fat — Saturated (g)	0.55
Fat — Monosaturated (g)	4.56
Fat — Polysaturated (g)	1.73
Cholesterol (mg)	0.00

Apple (1 medium)

Nutrition Facts

Calories	52.00
Protein (g)	0.26
Fat Total (g)	0.17
Carbohydrate (g)	13.81
Fiber — Total (g)	2.40
Sugar — Total (g)	10.39
Calcium (mg)	6.00
Iron (mg)	0.12
Magnesium (mg)	5.00
Phosphorus (mg)	11.00
Potassium (mg)	107.00
Sodium (mg)	1.00
Zinc (mg)	0.04
Copper (mg)	0.03
Manganese (mg)	0.04
Selenium (mg)	0.00
Vitamin C (mg)	4.60
Thiamin (mg)	0.02
Riboflavin (mg)	0.03
Niacin (mg)	0.09
Vitamin B6 (mg)	0.04
Folate — Total (mcg)	3.00
Food — Folate (mcg)	3.00
Folate — DFE (mcg_DEF)	3.00
Vitamin B12 (mcg)	0.00
Vitamin A (IU)	54.00
Retinol (mcg)	0.00
Vitamin E (mg)	0.18
Vitamin K (mcg)	2.20
Fat — Saturated (g)	0.03
Fat — Monosaturated (g)	0.01
Fat — Polysaturated (g)	0.05
Cholesterol (mg)	0.00

Pretzels (1 oz)

Nutrition Facts

Calories	108.01
Protein (g)	2.58
Fat Total (g)	0.99
Carbohydrate (g)	22.45
Fiber — Total (g)	0.91
Sugar — Total (g)	0.08
Calcium (mg)	10.21
Iron (mg)	1.22
Magnesium (mg)	9.92
Phosphorus (mg)	32.04
Potassium (mg)	41.39
Sodium (mg)	486.20
Zinc (mg)	0.24
Copper (mg)	0.07
Manganese (mg)	0.51
Selenium (mg)	1.64
Vitamin C (mg)	0.00
Thiamin (mg)	0.13
Riboflavin (mg)	0.18
Niacin (mg)	1.49
Vitamin B6 (mg)	0.03
Folate — Total (mcg)	48.48
Food — Folate (mcg)	23.53
Folate — DFE (mcg_DEF)	66.06
Vitamin B12 (mcg)	0.00
Vitamin A (IU)	0.00
Retinol (mcg)	0.00
Vitamin E (mg)	0.10
Vitamin K (mcg)	0.26
Fat — Saturated (g)	0.21
Fat — Monosaturated (g)	0.39
Fat — Polysaturated (g)	0.35
Cholesterol (mg)	0.00

References

Beijing College of Traditional Chinese Medicine, Shanghai College of Traditional Chinese Medicine, Nanjing College of Traditional Chinese Medicine (1987). *Chinese Acupuncture & Moxibustion.* Beijing: Foreign Languages Press.

Hammerschlag, R. (1997). *NIH consensus development conference on acupuncture.* Methodological and Ethical Issues in Acupuncture Research, 45 – 49.

Henkin, Y., Shai I., Zuk, R., et al. (2000). *Dietary treatment of hypercholesterolemia: Do dietitians do it better? A randomized, controlled trial.* American Journal of Medicine, 109, 549.

Jonas, S. (2004). *The "dynamic epidemiology" of obesity: knowledge to help improve our ability to manage the condition.* American Medical Athletics Association Journal, Summer.

Kirschbaum, B. (2000). *Atlas of Chinese Tongue Diagnosis.* Seattle: Eastland Press.

Lacey, C.F., Armstrong, L.L, Goldman, M.P., Lance, L.L. (2004). *Drug Information Handbook,* 11th Edition. Hudson, OH: Lexi-Comp Inc.

Lyttleton, J., Clavey, S. (2004). *Treatment of Infertility With Chinese Medicine.* New York: Churchill Livingstone.

NHLBI (2002). *Detection, evaluation, and treatment of high blood cholesterol in adults* (Adult Treatment Panel III), 2005, from www.nhlib.nih.gov/guidleines/hypertension/jnc7full.pdf.

Riddle, J. (1974). *Report of the New York communication on acupuncture.* American Journal of Chinese Medicine, 2 (3): 289 – 318.

Ulett, G.A., Han, S., Han, J.S. (1998). *Electroacupuncture: mechanisms and clinical application.* Biological Psychiatry, 44 (2): 129 – 138.

CASE NINE:
A 47-year-old woman with diabetes, hypertension, hyperlipidemia, and depression presenting for primary care

This case study summarizes the care provided in a primary care office over a period of three years for a woman with diabetes and hypertension.

FIRST ENCOUNTER

Chief complaint
47-year-old black female presents for initial comprehensive preventive exam. "I've chosen you for my primary care provider, and I have diabetes and hypertension. My last doctor changed my medication one month ago, and I need to check my blood pressure."

Present illnesses
Hypertension diagnosed three years ago. She was treated with a low-sodium diet and weight reduction for three months. When her blood pressure did not improve, treatment with hydrochlorothiazide 12.5 mg qd was initiated. Her blood pressure control remained suboptimal and Norvasc 5 mg was added six months ago. The Norvasc was increased to 10 mg four weeks ago, as her blood pressure was 140/90. She has not had any follow-up since the medication was increased. She takes the medication as prescribed and denies medication side effects. She adds salt at the table and eats foods high in salt. She drinks two cups of coffee per day and one can of caffeinated soda. She has never smoked cigarettes. Her last cholesterol was measured four weeks ago. She has her lab results with her. She denies history of chest pain, palpitations, dyspnea with exertion, orthopnea, paroxysmal nocturnal dyspnea, nocturia, edema, syncope, dizziness, or fatigue. No history of coronary artery disease, MI, elevated lipids.

Type 2 diabetes diagnosed one year ago when an elevated glucose was noted on a routine blood test. She reports that she is doing well with her diabetes because she didn't need insulin. She has not received formal nutrition counseling or any counseling with a diabetes educator. She is unable to describe the impact of diabetes on her general health.

She has been treated with diet and exercise therapy and was advised to lose weight. It has been difficult for her to lose weight because her busy schedule does not give her adequate time for exercise and healthy cooking. She never eats breakfast. Lunch usually consists of a sandwich with chips and a diet soda. Dinner is usually meat with a vegetable and rice, potato, or pasta. She usually snacks late at night on chips, pretzels, and popcorn. She does not perform home glucose monitoring. Denies polydipsia, polyphagia, polyuria, or symptoms of infection. She has never had pain, numbness, tingling, coldness, discoloration, varicose veins in her legs, or skin ulcers.

PAST HISTORY

Childhood illnesses
Chicken pox at age 5.
Denies measles, mumps, croup, pertussis, rheumatic fever, scarlet fever, or polio.

Adult illnesses
Hypertension for three years.
Diabetes for one year.
Obesity since early adulthood.

Psychiatric illnesses
Depression: She describes symptoms of depression since childhood. Her depression worsened after she had multiple procedures for gynecological problems and eventually a hysterectomy. She felt most depressed after her hysterectomy when she realized she could never bear children. At that time, she felt hopelessness and that she would be better off dead. She never attempted suicide or developed a plan. She has isolated herself from friends and family since breaking up with her last boyfriend eight years ago. She has minimal leisure activity except for watching television and reading.

At present, she denies homicidal or suicidal ideation. She sleeps well at night. She has not experienced a change in eating habits. She does not feel hopeless or helpless and is able to concentrate at work. She has never taken medication or received counseling for depression. She states that she is reluctant to see a therapist because African Americans rely on prayer, church, relationships, and family for counseling. She states "crazy people" need professionals. She is afraid that she will be ridiculed, labeled, and further isolated from her present support system if she agrees to treatment and counseling. She would only consider treatment for depression as a last resort.

Accidents and injuries
Denies.

Operations/hospitalizations
Tonsillectomy at age 9.
Myomectomy in her 20s.
Right oophorectomy in her 30s.
Total abdominal hysterectomy with left oophorectomy 17 years ago.

CURRENT HEALTH STATUS

Allergies
No known drug allergies.

Immunizations
Last tetanus shot was about eight years ago.
She never takes the flu vaccine.

Screening test
Last dental exam was one year ago.
Last pelvic exam was 17 years ago.
Last mammogram was two years ago.

Her previous medical provider checked her cholesterol four weeks ago. Other blood tests were performed at that time. She does not recall the results but has copies of her last blood test with her. She has never had any cardiac testing except for an electrocardiogram that was done as part of her presurgical testing for her hysterectomy.

Environmental hazards/use of safety measures
She drives on weekends and always uses seat belts. She has working smoke and carbon monoxide detectors at home.

Diet/exercise
See HPI.

Current medications
Norvasc 10 mg qd.
Hydrochlorothiazide 12.5 mg qd.

> *Norvasc (amlodipine) is a 1,4-dihydropyridine-derivative calcium-channel blocking agent with an intrinsically long duration of action. Amlodipine is used alone or in combination with other classes of antihypertensive agents in the management of hypertension. As monotherapy for the management of hypertension, the usual initial adult dosage of amlodipine is 2.5 – 5 mg once daily (McEvoy, 2005).*

> *Hydrochlorothiazide is a thiazide diuretic and antihypertensive agent. For the management of hypertension, the recommended initial adult hydrochlorothiazide dosage is 12.5 – 25 mg daily (McEvoy, 2005).*

Social/habits
She is employed as a manager at an investment firm for many years. After completing her master's in business administration, she was promoted to vice president at the firm and has maintained a good working relationship with her colleagues. She lives alone and does not have many friends except for one college friend who lives in another state. She lives in a residential neighborhood close to public transportation.

She denies tobacco or illicit drug use. She drinks alcohol socially during holidays and special occasions. She drinks two cups of coffee and one can of caffeinated soda/day. She does not participate in any regular exercise program. She normally sleeps seven to eight hours uninterrupted and does not require any sleep aids.

Family history
Paternal grandfather had colon cancer. Maternal grandmother and aunt both died of breast cancer at an "early age" (around their 50s). Father died at 72 years old from a silent myocardial infarction. He had uncontrolled type 2 diabetes and hypertension for 30 years. He was legally blind from diabetic retinopathy and had a bilateral above-the-knee amputation several years before his death. Mother is 74 years old. She is healthy, without any chronic diseases, and normal weight. Brother age 51 years old has uncontrolled type 2 diabetes, hypertension, obesity, depression, and coronary artery disease. Last year he had emergency coronary artery bypass graft surgery.

REVIEW OF SYSTEMS

General health
Reports usual health as "good." Has gained approximately 20 pounds since her hysterectomy 17 years ago. Denies fatigue, weakness, fever, and sweats.

Skin
No history of skin disease. Denies change in skin color, pigmentation, pruritus, rash, lesions.

Hair
No loss, changes in texture.

Head
Denies headache, head injury, dizziness, syncope, or vertigo.

Eyes
Reading glasses for two years. Last year, her eye exam included retinal and glaucoma screening that was negative. Denies double vision, eye pain, inflammation, and discharge.

Ears, nose, throat
Denies hearing loss, discharge, tinnitus, or vertigo, exposure to environmental noise.

Two to three upper respiratory infections per year usually resolve with fluids, rest, and over-the-counter cold preparations. Avoids preparations with sugar and reads labels for diabetes precautions. Denies nasal discharge, sinus pain, nasal obstruction, or epistaxis. Denies mouth pain, bleeding gums, toothache, sores or lesions in mouth, dysphagia, hoarseness, or sore throat. Brushes teeth twice daily and flosses three times a week.

Neck
Denies pain, limitation of motion, lumps, or swollen glands.

Breast
Denies pain, lump, nipple discharge, rash, swelling, or trauma. No surgery. Does not perform regular breast self-examination. Her last mammogram was two years ago with negative findings.

Respiratory
No history of lung disease, pneumonia, or positive TB testing. Denies wheezing and shortness of breath.

Cardiac
See adult history.

Gastrointestinal
Denies history of ulcers, liver or gallbladder disease, jaundice, appendicitis, or colitis. Appetite good with no recent change. Denies food intolerance, heartburn, indigestion, pain in abdomen, nausea, or vomiting. Bowel movement qd, soft brown, no rectal bleeding, pain, or hemorrhoids.

Urinary
No history of stones or urinary tract infections. Denies dysuria, frequency, urgency, nocturia, hesitancy, or straining.

Genitalia
Gravida 0. Menarche age 12. She was diagnosed in her early 20s with multiple fibroids and had several myomectomy procedures for removal of the fibroids. In her 30s she was diagnosed with a benign ovarian tumor and had a right oophorectomy. She continued to suffer with menorrhagia, was later diagnosed with multiple large fibroids, and had a total abdominal hysterectomy 17 years ago. She denied any history of oral contraceptive use. Not sexually active. Last HIV test was 17 years ago and was negative. Denied history of sexually transmitted infections or any interest in sexual relations since her hysterectomy and subsequent surgical menopause.

Peripheral vascular
See adult history.

Musculoskeletal
Mild aching bilaterally in knees usually after walking or standing for long periods, with some limitation in range of motion. Denies any past trauma, swelling, redness, deformity, stiffness, muscle pain, weakness, or past history of arthritis.

Neurological
Denied history of seizure disorder, stroke, syncope, numbness, tingling, weakness, tremor, and problems with coordination. Reports good memory.

Hematologic
Denies excessive bruising. Denies exposure to toxins and never had a blood transfusion.

Endocrine
She denies any problems with hot or cold environments. She denied any change in skin, appetite, or nervousness.

Psychiatric
See past medical history.

PHYSICAL EXAM

General survey
She was a well-appearing, moderately obese, middle-aged black female who walked and moved easily and responded quickly to questions. She wore no makeup and was neatly dressed.

Height (without shoes) 162.5 cm (5' 4")   Weight (undressed) 92 kg (202 lbs)
BMI: 33

Blood pressure: 146/88 right arm, sitting
140/94 right arm, lying
142/96 left arm, lying (wide cuff)

Heart rate: 76

Respiratory rate: 16, unlabored

Skin
Uniformly brown in color, warm, dry, intact, turgor good. There were no lesions, birthmarks, or edema. Hair, braided at shoulder length with thinning at the top, and normal texture. Nails, without clubbing or discoloration.

Head
Normocephalic, without lesions, lumps, or tenderness. Face, symmetric.

Eyes
Acuity by Snellen chart O.D. 20/20, O.S. 20/20. Visual fields full by confrontation. EOMs intact, without nystagmus. No ptosis, lid lag, or discharge. Corneal light reflex symmetric. Sclera white, without lesions or redness. PERRLA. *Fundi:* discs flat with sharp margins, without arterial narrowing, A-V nicking, or retinal hemorrhage.

Ears
Pinna; without lesions, discharge, or tenderness to palpation. Canals clear. Tympanic membrane pearly gray, landmarks intact, without perforation. Whispered words heard bilaterally. Weber midline without lateralization.

Nose
No deformities or tenderness to palpation. Nares patent. Mucosa pink without lesions. Septum midline, without perforation or sinus tenderness.

Mouth

Mucosa and gingivae pink, without lesions or bleeding. Teeth in good repair. Tongue symmetric, protruded midline, without tremor. Pharynx pink, without exudates. Uvula rises midline on phonation. Tonsils 1+. Gag reflex present.

Neck

Neck supple with full ROM. Symmetric, without masses, tenderness, lymphadenopathy. Trachea midline. Thyroid nonpalpable, nontender. No JVD. Carotid arteries 2+ = bilaterally, without bruits.

Lymph nodes

Negative tonsillar, posterior cervical, and epitrochlear nodes bilaterally. Several small inguinal nodes bilaterally that are soft and nontender.

Thorax and lungs

Nonlabored effort. Chest expansion symmetric. Breath sounds vesicular with no adventitious sounds.

Cardiovascular

S_1, S_2 present, without S_3, S_4, or murmurs. Apical impulse at 5th ICS left MCL, precordium, without abnormal pulsations.

Breasts

Large, pendulous, symmetric; without retraction, dimpling, discharge, or lesions. Without masses, tenderness, axillary, supra, or infraclavicular lymphadenopathy.

Abdomen

Abdomen soft, without masses, tenderness. Bowel sounds present. Liver span 7 cm in right MCL. Abdominal aorta palpable without lateralization, measuring approximately 2 cm. No abdominal bruits. No inguinal lymphadenopathy or CVA tenderness. Healed 7 cm vertical scar from umbilicus to lower abdomen, without keloid.

Genitalia/rectal

Deferred, as per patient request.

Peripheral vascular

Without redness, cyanosis, lesions, edema, varicosities, and calf tenderness. All peripheral pulses present, 2+ = bilaterally. Feet are symmetrically warm with normal pigmentation and hair distribution. Lower extremities and feet without stasis, rubor, ulcer, or thickened and ridged nails.

Musculoskeletal

Temporomandibular joint without slipping or crepitation. Spine without tenderness, full ROM, without kyphosis, lordosis, or scoliosis. Extremities symmetric with full ROM, without pain or crepitation.

Neurologic

Alert and cooperative, thought coherent, oriented x 3.
CN II-XII intact.
Sensory: Pinprick, light touch, vibration, intact. Foot exam with monofilament without decreased sensation. *Motor:* Normal strength, bulk, and tone. *Cerebellar:* Finger-to-nose intact. Romberg negative without pronator drift. *Gait:* Normal stance and cadence. DTRs 2+ all extremities, toes downgoing.

Mental status

Appearance, behavior, and speech appropriate. Remote and recent memories intact. Affect appropriate without evidence of hallucinations, delusions, without suicidal or homicidal ideation.

LABORATORY

For diabetic patients with hypertension, the initial laboratory examination should include serum creatinine, electrolytes, A1C test, fasting lipid profile, and urinary albumin excretion (this can be measured by semiquantitative methods as screening tests, by quantitative methods in timed urine samples, or as albumin-to-creatinine ratio in spot sample) (Arauz-Pacheco, Parrot, & Paskin, 2002).

Laboratory tests reviewed: Four weeks ago, the previous provider ordered laboratory tests, which included EKG, basic metabolic panel, chemistry panel, complete blood count with differential, urinalysis with microalbumin, and thyroid panel. I reviewed the results, which were within normal limits except for the glycosylated hemoglobin and lipid panel.

Glycosylated HGB 7.2%   Normal 4.5 – 5.7%

The HbA1c value reflects the average blood glucose concentration during the previous 10 to 12 weeks; a significant and sustained alteration in blood glucose concentrations can alter the HbA1c value in as little as three to four weeks (McCulloch, August 18, 2004).

Measurement of hemoglobin A1c (HbA1c) provides a better estimate of chronic glycemic control than measurements of fasting blood glucose (McCulloch, September 14, 2004).

Lipid Panel

Total Cholesterol	181	Normal 100 – 199 mg/dL
Triglycerides	78	Normal 0 – 199 mg/dL
HDL Cholesterol	53	Normal 35 – 150 mg/dL
LDL Cholesterol	112	Normal 0 – 129 mg/dL

The American Diabetes Association (ADA) recommends a target goal for serum LDL cholesterol of <100 mg/dL (2.6 mmol/L). Behavioral interventions should be initiated for serum LDL 100 mg/dL (2.6 mmol/L). Drug therapy should be started in patients who do not achieve this goal with lifestyle modifications (McCulloch & Rosenson, 2004).

IMPRESSION

47-year-old black woman with hypertension, type 2 diabetes, depression, surgical menopause, obesity, and family history of premature CAD presents for initial comprehensive examination.

Her hypertension, hyperlipidemia, and type 2 diabetes are not optimally controlled with diet and her present oral medications. She does not demonstrate adequate knowledge and actions of self-care management with regard to nutrition and exercise. She also demonstrates a knowledge deficit with regard to diabetes disease process, and short- and long-term complications of hyperglycemia. She is considered "Coronary Risk Equivalent" with >20% 10-year risk for a cardiac event, thus her diabetes, dyslipidemia, and hypertension necessitates aggressive management and setting her blood pressure below 120/80, LDL cholesterol below 100 mg/dL, and glycosylated hemoglobin below 6%.

Depression: For many years, she has exhibited evidence of clinical depression and has never received counseling or taken medications. She has been reluctant to initiate pharmacotherapy and psychotherapy because it is not consistent with her cultural values. During times of illness, she had been socialized to accept comfort, nurturing, and counseling from family and church elders. Consequently, she doesn't view her depression as a critical problem that requires professional intervention. Given her family history of poor health outcomes, an aggressive approach to her managing her depression is indicated. It is possible that her depression is impacting her ability to properly manage her hypertension and diabetes. Psychiatric care is indicated to prevent the morbidity and mortality associated with diabetes, hypertension, dyslipidemia, obesity, and depression.

> *African-American women utilized religion and spirituality most often for serious conditions such as cancer, heart disease, and depression. Furthermore, religion and spirituality are associated with health-seeking behaviors of African-American women (Dessio et al., 2004).*

> *Patients with type 2 diabetes often experience significant stress related to the many self-care responsibilities to optimize glycemic control (lifestyle modifications, medication, and self-monitoring of blood glucose). Concurrent depression may also interfere with self-care (McCulloch, November 29, 2004).*

PLAN

Medications

- Continue Norvasc 10 mg daily.
- Continue hydrochlorothiazide 12.5 mg daily.
- Add Vasotec 2.5 mg daily since potassium and creatinine are within normal limits. Will titrate to achieve goal blood pressure less than 130/80. Will monitor for side effects of cough and renal insufficiency by checking chemistry panel/comprehensive metabolic in two weeks.

> *Vasotec, enalaprilat and enalapril are angiotensin-converting enzyme (ACE) inhibitors. Enalapril is used alone or in combination with other classes of antihypertensive agents in the management of hypertension. Most experts recommend ACE inhibitors, angiotensin II receptor antagonists, beta-blockers, thiazide diuretics, or calcium-channel blockers as initial therapy in diabetic patients with hypertension (McEvoy, 2005). ACE inhibitors protect against the development of progressive nephropathy due to type 1 and 2 diabetes (Kaplan, Rose, & Bakris, 2005).*

- Add Lipitor 10 mg daily with dinner two weeks after starting Vasotec if patient tolerates Vasotec and ALT/AST are normal.

> *Diabetes mellitus is considered a CHD equivalent and, as mentioned above, both the CARE trial and the Heart Protection Study found significant improvement in outcomes with statin therapy even at LDL-cholesterol (LDL-C) values below 116 mg/dL (3.0 mmol/L). The statins are the only class of drugs to demonstrate clear improvements in overall mortality in primary and secondary prevention (Rosenson, 2004).*

> *Lipitor, atorvastatin calcium, a hydroxymethylglutaryl-CoA (HMG-CoA) reductase inhibitor (i.e., statin), is an antilipemic agent. Atorvastatin is used as an adjunct to dietary therapy to decrease elevated serum total and low-density lipoprotein (LDL) cholesterol, apolipoprotein B (apo B), and triglyceride concentrations, and to increase high-density lipoprotein (HDL) cholesterol concentrations in the treatment of primary hypercholesterolemia and mixed dyslipidemia, homozygous familial hypercholesterolemia, primary dysbetalipoproteinemia, and/or hypertriglyceridemia. The usual initial oral dosage of atorvastatin in adults for the management of primary hypercholesterolemia (heterozygous familial or nonfamilial) and mixed dyslipidemia is 10 or 20 mg once daily (McEvoy, 2005).*

- Initiate 81 mg aspirin daily.

> *Aspirin (75 to 162 mg/day) is recommended for primary prevention in any diabetic patient with an additional cardiovascular risk factor (e.g., age >40 years, cigarette*

smoking, hypertension, obesity, albuminuria, hyperlipidemia, or a family history of coronary heart disease) (McCulloch, November 29, 2004). Surgical menopause is also a risk factor.

Counseling

- Disease process and prognosis.
- Complications related to suboptimal diabetes control.
- Signs and symptoms of hyperglycemia and hypoglycemia.
- Medication instructions and adverse effects.
- Foot care.
- Weight reduction program: Nutrition — low fat, 4 gm sodium, high fiber, and 1800 diabetic diet for weight reduction and diabetic management.

    Dietary modification can improve many aspects of type 2 diabetes, including obesity, hypertension, and insulin release and responsiveness. The improvement in glycemic control is related both to the degree of caloric restriction and weight reduction (McCulloch, November 29, 2004).

- She can initiate nonaerobic exercise now, but moderate physical activity and aerobic exercise to be initiated after exercise stress test.

    Regular exercise is also beneficial in type 2 diabetes, independent of weight loss. It leads to improved glycemic control due to increased responsiveness to insulin; it can also delay the progression of impaired glucose tolerance to overt diabetes (McCulloch, November 29, 2004).

Screening tests

- Mammogram

    She has an intermediate family history risk of breast cancer, and her last mammogram was two years prior. She may also be at an increased risk for breast cancer because of both breast and colon cancer in her family and null parity. The third United States Preventive Services Task Force and the 2002 statement by the American Academy of Family Physicians recommend screening mammography every one to two years for women ages 40 and older (Fletcher, 2004).

Referrals

- Cardiologist — She has an increased risk of coronary artery disease because of her hypertension, diabetes, dyslipidemia, obesity, and family history. Her father died of a silent MI and her brother had a CABG at age 51, both related to suboptimal management of their hypertension and diabetes. Furthermore, her cardiac function needed to be evaluated before beginning an exercise program.
- Ophthalmologist — Retinal exam to screen for retinopathy.

    One of the main motivations for screening for diabetic retinopathy is the efficacy of laser photocoagulation surgery in preventing visual loss. Patients with type 2 diabetes should have an initial dilated and comprehensive eye examination by an ophthalmologist or optometrist shortly after the diagnosis of diabetes. An ophthalmologist or optometrist for type 1 and type 2 diabetics should repeat subsequent examinations annually (McCulloch, November 29, 2004).

- Podiatrist — Foot exam to screen for initial evaluation of neuropathic or vascular problems.

  Foot problems due to vascular and neurologic disease are a common and important source of morbidity in diabetic patients. Systematic screening examinations for neuropathic and vascular involvement of the lower extremities and careful inspection of feet may substantially reduce morbidity from foot problems (McCulloch, November 29, 2004).

- Psychiatrist — Preferably an African-American to help bridge the cultural barriers to treatment and the traditional cultural values.

  African-American patients reported higher levels of satisfaction with care from African-American health-care providers compared to those who received care from other health-care providers that were not race concordant (La Veist, Caroll, 2002).

- Nutritionist — To review the elements of an 1800 diabetic diet that is low fat, 4 gm sodium, and high fiber.

SUMMARY OF CARE THROUGH THE END OF YEAR TWO

During the following two years the patient continued care in my office. She lost 40 pounds. She followed a nutritious diet and maintained regular physical activity. Her blood pressure medications were titrated, blood pressure control was achieved with Vasoretic 10/12.5 mg qd, and the Norvasc was discontinued. Her blood pressure at the last appointment in year two was 114/72 and pulse 77. She denied any adverse effects from Vasoretic or any other symptoms. Her glycosylated hemoglobin at the end of the second year was 5.5%. She did not demonstrate any clinical evidence of diabetic retinopathy, neuropathy, nephropathy, or autonomic dysfunction. The patient did not experience adverse effects from Lipitor 10 mg qd. Her lipid profile after treatment with diet, exercise, and Lipitor was total cholesterol 165, HDL cholesterol 64, LDL cholesterol 76, and triglycerides 55.

  Vasoretic is an oral preparation that combines enalapril maleate with hydrochlorothiazide (McEvoy, 2005).

  Although ACE inhibitors are relatively ineffective as monotherapy in blacks, the addition of even a low dose of a thiazide diuretic to an ACE inhibitor leads to a fall in BP that is comparable to that seen in white patients (Kaplan & Rose, 2004).

She began and continued treatment with an African-American psychiatrist and a Psychiatric Nurse Practitioner. She became more social and emotionally healthy.

The psychiatrist began treatment with Zoloft 50 mg qd that was titrated to 150 mg over two months. The patient showed minimal improvement and Wellbutrin was added and titrated to 300 mg. Her depressive symptoms improved on this regimen. She increased socializing, and adhered to her diabetes self-care management program. Although she initially gained weight with the Zoloft and Wellbutrin, she was motivated to join a health club and began a regular exercise program.

  Zoloft (sertraline), a selective serotonin-reuptake inhibitor, is an antidepressant agent. Sertraline is used in the treatment of major depressive disorder. A major depressive episode implies a prominent and relatively persistent depressed or dysphoric mood that usually interferes with daily functioning (nearly every day for at least two weeks) (McEvoy, 2005).

  Wellbutrin (bupropion hydrochloride) is an aminoketone-derivative antidepressant agent that is chemically unrelated to tricyclic, tetracyclic, or other currently available antidepressants (e.g., selective serotonin-reuptake inhibitors), and also is chemically unrelated to nicotine or other agents currently used in the treatment of nicotine dependence. Bupropion hydrochloride is used in the treatment of major depressive disorder (McEvoy, 2005).

Summary of Care Provided
During Year Three Through Year Four

The patient canceled two appointments during a six-month period. I contacted the patient, who reported that she would not be able to continue her regular care because she had been laid-off from work, unable to find employment, and was unable to maintain her health insurance on COBRA. She reported that her medications were very costly and she was using her savings to pay for the medications. I agreed to continue to refill her medications until she found a new health-care provider. She reported that she had recently applied for Medicaid and planned to continue her medical care with a clinic that accepted Medicaid.

The patient obtained Medicaid and began receiving treatment in a clinic. She contacted me nine months later. She stated that she was more depressed than when we initially met. She had been unable to exercise and maintain her well-balanced diet. She has regained most of her weight, her blood pressure has been consistently over 140/90, and she had symptoms of hyperglycemia.

After obtaining consent from the patient and satisfying all the HIPPA requirements, I contacted an endocrinologist from my previous employment, who accepted her insurance, and presented her case. The endocrinologist agreed to see the patient with the diabetes management team. I helped the patient schedule an initial consultation within one week. I assured the patient that the team, which included a psychiatrist, would approach her care in a comprehensive manner.

One month later, I contacted the patient. She reported that her initial visit with the endocrinologist and a psychiatrist was positive. She reported feeling better and was back on course with her therapy and treatments. She was scheduled to start group therapy in one week and was looking forward to meeting other black women with similar issues.

References

Dessio, W., Wade, C., Chao, M., Kronenberg, F., Cushman, L.E., Kalmuss, D. (2004). *Religion, spirituality, and health-care choices of African-American women: results of a national survey.* Ethnicity and Diseases, Spring: 14 (2): 189 – 97.

Fletcher, S.W. (Dec. 29, 2004). *Screening for Breast Cancer.* Retrieved on Apr. 25, 2005. http://www.utdol.com/application/topic.asp?file=screenpm/3044&type=A&selectedTitle=1~1.

Kaplan, N.M., Rose, B.D. (Nov. 30, 2004). *ACE Inhibitors in the Treatment of Hypertension.* Retrieved on May 23, 2005. http://www.utdol.com/application/topic.asp? file=hyperten/10107&type=A&selectedTitle=2~211.

Kaplan, N.M., Rose, B.D., Bakris, G.L. (Jan. 20, 2005). *Treatment of Hypertension in Diabetes Mellitus.* Retrieved on Apr. 25, 2005. http://www.utdol.com/application/topic.asp?file=hyperten/14262&type=A&selectedTitle=33~115.

La Veist, T.A., Caroll, T., (2002). *Race of physician and satisfaction with care among African-American patients.* Journal of National Medical Association, Nov. 94 (11): 937 – 43.

McCulloch, D.K. (Sept. 14, 2004). *Treatment of Blood Glucose in Type 2 Diabetes Mellitus.* Retrieved on Feb. 21, 2005. http://www.utdol.com/application/topic.asp?file=diabetes/19865.

McCulloch, D.K. (Nov. 29, 2004). *Overview of Medical Care in Diabetes Mellitus.* Retrieved on Feb. 21, 2005. http://www.utdol.com/application/topic.asp?file=diabetes/10339&type=A&selectedTitle=10~112.

McCulloch, D.K., Rosenson, R.S. (Sept. 17, 2004). *Treatment of Dyslipidemia in Diabetes Mellitus.* Retrieved on May 10, 2005. http://www.utdol.com/application/topic.asp?file=diabetes/13693&type=A&selectedTitle=32~115.

McEvoy, G.K. (2005). *AHFS Drug Information Book 2004.* Bethesda, MD: American Society of Health Systems Pharmacist Inc.

Rosenson, R.S. (Sept. 17, 2004). *Overview of Treatment of Hypercholesterolemia.* Retrieved on Feb. 21, 2005. http://www.utdol.com/application/topic.asp?file=lipiddis/5110.

A 10-year-old with ADHD, inattentive type and congenital bicuspid aortic valve requiring social services/special education in the public school system

This case was selected because it presents the complexity of diagnosing and treating a child with common chronic conditions and comorbidity. In addition, as frequently encountered with children with Attention Deficit Hyperactivity Disorder and speech problems, the public school system does not provide the services that the student is entitled to by law. All too often, without a strong advocate, many children in special education do not access the entitled full range of services so that all eligible school-aged children and youth with disabilities receive a free appropriate public education.

REASON FOR ENCOUNTERS

10-year-old male who is easily distracted and not doing well in school and who has frequent headaches.

PAST MEDICAL HISTORY

Birth history: Born via NSVD at 26 weeks, 1 lb ½ oz. Remained in the hospital for four months. Discharged with referral to Early Intervention for high-risk developmental delay secondary to prematurity.

Past health problems/review of systems:
Cardiac: There is a history of bicuspid aortic valve without aortic stenosis. A click without a murmur was noted on routine physical at three years of age, and a referral to cardiology was made. Since that time, the child has seen the cardiologist every two years for echocardiograms, which have shown no change. There is no family history of bicuspid aortic valve. The child uses amoxicillin 50 mg/kg one hour prior to dental work. There is no history of asthma, seizures, or any GI conditions.

Congenital bicuspid aortic valve (BAV) is the most common congenital cardiac anomaly with an occurrence rate of 1% – 2% of the total population (Fedak et al., 2002), and is the most common cause of aortic stenosis in adults (Roberts & Ko, 2005). BAV is associated with other congenital anomalies, including coarctation of the aorta and patent ductus arteriosis. The important and potential clinical outcomes of BAV are valvular stenosis, regurgitation, infective endocarditis and aortic dilation, aneurysms, and dissections (Fedak et al., 2002).

The bicuspid valve may be functionally normal, however after the age of 10, calcification and thickening of the bicuspid valve can be detected on echocardiogram (Beppu et al., 1993). Progressive stenosis that requires surgery occurs in about 75 percent of patients, and the remainder of congenital BAV do not become functionally malformed (Lewin & Otto, 2005).

The peak incidence of symptoms is between the ages of 40 and 60 (Fenoglio et al., 1997). Once symptoms of angina, syncope, or heart failure develop, survival is less than five years if the valve is not replaced. Frequency of surgery for congenital BAV-caused aortic stenosis varies inversely with age (Roberts & Ko, 2005).

Most sudden deaths in adults are associated with a history of syncope; in comparison, the majority of children are asymptomatic (Lambert et al., 1974).

Because of these serious and life-threatening vascular sequela, patients with BAV require close cardiac monitoring. Serial assessment of the aortic valve using echocardiography is used to evaluate the functional status of the valve and the ventricles as well as anatomic measures of the aortic diameter and chamber dimensions.

Carlos was referred to the pediatric cardiologist when the click was first heard for continual monitoring of valvular and vascular status. In addition, with the risk for bacterial endocarditis, antibiotic prophylaxis is recommended to prevent this serious complication. According to the American Heart Association (AHA) (Dajani et al., 1997), BAV is considered a moderate risk for severe endocarditis. In addition, there is some evidence to support that an audible click (even without a murmur) can be indicative of a potential for an intermittent regurgitation. This adds to the risk profile for children with BAV and the need for antibiotic prophylaxis. The AHA-recommended standard prophylactic regimen is a single dose of oral amoxicillin one hour prior to the procedure. The pediatric dose is 50 mg/kg, not to exceed 2 grams.

Development: Early Intervention was initiated in the newborn nursery. Carlos had occupational and speech therapy from 0 to 3 years old, and transitioned to preschool special education for continued occupational and speech therapy.

Three-year history of headaches, no specialist consultation, mother gives acetaminophen 160 mg with poor effectiveness.

Immunizations: Up to date, including Hep A.

Allergies: None to food, none to medications.

FAMILY SOCIAL AND ENVIRONMENTAL HISTORY

Mother is 43 years old and bilingual (English and Spanish), father is 46 and speaks only Spanish. Parents are from Honduras, all three children were born in U.S., and brothers are 18 and 20. Carlos lives with mother, father, and two brothers in three-bedroom apartment in an upper Manhattan low-income project. Father did not continue past sixth grade, history of reading problems. Father has limited reading literacy (in Spanish); he can read instructions, signs, forms, but he does not read for pleasure. Apartment facilities are in working order including heat, hot water. Family receives AFDC (public assistance). Father does "odd jobs" and carpentry work. Mother does not work outside the home. Carlos spends summers in Honduras with his maternal grandparents. Child is insured with Community Premier Plus, a Medicaid-managed care plan.

FAMILY PAST MEDICAL HISTORY

- Mother has history of migraine headaches since her first pregnancy, controlled with medication.
- 18-year-old brother has seizure disorder (on Depakote with good control).
- Father has history of academic problems.
    LDs are more common in children with a family history of LDs.

- No significant family history of diabetes, hypertension, cancer, sudden unexplained death, cardiac disease including long QT syndrome or aortic valve disease, infective endocarditis, or respiratory illness.

HISTORY OF PRESENT ILLNESS

School failure and "spacing out" episodes: Mother and child come to see me because Carlos is doing very poorly in school (grade 5). Since third grade, Carlos has had difficulty with reading, increasingly falling behind his classmates.

> *Often, the first presenting complaint in the diagnostic process for LD is school failure (McInerny, 1995).*

Until recently, he was able to make progress in school, although he always had a problem with focus. Frequent periods in which he "daydreams" and stares blankly, usually during lessons in school and during homework. These periods last several minutes, during which time Carlos is not responsive. Questionable if Carlos is aware of these episodes.

> *It is important to distinguish between a seizure disorder and attention problems, in particular with a child who displays symptoms of both ADHD and staring spells.*

No repeated grades, but mother has been notified that promotion to sixth grade is in doubt. Teacher requested that child get an evaluation for ADHD.

He is in special "inclusion," and according to his IEP is supposed to get speech therapy during school hours. Mother reports that he does not.

> *Developmental language disorder is the most common developmental disability of childhood, occurring in 5 – 10% of children. Children who have an identified speech or language disability are placed in regular classrooms.*

> *The practice of "inclusion" has increased in public schools. Rather than removing the child for speech therapy, it is delivered in the classroom.*

He does not have many friends, but does identify one classmate as his best friend. According to mother, he has very little interaction with his classmates during the school day and no contact with classmates after class.

> *Children who have LDs have difficulty in social situations, have few or no friends, and are often unable to maintain friendships (Silver, 1989).*

Mother describes Carlos as shy and easy to parent, though he worries a lot. For example, he refuses to sleep over at his cousins' house.

Headaches: Three-year history of headaches, three times/week, nonprogressive, diffuse in nature, nonthrobbing, no nocturnal arousal, no change in personality, (+) emesis during the headache episode, denies aura, precipitated by hunger, occur at any time of the day, uses acetaminophen (160 mg/dose) with irregular effectiveness. Denies any symptoms associated with space-occupying brain lesions, (-) nocturnal awakening headache, (-) persistent vomiting, nonprogressive, (-) personality change, (-) recent abrupt onset, (-) confusion.

INTERVAL HISTORY

Elimination: Daily BM, (-) enuresis, (-) dysuria or urgency.

Sleep: Sleeps through the night, headaches do not awaken him, sleeps alone in own bed, goes to sleep at 9 p.m. and awakens easily for school at 7 a.m.

Nutrition: Good appetite, eats all four food groups, refuses to eat school lunch.

Development: Premature at 26 weeks, gross motor skills achieved within normal range but at the later limits, speech and occupational therapy in Early Intervention Program. Mother is not sure when the therapy stopped, but he has not had speech therapy for several years, although he was not discharged from special education services. He sat at 7 months, walked at 15 months, spoke words at 13 months and short phrases at about 30 months.

PHYSICAL EXAM

Shy, thin, soft-spoken, cooperative male. His vocabulary is normal, but with poorly articulated speech. He was not excessively active during the visit, but had limited attention to PNP directions. He transitions well between aspects of the PE and seems to like the constantly changing activities during the exam.

HR 93   RR 24   Temp 98.8   Weight 65 lbs. (25%)   Height 57" (75%)

General appearance: Alert, healthy looking, no distress.

Skin: Warm and dry to touch, good turgor, intact, no lesions.

Eyes: PERRL, (-) cover/uncover, conjunctiva clear, sclera white, discs normal, EOMs intact.

Ears: Large pinnas bilaterally, TMs bilaterally gray, (+) light reflex, (+) mobility, bony landmarks visualized.

Nose: Bilaterally patent, (-) discharge.

Throat: Tonsils +1, (-) erythema, (-) exudate, uvula midline, teeth without obvious caries.

Head: Normocephalic, hair evenly distributed.

Neck: Supple, FROM.

Nodes: (-) adenopathy.

Chest: Clear anterior and posterior, good aeration to bases, (-) wheeze.

Cardiovascular: S_1 and S_2 normally split, regular rhythm, with a click in the right second intercostal space without any cardiac murmur along the precordium or in the back. (+) and (=) femoral pulses.

Abdomen: Soft, nontender, (+) bowel sounds (not hyperactive), (-) masses, (-) HSM.

GU: Normal male external genitalia, testes bilaterally in scrotum, Tanner I.

Extremities: FROM for all extremities, normal gait, normal heel and toe walking, tandem walking.

Back: Spine without deformities.

Neurologic: CN II to XII intact, DTR upper and lower extremities +1, muscle strength equal right and left, finger-to-nose coordination WNL.

Speech: Language skills appear to WNL, very poor articulation.

Parent/child interaction: Comfortable mother/child interaction noted during the visit.

DIFFERENTIAL DIAGNOSIS FOR HEADACHE

Symptom	Migraine	Tension	Cluster
Location	Mostly unilateral	Bilateral	Always unilateral, usually begins around the eye
Characteristics	Gradual onset, moderate to severe	Pressure or tightness that waxes and wanes	Pain is abrupt, deep, continuous, excruciating
Patient appearance	Patient prefers a quiet, dark room	Patient may remain active	Patient remains active
Duration	4 – 72 hours	Variable	30 minutes
Associated symptoms	Nausea, vomiting, photophobia, may have aura	None	Lacrimation and red eye, stuffy nose

(adapted from Up to Date, 2005)

Headaches are more common in children who have a family history of headaches in parents and siblings, with an onset at early school age. Children who have headaches are more likely to have multiple physical symptoms, psychiatric symptoms, and headache in adulthood (Fearon & Hotopf, 2001).

Neuroimaging is not indicated for patients with migraine headache and a normal neurologic examination (Silberstein et al., 2000).

DIFFERENTIAL DIAGNOSIS FOR SCHOOL PROBLEMS AND "SPACING OUT"

Attention Deficit Hyperactivity (ADHD)	This diagnosis is based on a full ADHD evaluation

ADHD is among the most prevalent chronic health conditions affecting school-aged children. Prevalence rates between 5.5% to 12.7% (AAP, 2000).

In the Clinical Practice Guidelines (AAP, 2000), the recommendations for the evaluation of ADHD are as follows:

• In a child six to 12 years old who presents with inattention, hyperactivity, impulsivity, academic underachievement, or behavior problems, primary care clinicians should initiate an evaluation for ADHD (strength of evidence: good; strength of recommendation: strong).

• The diagnosis of ADHD requires that a child meet DSM-IV criteria (strength of evidence: good; strength of recommendation: strong).

• The assessment of ADHD requires evidence directly obtained from parents or caregivers regarding the core symptoms of ADHD in various settings, the age of onset, duration of symptoms, and degree of functional impairment (strength of evidence: good; strength of recommendation: strong).

- *The assessment of ADHD requires evidence directly obtained from the classroom teacher (or other school professional) regarding the core symptoms of ADHD, the duration of symptoms, the degree of functional impairment, and coexisting conditions. A physician should review any reports from a school-based multidisciplinary evaluation where they exist, which will include assessments from the teacher or other school-based professional (strength of evidence: good; strength of recommendation: strong).*

- *Evaluation of the child with ADHD should include assessment for coexisting conditions (strength of evidence: strong; strength of recommendation: strong).*

- *The diagnosis usually requires several visits (two to four) to make the full evaluation (AAP, 2000).*

Learning disability or slow learner	This condition is based on a psychoeducational evaluation, including academic achievement test and a reliable measure of intelligence

Learning disabilities (LDs) are a heterogeneous group of disorders associated with failure of the child to acquire, retrieve, and use information competently.

The primary deficit for children with LDs is difficulty with basic reading skills (i.e., dyslexia).

LDs are more common in children with a family history of LDs.

Often, the first presenting complaint in the diagnostic process for LD is school failure or complaint (McInerny, 1995).

In order to identify the cognitive deficits and abilities of the child, a psychoeducational and neuropsychological evaluation are indicated. This information is used to develop an individualized education program (IEP) for the child.

Comprehensive testing of the skills and abilities needed to learn include:

- *Reliable, stable, and valid measure of intellectual ability (IQ)*

- *Measures of aural, motor, and visual processing*

- *Measures of vocabulary and language development*

- *Measures of academic achievement*

- *Measures of attention regulation*

- *Assessment of social skills and emotional stability*

Language impairment	This diagnosis is based on a full battery of speech and language screening and diagnostic tests (part of the psychoeducational evaluation)

Developmental language disorder is the most common developmental disability of childhood, occurring in 5– 10% of children. It is recommended that children be evaluated in their dominant language and receive speech therapy in that language as well.

There is a relationship between a history of speech and language disorders and poor performance on writing tasks (Carter & Musher, 2005). Speech and language disorders persist into school age, adolescence, and adulthood.

Seizure disorder (pseudoabsence and absence seizure disorder)	This diagnosis is made by the pediatric neurologist

There is a higher incidence of seizures among relatives of children with seizures (Sharp, 2005). The presence of a seizure disorder is a precaution for the use of methylphenidate (Micromedex, 2005).

It is important to distinguish between a seizure disorder and attention problems, in particular with a child who displays symptoms of both ADHD and staring spells. The diagnosis of seizure disorder and the initiation of treatment are done by a pediatric neurologist. Often it is necessary to do a prolonged video-EEG monitoring (Williams et al., 2002).

Inappropriate parent/teacher expectations	

It has been my experience that the teacher expectations in elementary school vary. Some teachers recognize a wide range of normal age-appropriate behaviors and accept this variation in the classroom. Other teachers maintain a very narrow scope of expected student behaviors and do not tolerate nor adapt to children who fall outside their narrowly defined parameters. Because much of the input for the evaluation rests on the teacher assessment, it is very important to identify all professional and nonprofessional staff members who have extended interaction with the child, especially in group situations. In addition, it has been my experience that, in general, the parents in this community are very tolerant of their child's behavior and do not identify, recognize, nor have concerns about many of the "ADHD symptoms." For a child to meet criteria for the diagnosis of ADHD (or any of the subtypes), s/he must have a certain number of symptoms in the prescribed categories AND (among other stated criteria) have significant impairment in at least two settings. Often, there is discrepancy between home assessment and teacher assessment reports.

ADHD with learning disability	This diagnosis is based on a full ADHD evaluation plus psychoeducational evaluation

ADHD and LD are often comorbid conditions. It is estimated that the rate of ADHD in the LD population ranges from 12 to 80% (APA, 2000; AAP, 2000). Therefore, LD should always be considered and ruled out.

ADHD with comorbid anxiety	This diagnosis is based on a full ADHD evaluation plus psychiatric evaluation

ADHD commonly occurs in association with oppositional defiant disorder, conduct disorder, depression, anxiety disorder.

Oppositional defiant or conduct disorders coexist with ADHD in ~35% of children (AAP, 2000).

The coexistence of ADHD and mood disorders (e.g., major depressive disorder and dysthymia) is ~18% (AAP, 2000).

The coexisting association between ADHD and anxiety disorders has been estimated to be ~25% (AAP, 2000).

> *Although the primary care provider is not able to make psychiatric diagnosis, it is important to consider and examine (screen) for these comorbidities.*

SEIZURE DISORDER

I requested that Carlos maintain a headache diary and referred Carlos to the pediatric neurologist to rule out absence seizures and to evaluate the headaches and make recommendations for treatment. Consultation findings were migraine headache, precipitated by hypoglycemia, and no evidence of absence seizure or pseudoseizure.

Concurrently, I initiated the full ADHD evaluation, including specialist input for learning and speech problems and psychiatric comorbidities.

LEARNING DISABILITY

Because I was highly suspicious that there was a comorbid LD, I requested that the mother bring the child's most recent school evaluation. The IEP revealed that Carlos has speech and language problems and was to obtain speech therapy. Mother reports that Carlos used to receive speech therapy but no longer. Carlos concurs.

> *Public Law 94 – 142 (1975), the Individuals with Disabilities Education Act (IDEA) guarantees that children (aged 3 – 21) have a free and appropriate education, an education in the least restrictive environment, an assessment of needs that is racially and culturally unbiased, an individualized education plan (IEP), and due process for complaints to ensure these rights. A later amendment to this law, Public Law 101 – 476 (1990), gives parents the right to question the placement decisions. In this case, the mother and I questioned whether speech therapy is being given in the classroom and, if so, we question the adequacy of the service.*
>
> *The IDEA expects that children with disabilities will be educated with their nondisabled peers, to the maximum extent appropriate. The IEP is expected to be clear about a plan for special education, related to and including the duration, frequency, and location of the services.*

PSYCHIATRIC COMORBIDITY

The mother voiced some concern about excessive shyness and the inability to "sleep over" at the cousins' house. He did, however, go to Honduras every summer without his parents. I was not very suspicious of comorbid social or separation anxiety. The mother and child completed the DPS screen. Both the mother and child report versions of the DPS were negative for anxiety and mood disorders, and positive for ADHD.

> *The DPS-P (Lucas et al., 2001) (designed for parent completion) and the DPS-Y (designed for child completion) is used as the screening questionnaire. The DPS was tested by Honig (R21 MH63451) in an urban minority pediatric primary care practice and was found to be an effective screening questionnaire in this setting. It is available in both English and Spanish. The DPS has the advantage of being theoretically linked to the DSM-IV diagnostic criteria so that a positive score in one subscale is highly correlated with the DSM-IV diagnosis for that subscale. In the primary care context, a sophisticated and nearly diagnostic scale can provide pediatric practitioners with helpful and important information about the scope (by the magnitude of the score in each subscale) and the urgency (the subscale*

itself). The DPS report and the score can drive clinical decision-making for psychiatric intervention and whether the need for services is urgent or emergent.

Screening performance was calculated on large community and clinical samples of parents and children. Sensitivity and specificity ranged between 50 – 100% (Lucas et al., 2001).

During several weeks of evaluation, I obtained information from the teachers, school counselor, after-school teacher, and parents. I requested that the teacher and after-school teacher complete the SNAP IV Teacher Report, the Concentration Assessment Profile, and Pediatric Symptom Checklist (PSC). The mother was interviewed using open-ended questions, asked to complete a battery of questionnaires and rating scales, including SNAP IV Parent Report and PSC. Based on the above, Carlos met full criteria for Attention Deficit Hyperactivity Disorder: Inattentive type (ADHD/I).

ASSESSMENT AND PLAN

- Attention Deficit Hyperactivity Disorder: Inattentive type (ADHD/I)
- Migraine headache
- Articulation deficit
- Bicuspid aortic valve without aortic stenosis

Assessment	Plan of care
ADHD/Inattentive type	Education • Information about the disorder • Provide knowledge about the prevalence, etiology of ADHD • Treatments • Effects on learning, behavior, self-esteem • Discuss treatment options and combinations • Counseling family • Coordination with the school and advocacy for appropriate services • Linking child and family with other children with ADHD and/or other chronic disorder In collaboration with child, mother, and school, specify target outcomes • Improved academic performance • Decreased reports from teacher that Carlos did not pay attention • Increased independence in completion of homework (after-school program plus one hour after dinner) Classroom strategies • Seat assignment near teacher, away from window and friends • Allow frequent bathroom/stretch breaks • Send daily status report home to parents Behavior therapy • (+) reinforcement • Consequence (time-out) • Rewards system using tokens

	• Structure the environment • Outline expectations
	Initial medication therapy Titrate methylphenidate dosage, starting with 5 – 10 mg bid to tid • Specific schedule of increasing dosage over 2 – 4 weeks with incremental increase on weekends • Maintain phone contact weekly • Discontinue if any adverse or unusual effects/behavior and call PNP immediately • Never give after 3 p.m. (insomnia) Short-term side effects reviewed • Headaches (may increase slightly) • Bellyaches Side effects • Anorexia • Insomnia • Sluggishness Maintain record of side effects and dosage increase • Bring record to next visit in 2 – 3 weeks
ADHD/I responsive to medication and behavioral therapy	Follow-up for optimal maintenance dosage Optimal dosage determined for methylphenidate (10 mg bid) Dosage converted to long-acting Ritalin LA 20 mg od • After a full breakfast • Do not give after 12 noon • May sprinkle on food or swallow whole • Weekends, holidays advised Request follow-up assessments from teachers (SNAP medication effects, CAP given to mother) Continue rewards systems Return to clinic every four weeks to monitor weight and BP, counsel and reinforce behavioral therapy, monitor adherence to treatment plans, monitor effectiveness and dosage of medication, review periodic academic achievements, monitor symptoms in school.

The clinical guideline for the treatment of ADHD includes the following recommendations (AAP, 2000):

• Primary care clinicians should establish a treatment program that recognizes ADHD as a chronic condition.

- *The treating clinician, parents, and child, in collaboration with school personnel, should specify appropriate target outcomes to guide management.*

- *The clinician should recommend stimulant medication and/or behavior therapy as appropriate to improve target outcomes in children with ADHD.*

- *When the selected management for a child with ADHD has not met target outcomes, clinicians should evaluate the original diagnosis, use of all appropriate treatments, adherence to the treatment plan, and presence of coexisting conditions.*

- *The clinician should periodically provide a systematic follow-up for the child with ADHD. Monitoring should be directed to target outcomes and adverse effects, with information gathered from parents, teachers, and the child.*

As in most chronic illnesses that are managed in primary care, education is a key to the successful treatment and adherence to the behavioral and pharmacologic interventions.

As with other chronic illnesses, the treatment of ADHD requires the development of child-specific treatment plans (AAP, 2001).

Psychostimulant Therapy: Many studies have documented the efficacy of stimulants in reducing ADHD symptoms. For ADHD symptoms, medication management was more effective than behavioral treatment or standard community care. Adding behavioral treatment to medication management was not more effective than medication management for ADHD symptoms (Jensen et al., 1999). A single daily administration increases the likelihood of medication adherence. In addition, in order to get medication during the school day, special forms must be submitted to school, and the student needs to get a pass to the health office for the medication administration. This is disruptive to the student and brings unnecessary attention to a private medical matter. Long-acting methylphenidate preparations are available. In this case, Carlos' dosage was converted to long-acting methylphenidate.

According to his cardiologist, there is no contraindication for psychostimulant therapy and BAV. The American Heart Association Science (1999) recommends that before psychostimulant therapy is started, it should be determined if there is a personal history of palpitations, syncope or near syncope, and a family history of long QT syndrome or sudden, unexplained death. Because the cardiac effects of methylphenidate include mild tachycardia and increased heart rate, baseline rates and blood pressure should be within normal and should be closely monitored.

Stimulant medication dosage is not weight dependent. Titration for optimal dose uses the principle of "start low and titrate up" and continue after there is improved function in order to achieve the optimal benefit of the medication. Medication is recommended for symptoms. If there is a need for relief of symptoms only during school, a five-day schedule is recommended. I educate families to use the medication for symptom relief and to offer the child "drug holidays" on weekends, if possible, and during school vacation periods. Common side effects during initial treatment include: decreased appetite, insomnia, stomachache, headache, social withdrawal (Micromedex, 2005). Although there has been concern about growth delay, research does not support that psychostimulant therapy adversely affects the final adult height.

According to PDR (2005): "Ritalin® LA (methylphenidate hydrochloride) extended-release capsules are for oral administration once daily in the morning. Ritalin LA may be swallowed as whole capsules or alternatively may be administered by sprinkling the capsule contents on a small amount of applesauce (see specific instructions below). Ritalin LA capsules and/or their contents should not be crushed, chewed, or divided.

The capsules may be carefully opened and the beads sprinkled over a spoonful of applesauce. The applesauce should not be warm because it could affect the modified release properties of this formulation. The mixture of drug and applesauce should be consumed immediately in its entirety. The drug and applesauce mixture should not be stored for future use.

Behavior Therapy (AAP, 2001): Behavior therapy includes: 1) providing rewards for demonstrating the desired behavior (e.g., positive reinforcement) and 2) consequences for failure to do so (e.g., punishment). Repetitive application of the rewards and consequences gradually shapes behavior.

Effective behavioral techniques for children with Attention Deficit Hyperactivity Disorder

Technique	Description	Example
Positive reinforcement	Providing rewards or privileges contingent on the child's performance.	Child completes an assignment and is permitted to play on the computer.
Time-out	Removing access to positive reinforcement contingent on performance of unwanted or problem behavior.	Child hits sibling impulsively and is required to sit for five minutes in the corner of the room.
Response cost	Withdrawing rewards or privileges contingent on the performance of unwanted or problem behavior.	Child loses free-time privileges for not completing homework.
Token economy	Combining positive reinforcement and response cost. The child earns rewards and privileges contingent on performing desired behaviors and loses the rewards and privileges based on undesirable behavior.	Child earns stars for completing assignments and loses stars for getting out of seat. The child cashes in the sum of stars at the end of the week for a prize.

From AAP (2001)

Articulation deficit with inadequate special education services	Make all requests to Board of Education in writing
	Send all requests certified mail, return receipt requested
	Assist the mother with written requests for • Re-evaluation of the special education services and goals for Carlos • Copies of previous IEPs from the school • Most recent progress report for Carlos

184

	Instruct mother to send all requests in writing, return receipt requested
	Encourage mother to document all contacts (meetings and conversations) with teacher, team members, educational administrators
	• Personal journal
	• Compile all written information and forms
	• Bring all documents to next visit
	• Discuss parents' rights
	• Refer mother to parent advocacy literature and Internet references
	Review parents' rights
	• Right to review child's records including IEP and evaluations
	• Right to informed consent for evaluations and re-evaluations
	• Right to written notice when the school decides to refuse or start an evaluation
	• Right to notice of procedural due process rights upon re-evaluation, when district receives a letter from the parent requesting an impartial hearing
	(From: Advocates for Children http://www.insideschools.org/st/ST_specialed.php)
	Give written materials and Websites re: parents' rights, evaluation and re-evaluation procedures, Federal and NYS regulations.
	Give list of advocacy organizations and Websites to mother.

I identified appropriate Websites for mother that offer accurate and up-to-date information and can assist as an informational support resource. I used the evaluation tool for Website evaluation for content and literacy level.

The Individualized Education Plan (IEP) is a document report of an interdisciplinary team (regular education teacher, special education teacher, speech pathologist, parent, etc.) that outlines the disability, identifies the services that will be provided (including where, how long, and how frequent), and outlines the yearly goals for progress.

"Need for an official record for personal journal. May be useful, if the school does not respond within the required time frame mandated by law. Under NYS regulations, a child should receive services within 65 school days from the day of the referral."

"Once the evaluation is complete, parent is invited to the team meeting to discuss and determine the IEP. Parents are permitted to bring an advocate to these meetings. If the meeting is held and the recommendations are not satisfactory to the parent, she/he may contest the recommendations." (From: Advocates for Children http://www.insideschools.org/st/ST_specialed.php)

If the mother believes that the evaluation is inadequate, she may request a private evaluation at the Board of Education's expense.

EXCERPT TAKEN FROM NATIONAL DISSEMINATION CENTER FOR CHILDREN WITH DISABILITIES 2ND EDITION (2000) AND GIVEN TO MOTHER

"The first time your child is evaluated is called an initial evaluation (Section 300.531). Evaluations must also be conducted at least every three years (generally called a triennial evaluation) after your child has been placed in special education [Section 300.536(b)]. Re-evaluations can also occur more frequently if conditions warrant, or if you or your child's teacher requests a re-evaluation [Section 300.536(b)]. Informed parental consent is also necessary for re-evaluations [Section 300.505(a)(1)(i)].

Two general purposes of the IEP are (1) to establish measurable annual goals, including benchmarks or short-term objectives, for the child; and (2) to state the special education and related services and supplementary aids and services that the public agency will provide to, or on behalf of, the child. The regulations state that the State Education Agency (SEA) must ensure that each public agency develops and implements an IEP for each child with a disability served by that agency (Section 300.341).

While the law requires that this review and revision of the IEP take place at least once a year, you as parents may request a review or revision of your child's IEP at any time. If you feel that your child is not progressing toward the annual goals as he or she should, or you feel that he or she has achieved the goals and that new ones need to be written, you may contact the school and request that the IEP team review and revise your child's IEP as appropriate. Because of the law's new requirement that parents be regularly informed of their child's progress toward the annual goals and the extent to which that progress is sufficient to enable the child to achieve the goals by the end of the year [Section 300.347(a)(7)(ii)], parents will have the ability to gauge their child's progress more closely than ever before."

Migraine headache triggered by hypoglycemia	Avoid skipping meals. Avoid caffeinated drinks. Avoid chocolate. Keep a snack in book bag. Maintain a headache diary. • Time of onset • Precipitating events • Time of resolution • Treatment Bring diary to each primary care visit to review triggers, identify new triggers, to evaluate medication management. Acetaminophen 325 mg q4h prn for pain or Ibuprofen 200 mg q6h prn for pain. Darken the room.

Mother was giving an ineffective dose of acetaminophen. Acetaminophen dosage (10 – 15 mg/kg/dose) for Carlos's weight is between 300 mg and 443 mg/dose. The frequency of Carlos's headache has remained consistent, but the relief time is improved so that the headache does not interfere with his school and social activities.

Bicuspid aortic valve without aortic stenosis	Assure cardiac specialist evaluation every two years. Request summary of cardiac evaluation and results of serial assessment of aortic valve.

	Request echocardiogram results for primary care record.
	Continue antibiotic prophylaxis.
	Review dental and other procedures for which antibiotic prophylaxis is recommended.
	Review prophylactic regimen and dosage.
	Prescription given for amoxicillin 1500 gm (50 mg/kg).
	Pocket guide in Spanish given to mother with current dosage.

Wallet card reinforces the information for families and other health professionals. It outlines the diagnosis, prophylaxis dose, and the procedures that require endocarditis prophylaxis (adapted from Dajani et al., 1997).

CONTINUITY OF CARE

Carlos's schoolwork has improved. School reports from teacher reveal that he is more attentive to his assignments. Mother reports that homework time is less stressful and that Carlos is completing his homework in a more timely way. As far as the speech disability and school services, a re-evaluation is being scheduled. I have offered to advocate on behalf of the child. The procedure makes the provision for an outsider to attend the meeting as an advocate. Once the evaluation is complete, I will attend the interdisciplinary conference to hear the team's recommendations regarding eligibility for services and the outline of services to be provided.

References

American Academy of Pediatrics, Committee on Quality Improvement and Subcommittee on Attention Deficit Hyperactivity Disorder (2000). *Clinical practice guidelines: diagnosis and evaluation of the child with attention deficit hyperactivity disorder.* Pediatrics, 105 (5): 1158 – 1170.

American Psychiatric Association (2000). *Learning disorders.* In: M.E. First (Ed.), Diagnostic and Statistical Manual — Text Revision (DSM-IV-TR, 2000), 4th ed. Washington, D.C.: American Psychiatric Association.

Beppu, S., Suzuki, S., Matsuda, H., et al. (1993). *Rapidity of progression of aortic stenosis in patients with congenital bicuspid aortic valves.* American Journal of Cardiology, 71, 322.

Carter, J., Musher, K. (2005). *Evaluation and treatment of speech and language impairment in children.* Up to Date accessed on Mar. 18, 2005 at: http://www.uptodateonline.com.

Dajani, A.S., Taubert, K.A., Wilson, W., Bolger, A.F., Bayer, A., Ferrieri, P., Gewitz, M.H., Shulman, S.T., Nouri, S., Newburger, J.W., Hutto, C., Pallasch, T.J., Gage, T.W., Levison, M.E., Peter, G., Zuccaro Jr., G. (1997). *Prevention of bacterial endocarditis. Recommendations by the American Heart Association.* Journal of the American Medical Association, 277, 1794 – 1801.

Fearon, P., Hotopf, M. (2001). *Relation between headache in childhood and physical and psychiatric symptoms in adulthood: national birth cohort study.* British Medical Journal, 322 (7295): 1145.

Fedak, P.W.M., Verma, S., David, T.E., Leask, R.L., Weisel, R.D., Butany, J. (2002). *Clinical and pathophysiological implications of a bicuspid aortic valve.* Circulation, 106, 900 – 904.

Feigin, J.Z. *Clinical features, evaluation, and diagnosis of learning disabilities in children.* Up to Date accessed on Mar. 15, 2005 at: http://www.uptodateonline.com.

Fenoglio, J.J., McAllister, H.A., DeCastro, C.M., et al. (1997). *Congenital bicuspid aortic valve after age 20.* American Journal of Cardiology, 39, 164.

Gutges, H., Atkins, D., Barst, R., Buck, M., Franklin, W., Humes, R., Rngel, R., Shaddy, R., Taubert, K.A. (1999). *Cardiovascular monitoring of children and adolescents receiving psychotropic drugs: a statement for healthcare professionals from the Committee on Congenital Cardiac Defects, Council on Cardiovascular Disease in the Young, American Heart Association.* Circulation, 99, 979 – 982.

Jensen, P., Arnold, L., Richters, J. (1999). *14-month randomized clinical trial of treatment strategies for attention deficit hyperactivity disorder.* Archives of General Psychiatry, 56, 1073 – 1086.

Lambert, E.C., Menon, V.A., Wagner, H.R., et al. (1974). *Sudden unexpected death from cardiovascular disease in children: a cooperative international study.* American Journal of Cardiology, 34, 89.

Lewin, M.B., Otto, C.M. (2005). *The bicuspid aortic valve: adverse outcomes from infancy to old age.* Circulation, 111, 832.

Lewis, B.A., O'Donnell, B., Freebairn, L.A., Taylor, H.G. (1998). *Spoken language and written expression interplay of delays.* American Journal of Speech and Language Pathology, 7, 77.

Lucas, C.P., Zhang, H., Fisher, P.W., Shaffer, D., Regier, D.A., Narrow, W.E., et al. (2001). *The DISC Predictive Scales (DPS): efficiently screening for diagnoses.* Journal of the American Academy of Child & Adolescent Psychiatry, 40 (4).

McInerny, T.K. (1995). *Children who have difficulty in school: a primary pediatrician's approach.* Pediatrics in Review, 16 (9): 325 – 32.

Micromedex (2005). Accessed on Mar. 18, 2005 at http://p70salk.cpmc.columbia.edu.osiyou.cc.columbia.edu:2048/mdxcgi/mdxhtml.exe?&tmpl=mdxhome.tm1&SCRNAME=mdxhome&CTL=/mdx/mdxcgi/megat.sys.

National Dissemination Center for Children with Disabilities (2nd ed., 2000). *Questions and answers about IDEA.* News Digest 21 (ND21). Accessed on Apr. 2, 2005 at http://www.nichcy.org/pubs/newsdig/nd21txt.htm.

Roberts, W.C., Ko, J.M. (2005). *Frequency by decades of unicuspid, bicuspid, and tricuspid aortic valves in adults having isolated aortic valve replacement for aortic stenosis, with or without associated aortic regurgitation.* Circulation, 111, 920.

Sharp, B.R. *Differential diagnosis of seizures in children.* Up to Date accessed on Mar. 15, 2005 at http://www.uptodateonline.com.

Silberstein, S.D., Rosenberg, J. (2000). *Multispecialty consensus on diagnosis and treatment of headache.* Neurology 54, 1553. Full text of guidelines available at www.neurology.org.

Silver, L.B. (1989). *Learning disabilities.* Journal of American Academy of Child and Adolescent Psychiatry, 28, 309.

The Individuals with Disabilities Education Act (1997). Accessed on Apr. 2, 2005 at http://www.ed.gov/offices/OSERS/Policy/IDEA/the_law.html.

Williams, J., Griebel, M.L., Sharp, G.B., Lange, B., Phillips, T., DelosReyes, E., Bates, S., Schulz, E.G., Simpson, P. (2002). *Differentiating between seizures and attention deficit hyperactivity disorder (ADHD) in a pediatric population.* Clinical Pediatrics, 41, 565 – 568.

Appendices

Academic progression of the DrNP post-BS in nursing

Year 1	Year 2	Year 3	Year 4
Advanced Physiology	Diagnosis and Management of Illness I	Legal and Ethical Issues	Full-Time Residency
Pathophysiology	Practicum in Primary Care I	Advanced Seminar in Clinical Genetics	Clinical Seminars
Advanced Pharmacology	Seminar in Primary Care I	Informatics and Evidence-Based Practice	Portfolio Development
Incorporating Genetics into Advanced Nursing Practice	Diagnosis and Management of Illness II	Practice Management	
Health and Social Policy: Context for Practice	Practicum in Primary Care II	Research Methods	
Assessing Clinical Evidence	Seminar in Primary Care II	Principles of Epidemiology and Environmental Health	
Introduction to Primary Care	Integration Practicum	Chronic Illness Management	
Advanced Clinical Assessment		Doctor of Nursing Practice I Practicum Clinical Applications	
Practicum in Advanced Clinical Assessment			
		Doctor of Nursing Practice II Practicum Clinical Applications	
	MS Conferred		
	Eligible for Professional Certification	Oral and Written Comprehensive Exams	
			DrNP Conferred

Competencies of a Doctor of Nursing Practice (DrNP)

The DrNP graduate demonstrates expertise in the provision, coordination, and direction of care to patients, including those who present in healthy states and those who present with complex, chronic, and/or comorbid conditions, across clinical sites and over time. DrNP competencies build upon established competencies at the master's degree level and national certification.

DrNP graduates:

- Provide health promotion, anticipatory guidance, counseling, and disease prevention services to healthy or sick patients in any clinical setting based on age, developmental stage, family history, ethnicity, and individual risk, including genetic profile.

- Apply principles of epidemiology, environmental health, and biostatistics to identify population or geographically based risks to health of specific patients, and take action to reduce their risk.

- Formulate diagnostic strategies to deal with ambiguous or incomplete data in developing differential diagnosis for patients that present with new conditions and those with complex illnesses, comorbid conditions, and potential multiple diagnoses with attention to scientific evidence, safety, cost, invasiveness, simplicity, acceptability, adherence, and efficacy in all clinical settings.

- Determine the need for emergency evaluation and/or inpatient admission, and manage/co-manage and coordinate the care of patients in the emergency, acute, and subacute setting.

- Identify and select appropriate interventions that incorporate cultural values that meet the needs of specific patients at all levels of acuity in the most appropriate setting.

- Establish and utilize a collaborative network of specialists while maintaining primary responsibility for patient care; and accept referrals from other health professionals and agencies to provide optimum care.

- Manage chronic illness utilizing specialists, other disciplines, community resources, and family, to provide a seamless flow of patient data and continuity of care when the focus of care shifts among office, hospital, home, chronic care facility, or community settings.

- Identify gaps in access and/or reimbursement that compromise patients' optimal care and apply current knowledge of the organization and financing of health-care systems in order to ameliorate negative impact and/or reduce barriers to patient access.

- Introduce and guide the process of planning end-of-life care by facilitating understanding of diagnoses and prognosis, clarifying patient desires and priorities, promoting informed choices through discussion with patient, family, and members of the health-care team.

- Utilize the principles of legal and ethical decision-making to identify and analyze dilemmas that arise in patient care, interprofessional relationships, research, and practice management; take action to resolve the issues.

- Utilize and synthesize evidence from practice and patient databases, perform data mining, and analyze data to generate evidence from practice to improve patient care.